T2 For two people. A Deck
Twin bedded cabins, with a large window, two wardrobe units, chest of drawers/bedside table, one armchair, dressing table with over-lighted mirror. En-suite toilet, shower and wash basin.

T3 For three people. A Deck
Similar in size and layout to T2 cabins, but with one bed replaced by a lower and fold-away upper berth combination. Large window, triple wardrobe unit, chest of drawers/bedside table, one armchair, dressing table with over-lighted mirror. En-suite toilet, shower and wash basin.
Alternative grade for reduced occupancy: T2 Twin.

T2H For two people. A Deck
With lower and fold-away upper berth, large window, one or two wardrobe units, one armchair and a dressing table with over-lighted mirror. En-suite toilet, shower and wash basin.
Alternative grade for single occupancy: T1 Single

T4 For four people. A Deck
With two lower and fold-away upper berths, large window, four single wardrobes, two chests of drawers, two armchairs and a dressing table with over-lighted mirror. En-suite toilet, shower and wash basin.
Alternative grade for reduced occupancy: T2 Twin.

T2S For two people. B Deck
Larger cabin with porthole, twin beds, two wardrobe units, two chests of drawers, one armchair, large dressing table with over-lighted mirror, twin settee and coffee table. En-suite toilet, shower and wash basin.

T2HS For two people. B Deck
Slightly smaller than T2S cabins, with lower and fold-away upper berth unit, porthole, two wardrobe units, two chests of drawers, one armchair, dressing table with over-lighted mirror and small table. En-suite toilet, shower and wash basin.
Alternative grade for single occupancy: T1S Superior Single.

T4S For four people. B Deck
Porthole, two lower and fold-away upper berth units, four wardrobe units, two chests of drawers, one armchair, dressing table with over-lighted mirror, twin settee and coffee table. En-suite toilet, shower and wash basin.
Alternative grade for reduced occupancy: T2S Superior Twin.

Promenade Deck
Larger cabin with window, two lower and fold-away upper berth units, two wardrobe units, two chests of drawers, two armchairs, good sized dressing table with over-lighted mirror and small table. Large en-suite facilities with toilet, shower and wash basin.
Alternative grade for reduced occupancy: T2S Superior Twin.

Budget Accommodation

2Bo For two people. C Deck
Porthole, lower and fold-away upper berth, two half-height wardrobes, stool and chest of drawers. Washbasin.

2Biw For two people. C Deck
No natural light, lower and fold-away upper berth, two half-height wardrobes, stool and chest of drawers. En-suite toilet, shower and wash basin.

2Bi For two people. C Deck.
No natural light, lower and fold-away upper berth, two half-height wardrobes, stool and chest of drawers. Wash basin.

4B0 For four people. C Deck.
Porthole, two lower and fold-away upper berths, four half-height wardrobes, two stools and two chests of drawers. Wash basin.
Alternative grade ſ Budget Twin.

Accomodation plan for *St Helena* ous types of cabins available. *[RMS St Helen* ›llection]

CONTENTS

Ard Coasters – the fleet and history of P. MacCallum and Sons Ltd. *Roy Fenton* 2
British tramp shipping 1914-1939 - case studies in fleet rebuilding and renewal *Malcolm Cooper* 15
Every picture tells a story 44
Maracaibo to the Thames 45
Aberdeen liners were in for the long haul *Peter Myers* 49
A dozen cool beauties *Tony Breach* 56
Sources and acknowledgements 64
Paddling in the North West 65
Crossed the bar – obituaries of two Ships in Focus contributors 71
From sail to steam in the Belfast coal trade *Ian Wilson* 72
Margaronis family ship owning *Malcolm Cranfield* 79
Remembering *Khalij Crystal* *Tony Breach* 92
Putting the Record straight 94
Euxine Shipping Co. Ltd. *Ken Garrett* 101
A new ship for St. Helena *Andrew Bell* 117
Steel sailers to steam coasters: the ships of Williamsons of Workington *Roy Fenton* 122
Whale factory ships feedback 141
Index to ships 142

Ships in Focus Publications

Correspondence and editorial:
Roy Fenton
18 Durrington Avenue
London SW20 8NT
020 8879 3527
roy@rfenton.co.uk

Orders and photographic:
John & Marion Clarkson
18 Franklands, Longton
Preston PR4 5PD
01772 612855
shipsinfocus@btinternet.com

Printed by Amadeus Press Ltd., Cleckheaton, Yorkshire.
Designed by Hugh Smallwood, John Clarkson and Roy Fenton.

SHIPS IN FOCUS RECORD
ISBN 978-0-9928264-2-0

RECORD 2018

We are delighted to report that our enlarged annual, 'Record 2017', proved both popular with readers and successful in sales terms. Not only that, but our regular contributors have come up with so much interesting material that we have expanded 'Record 2018' from 128 to 144 pages in order to fit it all in. We have also aimed for a similar mix of articles, with features on individual ships (both fairly ancient and fairly modern), various ship types, ship owners and a shipbuilder.

The feature on Williamson's Workington shipbuilding and ship owning was compiled from work begun as the basis of a book on iron and steel shipbuilding in Cumberland. A dearth of background information has halted this project, but it is one worth pursuing, not least because this area's not insubstantial shipbuilding output has been ignored by all but a few local researchers. Harrington, Maryport, Whitehaven and Workington were all centres of iron and steel shipbuilding, also having coal and iron production facilities near at hand, yet this could hardly be guessed at from Cumberland's coverage in shipbuilding histories. The ships built at these yards are straightforward enough to research, but if anyone – especially those based locally – can shed light on these yards' owners and circumstances, we would be delighted to push this project forward.

Based on a talk he gave, Andrew Bell's article on designing the second *St. Helena* is timely in view of the ship's withdrawal from service in 2018, and is also particularly relevant in view of Andrew's close association with the ship from concept onwards.

This edition includes a very much extended 'Putting the Record Straight'. This is not just because there are comments on 'Record' 2017, but because some feedback from earlier 'Records' simply got mislaid and overlooked. We know some loyal readers have every edition, but (blatant plug coming up) if not then we would mention that all but two previous editions are still available: see our website.

Our readers should be aware that, at the time of writing, the future of 'Record' in its existing form is uncertain. Compiling the enlarged editions for 2017 and 2018 has been hugely satisfying, but also enormously time consuming. With the editors' ages growing just as their attention spans decrease, the investment in effort required cannot easily be justified, given that we have an ambitious programme of new books to publish, with at least four at various stages of preparation. If another 'Record' is produced, we will certainly let you know.

It only remains to thank all readers and contributors for their support of 'Record' over the years, and to hope that you enjoy this edition.

John Clarkson　　　Roy Fenton

October 2018

The veteran coaster *Glenaan* (332/1884) was owned by the Antrim Iron Ore Co. Ltd. from 1915 to 1932. Her story is told in this issue's article on the Belfast coal trade, which also has an even older photograph of her as Kelly's *Cultra*. *[Bristol Series/ J. and M. Clarkson]*

Front cover: *Zealandic [David E. Kirby/Russell Priest collection]* See page 92.
Back cover: *Galacum [World Ship Society Ltd.]* See page 138.
Fernmoor [Ships in Focus] See page 42.
Front end papers: general arrangement drawings of *St. Helena*. See pages 117 to 121.
Back end papers: funnels and house flags of companies featured in this issue.

ARD COASTERS

The fleet and history of P. MacCallum and Sons Ltd.

Roy Fenton

Although their history is intertwined with that of another and much larger Scottish fleet, that of Lang and Fulton, the Greenock-registered coasters with Ard names of P. MacCallum and Sons constituted a discrete unit with some interesting, unusual and long-lived vessels which were largely designed for carrying steel. The MacCallum company was actually older than that of Lang and Fulton, but by 1913 the latter had a significant fleet of deep-sea steamers, and the MacCallum company benefited from their experience as ship managers. Although ship owning began as very much an adjunct to MacCallum's core business, at times over the fleet's 60 years their ships produced the majority of the company's profits.

Founding father of the business was James MacCallum (1740-1804), son of a herring fisherman on the Argyllshire shore of the Kyles of Bute. The young James moved to Greenock, where in his twenties he began a hardware business mainly supplying nails to boat and ship builders in what was then Scotland's largest port. James' son Peter (1771-1854) continued and expanded the business, becoming a major supplier of nails and bolts to builders of wooden ships on both sides of the Clyde, and even making ventures into owning small vessels. On his death his sons, who in 1838 had been taken into partnership in Peter MacCallum and Sons, recognised the growing importance of iron shipbuilding, and moved the business into the supply of iron plate, major customers becoming Scott's Shipbuilding and Engineering Company who were amongst the pioneers of iron shipbuilding on the Clyde. From then the business expanded massively, with Peter MacCallum and Sons operating as merchants, buying iron and later steel from various manufacturers on behalf of their shipbuilding clients. Significantly for the future direction of the company, John Lang, a nephew of Peter MacCallum's sons, joined the company in the 1850s, becoming the senior partner in 1874. Chief Clerk James Fulton was also to become a partner. The MacCallum, Lang and Fulton families' fortunes were now firmly intertwined, especially with John Lang's son Peter MacCallum Lang marrying James Fulton's daughter. Whilst continuing to manage Peter MacCallum and Sons, John Lang and James Fulton also began what became a significant ship owning business by taking shares in the wooden ship *Lady Clarendon* (1,331/1853) in 1876.

Coaster owning

Peter MacCallum and Sons took the precaution of moving from a partnership to a limited liability company in 1907, by when they were buying steel from works in Scotland, Wales and England and supplying shipbuilders throughout Great Britain and as far afield as Norway and Hong Kong. During 1911, for instance, the company purchased over 130,000 tons of steel. With large quantities being bought from Port Talbot for resale to the yards of Russell and Company in Port Glasgow and Greenock and Workman, Clark in Belfast, Ard Coasters Ltd. was formed in 1913 to carry plate from South Wales to the Clyde and Belfast. Lang and Fulton Ltd., who acted as managers, were major shareholders, with the Port Talbot Steel Company, Workman, Clark and Russell and Company all having substantial holdings. Three large coasters were ordered from the Greenock yard of George Brown and Company, *Ardgarth*, *Ardglass* (1) and *Ardgour*. Their names were in line with those used by Lang and Fulton Ltd., but may have been inspired by knowledge that founder James MacCallum's family home was Ardgoil Farm near Ormidale in Argyllshire. The builders were told to design ships specifically for steel carrying, and a hatch of 77 feet allowed loading of 120-feet steel bars into the hold which extended beneath the bridge and the deck officers' accommodation. Steel cargoes were loaded by long, six-ton steel derricks and were placed in the centre of the hold where transverse frames helped to hold them in place.

Having three newly-built coasters trading by the outbreak of the First World War, the company might have expected to do particularly well out of the conflict. However, two of the coasters were requisitioned by the Government and a third, *Ardglass*, sunk by a U-boat in May 1917, so profits from ship owning, at £23,000 in 1916 but only £656 in 1917 were not as good as might be expected. Nevertheless, they were better than those from steel trading. Purchases of steel in 1914 hit a record 226,000 tons, but then fell off seriously as the Admiralty took powers to divert steel output to warship production, whilst the Ministry of Munitions took over all steel production in June 1915.

Despite this gloomy picture, further coasters were ordered during 1915, *Ardgarvel* (1) and *Ardgantock* (1) from Fergusons' yard at Port Glasgow, although they were not delivered until January and December 1917, and *Ardgantock*

One of the first three ships ordered, *Ardgour,* delivered in March 1914. *[David Hocquard collection]*

Delivered in November 1918, *Ardgirvan* was sold within a year, owners becoming the European Gas Co. Ltd. who renamed her *Bolbec.* In 1926 she was sold on to Swansea owners, Harries Brothers, in whose colours she is seen here. Despite sinking following a collision in 1943, she was refloated, refurbished and steamed on until 1958. *[World Ship Society Ltd.]*

was lost when only two months old in February 1918 when she collided with a destroyer. Two even larger ships, the 230-feet, engines-amidships *Ardgartan* and *Ardgirvan* were ordered from the Ardrossan Dockyard and Shipbuilding Co. Ltd. and registered during July and October 1919 respectively, although the former disappeared in 1919 and the latter was sold the same year, undoubtedly at a substantial profit. A third coaster from Ardrossan, this time 200-feet long, the second *Ardgantock* was delivered in 1919, having been laid down for the Shipping Controller (who may well have taken over her order from MacCallums). To complete this list of deliveries, the 200-foot *Ardglass* (2) was completed by Fullertons in October 1919, having spent over two years fitting out whilst priority was given to naval work. Both were to have satisfyingly long careers. Somewhat surprisingly, as all other ships were built specifically to their order, the company bought two 200-feet steamers from London owners in 1920, becoming the *Ardgryfe* and *Ardgarroch*.

The second *Ardgantock*. Sold in 1955, she lasted until 1958 under British ownership. *[Fotoflite incorporating Skyfotos]*

Although not built for MacCallum, *Ardgryfe* was clearly suitable for their trades, giving over 40 years of service, and being their last steamer when sold to breakers in 1959. *[B. and A. Feilden/J. and M. Clarkson]*

Ard Coasters Ltd. had a short existence, being wound up in October 1918 and its ships transferred to Peter MacCallum and Sons Ltd. This may have been part of a larger plan on behalf of Lang and Fulton who at the same time decided to sell off their deep-sea fleet at the astronomic prices then current for ships. Its principals continuing to operate Peter MacCallum and Co. Ltd. as steel merchants with the fleet of seven coasters which remained after losses and sales. With one interesting exception, there were to be no further acquisitions of ships until 1953.

Surviving the recession

Industrial and economic developments during the First World War had profound effects on MacCallum's business. Shipbuilders began to deal direct with steel producers, cutting out middlemen, a process that continued as shipbuilders and steel companies became vertically integrated, the resulting acquisitions included David Colville and Company by Harland and Wolff, and Lithgow's purchase of the Calderbank Steel Works. These and other mergers meant that shipyards bought largely from their associated steel works and bypassed the merchants such as MacCallum. However, the effects of these changes were not apparent at once, as immediate post-war years saw a boom in shipbuilding largely due to a shortage of ships and consequent massive inflation of freight rates. To help meet the demand, MacCallums bought steel not only from Port Talbot, but also surplus steel which the Ministry of Munitions had ordered during wartime, and steel from the USA which came significantly cheaper than Scottish steel. As a result, record profits of almost £26,000 were made in 1919, but in 1920 this turned into a loss of almost £7,000. Although this was put down to payments of Excessive Profits Duty, poor trading had an effect. Freight rates had fallen, so income from the shipping business fell dramatically from £41,000 in 1919 to under £26,000. By 1921 the British economy was moving into recession with freight rates plunging and shipbuilding orders cancelled with inevitable effects on steel merchants. However, MacCallum's shipping bucked the trend and its income rose to £37,500, largely because the ships were busy importing steel from the continent where steelworks in Belgium, France, Germany and Luxemburg were able to quote much lower prices than their British competitors. In 1922, almost two thirds of MacCallum's steel was bought from continental works. This work was shortlived, as recession deepened, and as a result the two oldest ships, *Ardgarth* and *Ardgour*, were sold in 1923. The 1917-built *Ardgarvel* followed in 1927, leaving a fleet of just four ships. As recession turned into depression, MacCallums stopped buying steel altogether from 1931 to 1933, meaning that the fleet was largely laid up through lack of work. Reduction in its size saw *Ardglass* (2) sold in 1935 and *Ardgarroch* follow in 1936. Even this did not bring the shipping side of the business back into profit as repair bills for the two ageing ships were heavy, whilst an agreement to time charter *Ardgryfe* to trade between London and Antwerp from 1936 to 1938 meant she could not benefit from a general, modest rise in freight rates.

The Kindiesel exercise

The exception to the run down of the fleet between the wars was the financing and building of *Kindiesel*. Although by no means universal (as Williamson's unflinching loyalty to the steam engine showed), owners and builders of coasters plus their engine suppliers were increasingly considering the adoption of the diesel engine. Marine engineers John G. Kincaid and Company were designing a small oil engine and to test a prototype they approached MacCallums suggesting a joint venture to fund a company to build a coaster fitted with this machinery. The Kindiesel Shipping Co. Ltd. was formed in 1936 with a capital of £12,500, most subscribed by Kincaid and MacCallums with the latter managing the ship. *Kindiesel* was delivered from Ardrossan in 1936 and, like many new and innovative motor ships, she initially spent considerable periods out of action with machinery problems. She lost some one and a half months work during her first 13 months, so that her owning company posted a loss of £285. When working, Kindiesel mainly carried coal, fertiliser, scrap metal and china clay, her first half year's

As part of MacCallum's response to recession, *Ardglass* (2) was sold to Monroe Brothers of Liverpool in 1935, and appears to have retained her grey hull as *Kyle Castle*. Sister *Ardgantock* (2) was also sold to Monroe Brothers and - after *Kyle Castle* was sold to Greek owners in 1949 - took the same name, although it was spelt *Kylecastle*. The former *Ardglass* lasted as *Thetis* until late in 1959. *[B. and A. Feilden/J. and M. Clarkson]*

service seeing her trading largely between Scottish ports with occasional voyages south to Charlestown and Teignmouth and making one visit to Antwerp with clay. The next year's trading saw losses through mechanical problems marginally reduced to 30 days, and at the end of this period she returned to Ardrossan for an extended overhaul which succeeded in almost eliminating her breakdowns. However, even this did not result in profitable employment and, in the six months following her return to service in March 1939, the owning company lost £150. The disappointing result was not blamed on her machinery, but on the fact that at just 142 feet she was too small to be profitable in the coastal trade. After further losses, she was sold in January 1942 for £14,000, rather more than her building cost.

Second World War

The Second World War saw the government better prepared than they had been in the First World War, quickly introducing controls on shipping and, hurting McCallum's business more, on supply of steel. Added to this four senior managers who were reservists were called up for war service. *Ardgantock* (2) was almost immediately requisitioned as an armed store carrier, and remained under Admiralty control for six years. *Ardgryfe* was not called up until June 1941, and although McCallums continued to run her, the Ministry of War Transport dictated her service, which mostly involved moving coal. There was no lack of work for those remaining in the Shipping Department, however, as several vessels were operated for the for the Ministry. *Margo* was a requisitioned foreign vessel and is listed by 'Lloyd's Register' as being managed on behalf of the Ministry of War Transport as was the new building *Empire Bank*. Management of the latter was transferred in 1942

Kindiesel in Norwegian ownership as *Senator* between 1956 and her loss in 1969. *[Roy Fenton collection]*

Left; *Ardgryfe* steamed on for MacCallums, right through the Second World War and through to 1959. However, she began to look her age, and in this photograph her signal post is decidedly bent. *[World Ship Society Ltd.]*

Bottom; The motorship *Ardglen* had a rather conventional layout, with her bridge amidships. *[Fotoflite incorporating Skyfotos]*

to Metcalf Motor Coasters Ltd., who later bought her, but *Margo* remained with MacCallum. Quite how much work was obtained from the 1895-built steamer is debatable, as her fate after the war was to be scuttled with a cargo of poison gas. The Swedish steamer *Nördost* is listed in company records as being managed, but no confirmation of this can be found in register books or registration papers, and it is likely that the company acted as agents for her as they did for a number of other coasters which were working at the Clyde Emergency Port: Zillah's *Ophir* (469/1907), Fisher's *Strait Fisher* (573/1917), Metcalf's *Ann M* (169/1926), *David M* (350/1933) and *Ngakoa* (494/1938).

Post-war motorships

With Government controls on steel supplies which had been imposed during the war still in place, a world-wide shortage of steel, and a Labour Government determined to nationalise the steel industry, MacCallum's core business languished post-war, and for a number of years the shipping department contributed most of its profits. This encouraged the company to put money into a reserve fund for investment in new ships, and in 1951 they ordered from James Lamont and Company at Port Glasgow the motor vessel *Ardglen*. However, on her delivery in March 1953 freight rates had fallen, and that year MacCallum's shipping business recorded its first post-war loss. In response, *Ardglen* was time chartered and after crossing the North Atlantic traded successfully in Canadian waters for a number of years.

Despite her 36 years, the steamer *Ardgantock* (2) found a buyer in 1955: Monroe Brothers of Liverpool, who had bought *Ardglass* (2) in 1935, and this sale encouraged the ordering of a second motor coaster from Port Glasgow. The *Ardgarry* was delivered in May 1957 and also went on time charter to Canada. Alongside these two motor ships, MacCallums still ran the 1918-built steamer *Ardgryfe* until her sale for scrap in 1959.

MacCallums fleet had suffered just one previous loss in peacetime when in April 1919 the *Ardgartan* disappeared after leaving Swansea with coal for Brest. The fate of *Ardgarry*, McCallum's 13th ship, was to be eerily similar. Having just returned from Canada to work on the British coast during the winter, she left Swansea on 28th December 1962 with coal, this time for Rouen. Casualty returns simply record her as having disappeared, yet more information emerged at her official enquiry. Entering the English Channel in winds which were reaching Force 11, she

Ardgarry of 1957 (left) had her bridge aft but, following the trend of other 1950s motor coasters, retained the raised quarter deck design inherited from the steam coaster. *[Fotoflite incorporating Skyfotos]*

Ardgarvel (bottom) was almost a repeat of *Ardgarry* with an extra deck to her superstructure. *[Ships in Focus]*

overtook the motor coaster *Hollandia* (327/1951). *Ardgarry* was seen to suddenly alter course by 90 degrees across the Dutchman's bows, also sending out an SOS signal. Watching her masthead lights it was apparent to those on watch on *Hollandia* that she had capsized to starboard. None of her crew survived, although lifeboats were washed up in the Scillies and in Cornwall. In the absence of evidence, the subsequent enquiry assumed that an engine breakdown or steering failure had lead to her broaching, after which a large wave had hit her broadside on, causing her cargo to shift so that she capsized. The enquiry found that *Ardgarry* had been well maintained. MacCallums immediately ordered a replacement from Lamonts; but although scheduled for delivery in October 1964, *Ardgarvel* did not arrive until January 1965.

Last years in shipping

During the 1960s the profits from the shipping business became unpredictable, with a loss of nearly £2,500 on the voyage account in 1967 contrasting with profits of about £17,000 in 1965 and 1969. The familiar arguments were made about the decline of coastwise trade, and of competition from family-owned Dutch and other motor coasters with low overheads. An attempt was made to develop an association with John Stewart and Co. (Shipping) Ltd., established operators of coasters with names beginning 'Yew', and a joint chartering operation was set up. But after for only a year this ended in April 1972, by which time the 20-year-old *Ardglen* had been sold and MacCallums were left with just the *Ardgarvel*. There was an intention to build a larger replacement for *Ardglen*, but the estimated cost of £1,250,000 meant the scheme was stillborn.

The prohibitive cost was not the only factor in the decision. It was becoming more difficult to recruit and retain crews, despite MacCallum's record of paying salaries well above recommended rates. There was also a feeling in the shipping department that the standard of officers and deck crews had declined, and they foresaw that British short-sea ship owners would find recruitment increasing difficult, a forecast which was to prove all too correct. During 1974 *Ardgarvel* experienced continuing trouble with her machinery, with two pistons requiring replacement and

repairs necessary to her tail shaft. But the worst blow was the 1973 hike in oil prices by OPEC, which not only raised fuel costs but also reduced charter rates by about two thirds. As a result of the bleak outlook, MacCallums decided to quit shipping after over 60 years, selling the *Ardgarvel* in November 1974.

MacCallum's original core business as steel merchants faced problems post-war with two attempts by Labour governments to nationalise the steel industry, which then had little need for steel merchants. The company's response was to move into steel stockholding, in which it was moderately successful, although its primary market, the British shipbuilding industry, was facing a protracted but ultimately almost complete decline. With money in their erstwhile ship replacement fund, the company now looked to diversify, acquiring an engineering works at Bo'ness on the Forth and an electrical engineering business at home in Greenock, which were run alongside their steel stockholding in the latter town. An odd twist was the renaming of the company Lang and Fulton Ltd. as which it survives into the 21st century, currently making and marketing steel fencing, flooring and gratings and based in Edinburgh. Their shipping background has not been forgotten: their website features photographs of two of Lang and Fulton's sailing ships and one of the launch of *Ardgarvel* (2).

MacCallum's close association with Lang and Fulton facilitated their move into ship owning in 1913. Although this began simply to expedite delivery of steel to its customers, it became a major part of their overall operation, and at times delivered most of the company's profits. Their coasters were well maintained and their crews relatively well rewarded, and the company's reputation saw them manage the innovative if disappointing *Kindiesel* and successfully charter their ships when their own trade was dull. Although it totalled just some 15 ships, the Ard fleet of Greenock has a history which deserves to be recorded.

The author would like to express his reliance, with permission, in compiling this account upon the excellent 'A Bed of Nails: the history of P MacCallum & Sons Ltd. of Greenock 1781-1981' compiled on behalf of the company by two eminent industrial historians, John R. Hume and Michael S. Moss.

A second look at *Ardgarvel*, sailing from Preston, now looking rather drab in an all-grey livery, with her derricks unshipped. *[J. and M. Clarkson]*

Fleet list

1. ARDGARTH 1913-1923
O.N. 135331 770g 350n.
200.2 x 29.1 x 12.8 feet.
T. 3-cyl. by Ross and Duncan, Glasgow; 95 NHP, 10 knots.
22.8.1913: Launched by George Brown and Company, Greenock (Yard No. 83).
24.9.1913: Registered in the ownership of Ard Coasters Ltd. (Lang and Fulton Ltd., managers), Greenock as ARDGARTH.
27.3.1915 to 19.4.1918: Requisitioned by the British government.
1918: Transferred to Peter MacCallum and Sons Ltd. (Lang and Fulton Ltd., managers), Greenock.
1923: Sold to Sollas Lines Ltd. (Richards, Longstaff and Co. Ltd., managers), London and renamed YORKMINSTER.
2.1925: Sold to the Sowards Coal Company (W.J. Driver, manager), Kingston, Ontario, Canada and renamed PATDORIS.
1930: Transferred to John F. Sowards, Kingston.
1944: Sold to the Toronto General Trusts Corporation, Toronto, Canada.
6.1945: Sold to the Maple Leaf Steamship Co. Ltd., Montreal, Quebec, Canada (F.L. Fraser, Havana, Cuba, manager).
1956: Registered in Panama.
1961: Deleted from 'Lloyd's Register'.

Ardgarth in Canadian ownership as *Patdoris*, with cut down mast and additional ventilators. *[William Schell]*

2. ARDGLASS (1) 1914-1917
O.N. 135336 778g 373n.
200.0 x 29.1 x 12.8 feet.
T. 3-cyl. by Ross and Duncan, Govan; 96 NHP, 675 IHP, 10½ knots.
27.11.1913: Launched by George Brown and

Company, Greenock (Yard No. 84).
2.1.1914: Registered in the ownership of Ard Coasters Ltd. (Lang and Fulton Ltd., managers), Greenock as ARDGLASS.
28.3.1917: Captured by the German submarine UC 65 and sunk by bombs in St. George's Channel, four miles east of the South Arklow Light Vessel in position 52.41N, 05.51W whilst on a voyage from Port Talbot to Belfast with a cargo of steel.
2.4.1917: Register closed.

3. ARDGOUR 1914-1923
O.N. 137041 778g 373n.
200.0 x 29.1 x 12.8 feet.
T. 3-cyl. by Ross and Duncan, Govan; 95 NHP, 10 knots.
1937: 4SCSA 6-cyl. oil engine made in 1935 by Motorenwerke Mannheim A.G., Mannheim, Germany.
12.2.1914: Launched by George Brown and Company, Greenock (Yard No. 85).
3.1914: Completed.
20.3.1914: Registered in the ownership of Ard Coasters Ltd. (Lang and Fulton Ltd., managers), Greenock as ARDGOUR.
6.8.1914 to 18.8.1914: Requisitioned by the British Government as a collier and Expeditionary Force transport.
10.10.1918: Transferred to Peter MacCallum and Sons Ltd. (Lang and Fulton Ltd., managers), Greenock.
25.10.1923: Sold to Sollas Lines Ltd. (Richards, Longstaff and Co. Ltd., managers), London.
14.12.1923: Renamed YORKDALE.
29.6.1925: Owners became Northminster Steam Ship Co. Ltd. (Richards, Longstaff and Co. Ltd., managers), London.
29.1.1929: Sold to Kilvey Shipping Co. Ltd. (Alfred J.L. Couston, of J.E. Fisher and Co. Ltd., managers), Swansea.
3.1930: Sold to Polski Przemysl Ryzowy W. Krakowie Spolka z Odpowledzialnoscia, Krakow, Poland.
1931: Owners became 'Polryz' S.Z.O.O. (Pantswowe Przedsieborstwo Zegluga Polska, managers), Gdynia, Poland and renamed KOPERNIK.
1933: Managers 'Zegluga Polska' Spolka Akcyjna.
1934: Sold to Onofrio Jacomino, Torre del Greco, Italy and renamed CARLOTTA.
1937: Fitted with oil engine.
19.6.1942: Mined and sunk south of Cattaro, 12 miles off Cape Platamone, whilst on a voyage from Antivari to Ragusa, Italy.

4. ARDGARVEL (1) 1917-1927
O.N. 137049 834g 410n.
200.2 x 30.2 x 12.8 feet.
T. 3-cyl. by Ferguson Brothers (Port Glasgow) Ltd., Port Glasgow; 90 NHP, 600 IHP, 10 knots.
21.11.1916: Launched by Ferguson Brothers (Port Glasgow) Ltd., Port Glasgow (Yard No. 221).
2.7.1917: Registered in the ownership of Ard Coasters Ltd. (Lang and Fulton Ltd., managers), Greenock as ARDGARVEL.

Ardgarvel as the Canadian *Chilliwack*, with extended derricks. *[William A. Schell]*

Ardgour, built especially for the ship-steel trade. *[Lang and Fulton]*

10.10.1918: Transferred to Peter MacCallum and Sons Ltd. (Lang and Fulton Ltd., managers), Greenock.
10.2.1927: Sold to J.H. Welsford and Co. Ltd., Liverpool.
24.2.1927: Sold to Union Steamships Ltd., Vancouver, British Columbia.
29.8.1927: Renamed CHILLIWACK.
8.11.1954: Register closed on sale to the Micronesia Metal and Equipment Co. Inc., Saipan, Marianas Islands and renamed IRON SHIELD under the United States flag, in United Nations' service.
18.3.1955: Delivered to Sumitomo Shoji Kaisha Ltd., Osaka, Japan for breaking up.

Ardgantock (2) aground at Whitby, 12th March 1936. *[J. and M. Clarkson collection]*

5. ARDGANTOCK (1) 1917-1918
O.N. 137057 841g 416n.
200.3 x 30.2 x 12.8 feet.
T. 3-cyl. by Ferguson Brothers (Port Glasgow) Ltd., Port Glasgow; 89.8 NHP, 600 IHP, 10 knots.
12.1917: Completed by Ferguson Brothers (Port Glasgow) Ltd., Port Glasgow (Yard No. 222).
7.12.1917: Registered in the ownership of Ard Coasters Ltd. (Lang and Fulton Ltd., managers), Greenock as ARDGANTOCK.
18.2.1918: Sank following a collision with the destroyer HMS TARTAR off West Hartlepool whilst on a voyage from London to Inverness with a cargo of navigation buoys. This was settled as a war loss, so it was probably a collision whilst in convoy.
3.4.1918: Register closed.

6. ARDGARTAN 1918-1919
O.N. 142261 1,345g 813n.
229.8 x 35.8 x 15.6 feet.
T. 3-cyl. by Ross and Duncan, Govan; 110 NHP, 850 IHP, 9½ knots.
7.6.1918: Launched by the Campbeltown Shipbuilding Co. Ltd., Campbeltown (Yard No. 106).
6.7.1918: Registered in the ownership of the Steamship Ardgartan Co. Ltd. (Lang and Fulton Ltd., managers), Greenock as ARDGARTAN.
12.4.1919: Left Swansea for Brest with a cargo of coal and disappeared.
23.7.1919: Posted missing.
24.10.1919: Register closed.

7. ARDGIRVAN 1918-1919
O.N. 142265 1,342g 1,029n.
230.0 x 35.8 x 15.5 feet.
T. 3-cyl. by Ross and Duncan, Glasgow.
24.9.1918: Launched by the Campbeltown Shipbuilding Co. Ltd., Campbeltown (Yard No. 108).
19.10.1918: Registered in the ownership of the Steamship Ardgartan Co. Ltd. (Lang and Fulton Ltd., managers), Glasgow as ARDGIRVAN.
1919: Sold to the European Gas Co. Ltd. (H.A. Brightman and Co., managers), London and renamed BOLBEC.
1926: Acquired by Harries Brothers and Company, Swansea.
9.1.1943: Sank following a collision with the Dutch steamer JOBSHAVEN (3,528/1916) in position 51.29.15 north, 00.52.16 east whilst on a voyage from Grimsby to Portsmouth with a cargo of coal.
16.9.1943: Refloated and declared a constructive total loss.
16.1.1945: Arrived on the Tyne for repair.
18.1.1958: Arrived at Rotterdam for breaking up by N.V. Verenigde Utrechtse Ijzerhandel, Utrecht.

8. ARDGANTOCK (2) 1919-1955
O.N. 142271 848g 415n.
200.1 x 30.2 x 12.6 feet.
T. 3-cyl. by Aitchison, Blair and Co. Ltd., Clydebank.
6.3.1919: Launched by the Ardrossan Dry Dock and Shipbuilding Co. Ltd., Ardrossan (Yard No. 303).
She had been laid down for the Shipping Controller as WAR TUMMEL.
30.5.1919: Registered in the ownership of Peter MacCallum and Sons Ltd. (Lang and Fulton Ltd., managers), Greenock as ARDGANTOCK.
6.1919: Completed.
2.9.1939: Requisitioned by the British Government as an Armament Store Carrier until 29.9.1945.
1955: Sold to the Kyle Shipping Co. Ltd. (Monroe Brothers, managers), Liverpool and renamed KYLECASTLE.
19.4.1958: Arrived at Barrow to be broken up by T.W. Ward Ltd.

9. ARDGLASS (2) 1919-1935
O.N. 142275 845g 424n.
200.6 x 30.1 x 12.9 feet.
T. 3-cyl. by Aitchison, Blair Ltd., Clydebank.
30.6.1917: Launched by John Fullerton and

Ardgantock (2) post-war (top); note the accommodation aft for DEMS gunners retained to the end of her days, and as *Kylecastle* (middle and bottom). *[W.H. Brown/ World Ship Photo Library; Skyfotos/Roy Fenton collection; World Ship Society Ltd.]*

Company, Paisley (Yard No. 264).
1.10.1919: Registered in the ownership of Peter MacCallum and Sons Ltd. (Lang and Fulton Ltd., managers), Glasgow as ARDGLASS.
16.3.1935: Sold to Monroe Brothers Ltd., Liverpool.
13.5.1935: Renamed KYLE CASTLE.
1.12.1936: Owners became the Kyle Shipping Co. Ltd. (Monroe Brothers, managers), Liverpool.
16.10.1937: Owners became the Walton Steamship Co. Ltd. (F.L. Dawson and Co. Ltd., managers), Newcastle-upon-Tyne.
12.1949: Sold to Elias Macris and John Fonaris, Athens, Greece and renamed THETIS.
1950: Owners became Macris Brothers and J. Fonaris, Athens.
12.1959: Breaking up began in Greece.

10. ARDGRYFE 1920-1959
O.N. 142318 964g 481n.
200.4 x 31.2 x 13.2 feet.
T. 3-cyl. by Aitchison, Blair Ltd., Glasgow; 106 NHP, 850 IHP, 10 knots.
3.1918: Completed by the Ardrossan Dockyard and Shipbuilding Co. Ltd., Ardrossan (Yard No. 270).

Ardglass (2) on 8th April 1932 (top). *[Ships in Focus]*
Ardglass as *Kyle Castle* on 8th February 1949 whilst in the ownership of the Walton Steamship Co. Ltd. (middle). From close examination of this photograph and others of the same vessel her name appears to be displayed as *Kylecastle*. *[World Ship Society Ltd.]*
Seen in May 1957 *Ardgryfe* spent a long period of time laid-up in Morpeth Dock, Birkenhead (bottom). *[Ships in Focus]*

1.3.1918: Registered in the ownership of Mead, Son and Hussey, London as ST. DUNSTANS HILL.
14.4.1920: Acquired by Peter MacCallum and Sons Ltd. (Lang and Fulton Ltd., managers), Greenock and renamed ARDGRYFE.
23.6.1941: Requisitioned by the British Government until 23.2.1946.
2.12.1959: Arrived at Preston from Birkenhead in tow of MARIE LAMEY to be broken up by T.W. Ward Ltd.

11. ARDGARROCH 1920-1936
O.N. 142743 968g 501n.
200.2 x 31.2 x 13.2 feet.
T. 3-cyl. by Aitchison, Blair Ltd., Clydebank; 106 NHP, 850 IHP, 10 knots.
13.12.1918: Completed by the Ardrossan Dry Dock and Shipbuilding Co. Ltd., Ardrossan (Yard No. 271).
13.12.1918: Registered in the ownership of Mead, Son and Hussey, London as PORTLAND HOUSE.
15.4.1920: Acquired by Peter MacCallum and Sons Ltd. (Lang and Fulton Ltd., managers), Greenock.
12.5.1920: Renamed ARDGARROCH.
18.8.1936: Sold to the Mersey Ports Stevedoring Co. Ltd. (William J. McKnight, manager), Liverpool.
2.9.1937: Sold to the Bristol Steam Navigation Co. Ltd., Bristol.
5.11.1937: Renamed CAPITO.
7.1950: Sold to the Société Navale Caennaise (G. Lamy et Compagnie, managers), Caen, France and renamed NEREE.
29.11.1952: Arrived on the Thames to be broken up by T.W. Ward Ltd.
2.12.1952: Work began at Grays, Essex.

12. ARDGLEN 1953-1972
O.N. 185762 1,044g 496n.
221.4 x 34.4 x 13. 8 feet.
6-cyl. 2SCSA oil engine by British Polar Engines Ltd., Glasgow; 171 NHP, 10½ knots.
19.12.1952: Launched by James Lamont and Co. Ltd., Port Glasgow (Yard No. 377).
11.3.1953: Registered in the ownership of Peter MacCallum and Sons Ltd., Greenock as ARDGLEN.
1972: Sold to Hortiatis Shipping Co. Ltd., Famagusta, Cyprus (G. Dalacouras and J. Alexiou, Piraeus, Greece) and renamed NENI.
1973: Sold to Kalthos Shipping Company, Famagusta, Cyprus (Provasion Marine and Trading Co. S.A., Piraeus) and renamed MARIANTHI.
1976: Sold to Kalpomare Shipping Co. Ltd., Limassol, Cyprus (Kalpogiannakis Shipping Lines Co. Ltd., Piraeus) and renamed KALPOGIORGOS.
1977: Renamed ARDGLEN
1977: Sold to Evrytos Shipping Corporation, Panama and renamed LITTLE NOTA.

Ardgryfe on Ward's grid-iron at Preston awaiting demolition. *[J. and M. Clarkson]*

Ardgarroch (above), and following sale to France and with a new bridge, as *Neree* (below). *[The Bristol Series; Fotoflite incorporating Skyfotos/Roy Fenton collection].*

1978: Sold to Oman Shipping Lines, Dubai, United Arab Republic and renamed LUBNA.
1.9.1982: Breaking up began at Gadani Beach by Karachi Shipyard and Engineering Works Ltd. She had been laid up at Karachi in damaged condition since 1978.

13. ARDGARRY 1957-1962
O.N. 185785 1,074g 507n.
221.3 x 34.4 x 13.7 feet.
8-cyl. 2SCSA oil engine by H. Widdop and Co. Ltd., Keighley; 10½ knots.
16.1.1957: Launched by James Lamont and Co. Ltd., Port Glasgow (Yard No. 388).
14.5.1957: Registered in the ownership of Peter MacCallum and Sons Ltd., Greenock as ARDGARRY.
29.12.1962: Foundered in the English Channel whilst on a voyage from Swansea to Rouen with a cargo of coal.

14. ARDGARVEL (2) 1965-1975
O.N. 306955 1,121g 486n.
223.0 x 35.5 x 14.5 feet.
4-cyl. 2SCSA oil engine by British Polar Engines Ltd., Glasgow; 1,100 BHP, 11 knots.
24.9.1964: Launched by James Lamont and Co. Ltd., Port Glasgow (Yard No. 402).
25.1.1965: Registered in the ownership of Peter MacCallum and Sons Ltd., Greenock as ARDGARVEL
1975: Sold to Henry W. Peabody Grain Ltd. (Fife Shipping Co. Ltd.), London, renamed BALMERINO and later registered in Singapore.
1977: Manager became Crescent Shipping Ltd., Rochester.
1977: Sold to Marpro Ltd., London and renamed MARIYOS HOPE.
1980: Sold to Concord Credit (N.S.G. Exports Ltd., managers), London, renamed ANGELINA S and registered in Georgetown, Cayman Islands.
1982: Sold to Balm Maritime Co. Ltd., Limassol, Cyprus, renamed DIANA and registered in San Lorenzo, Honduras.
1987: Renamed RAMKO and registered in Colombo, Sri Lanka.
1989: Sold to Abdul Rahman Hijazi, renamed ARADOUS I and registered in Kingstown, St. Vincent and the Grenadines.
1989: Sold to Agusta Campania Naviera (Seadoll Chartering Co. Ltd., managers), Limassol, Cyprus, renamed TADMOR and registered in San Lorenzo, Honduras.
1992: Converted to a livestock carrier with tonnages 397g 164n.
1997: Renamed LAILA H. Laid up at Valletta, Malta.
18.9.2001: Arrived at Aliaga, Turkey for demolition by Ege Gemi Sokum Sanayi Ve Ticaret A.S.

Ardglen at Liverpool (top). *[J. and M. Clarkson]*
Ardgarry (upper middle). *[Fotoflite incorporating Skyfotos/Roy Fenton collection]*
Ardgarvel arriving at Birkenhead after being sold and renamed *Balmerino* (lower middle). *[Ships in Focus]*
Mariyos Hope, ex *Ardgarvel* sailing from Preston 7th October 1978 (bottom). *[J. and M. Clarkson]*

Managed for the Kindiesel Shipping Co. Ltd.

KINDIESEL 1936-1942
O.N. 165219 339g 180g.
142.7 x 25.1 x 9.2 feet.
4-cyl. 2SCSA oil engine by J.G. Kincaid and Co. Ltd., Greenock; 47 NHP, 300 BHP, 400 IHP, 9 knots.
15.7.1936: Launched by the Ardrossan Dockyard Ltd., Ardrossan (Yard No. 361).
25.8.1936: Registered in the ownership of the Kindiesel Shipping Co. Ltd. (Peter MacCallum and Sons Ltd., managers), Greenock as KINDIESEL.
10.1.1942: Sold to Lovering and Sons Ltd., Cardiff.
7.11.1951: Register closed on sale to Skibs A/S Karlander (Egil Paulsen), Fredrikstad, Norway and renamed SLETTER.
1956: Sold to Trygve Klovning, Haugesund, Norway and renamed SENATOR.
1959: Sold to Abraham Bjellebø, Haugesund.
1966: Sold to Gunnar Årseth Partrederi, Ålesund, Norway.
31.1.1969: Wrecked off Vinga Light, Göteborg Archipelago, Sweden following engine trouble whilst on a voyage from Göteborg to Helsingborg in ballast.

Managed for the Ministry of War Transport

1. MARGO 1940-1947
O.N. 168621 1,2452g 736n.
232.8 x 34.4 x 13.8 feet.
T. 3-cyl. by Flensburger Schiffsbau Gesellschaft, Flensburg, Germany; 106 NHP, 500 IHP, 8½ knots.
6.3.1895: Launched by Flensburger Schiffsbau Gesellschaft, Flensburg (Yard No. 153).
30.3.1895: Completed for A.G. Dampfschiffs-Rhederei von 1889, Hamburg, Germany as GUTRUNE
26.4.1902: Sold to Woermann Linie K.G., Hamburg and renamed LINDA WOERMANN.
8.1914: Laid up at Beira.
23.2.1916: Seized by the Portuguese Government, subsequently transferred to Transportes Maritimos do Estado, Lisbon and renamed PUNGUÉ.
1925: Sold to S. Benoliel & Azancot, Lisbon and renamed LUNA
1927: Sold to Société Anonyme Coöpérative de Navigation, Marseille, France and renamed VILLE D'ALEXANDRETTE.
1.1929: Sold to Slobodna Bokeska Plovidba, Tivat, Yugoslavia and renamed ANTON IVOVIC.
7.1934: Sold to Alfred Kalm, Tallinn, Estonia and renamed MARGO.
7.9.1934: Beached in Tallinn Roads following outbreak of fire in her timber cargo whilst on a voyage from Parnu to Tallinn.
9.9.1934: Fire extinguished. Later settled as a compromised total loss, repaired and returned to service.

Norwegian *Sletter,* the former *Kindiesel. [J. and M. Clarkson]*

25.12.1940: Registered at Cardiff in the ownership of the Ministry of Shipping, London (Peter MacCallum and Co. Ltd., Greenock, managers) as MARGO.
20.3.1946: Owners became the Ministry of Transport, London.
3.11.1947: Scuttled west south west of Brest in position 47.36 north, 09.31 west with a cargo of 1,259 tons of poison gas ammunition.
10.2.1948: Register closed.

2. EMPIRE BANK 1941-1942
O.N. 167107 402g 183n.
143.6 x 26.1 x 9.9 feet.
7-cyl. 2SCSA oil engine by Crossley Brothers Ltd., Manchester; 9 knots, 385 NHP,
12.4.1941: Launched by Henry Scarr Ltd., Hessle (Yard No. 417).
25.7.1941: Registered in the ownership of the Ministry of War Transport, London (Peter MacCallum and Sons Ltd., Greenock, managers) as EMPIRE BANK.
8.1941: Completed.
1942: Managers became Metcalf Motor Coasters Ltd., London.
1945: Acquired by Metcalf Motor Coasters Ltd., London.
3.10.1946: Renamed ROSE-JULIE M.
13.7.1955: Transferred to Mac Shipping Co. Ltd., Glasgow (Thomas J. Metcalf, London, manager).
1.1966: Arrived at Queenborough for demolition.
19.3.1968: Register closed.

Although in their records as being managed by MacCallum during the Second World War, the following vessel was never registered in the UK.

3. NORDÖST 1942-1943
1,035g 537n.
216.2 x 34.6 x 15.5 feet.
T. 3-cyl. by C.A. Kuipers, Rotterdam, Netherlands; 83 NHP, 9 knots.
4.1919: Completed by De Haan & Oerlemans, Heusden, Netherlands (Yard No. 52) for A/S Det Dansk-Franske Dampskibsselskab (A.N. Petersen, manager), Copenhagen, Denmark as LIFLAND
1920: Sold to Rederi A/B Nord & Östersjöfart (Axel Nordström, manager), Göteborg, Sweden and renamed NORDÖST.
1945: Transferred to Nordströms Rederi A/B (Axel Nordström, manager), Göteborg.
6.1955: Sold to A/B Väring, Stockholm, Sweden.
9.1955: Sold for demolition and broken up at Travemünde by Alnwick Harmstorf Bergungs-Reederei.

Empire Bank on the Thames as *Rose-Julie M,* in the ownership of Metcalf Motor Coasters Ltd. *[World Ship Society Ltd.]*

BRITISH TRAMP SHIPPING 1914-1939: CASE STUDIES IN FLEET REBUILDING AND RENEWAL

Malcolm Cooper

The three decades before the outbreak of the First World War witnessed a quantum increase in British steam tramp ownership. This growth was primarily stimulated by the development of the international economy, embracing both industrialisation in developed countries and a widening import-export network between them and primary producers of such commodities as food, fuel and forest products. Within the industry itself, the most significant trigger was the advent in the mid-1880s of the triple-expansion engine and the replacement of iron by steel hulls which together enabled larger and more economical steamers to drive sailing vessels from one long-distance ocean trade after another. Although the tramp trades themselves were becoming increasingly cyclical, with longer troughs and shorter albeit sharper peaks, and although competition from foreign fleets was mounting, the United Kingdom maintained a significant sectoral leadership, playing host to some of the largest fleets in the world.

The largest British tramp fleets owed their growth to a combination of strong management and wide access to capital. These factors were mutually reinforcing, the consistent provision of good dividends stimulating a widening appetite for shares in new vessels among strongly localized investment communities. Profitability itself was anchored in the massive British coal export trade, a factor which led some shipowners to pursue vertical integration via direct investment in domestic collieries. With outwards voyages thus underwritten, British shipowners were able to offer competitive rates on the large import trades, most notably those of grain from the Black Sea and South America. Finally, the position of London as the primary international centre for ship chartering, broking and insurance, assisted British owners in winning and retaining a large market share in the cross trades around the globe, even in the face of growing competition from the fleets of such countries as Norway, Greece and, in the Pacific, Japan. The result of all these factors for the tramp sector leaders was generally good profitability leading to steady fleet growth and renewal. The vessels themselves grew larger and their engines more powerful, but design innovation was unspectacular, experiments like the Doxford Turret ship being driven as much by efforts to get around port and canal charges levied on measurement tonnage as by operational efficiency gains.

The entire picture changed after war began in August 1914. Vessel losses to enemy action, largely through submarine attack, were extremely heavy. Most large firms lost at least half of their fleet, some even more. The uncertainties of the war itself made the replacement of these losses a difficult issue, one that was made more complex by the progressive inflation in second-hand values and new-building prices, and often uneven match-ups between the latter and war loss insurance receipts. The arrival of peace in November 1918 brought not relief but a fresh set of challenges. Artificially high freight rates, themselves partly the result of port congestion and fleet dislocation, attracted a wave of speculative investment which drove vessel prices even higher. This promised new dawn for shipping investment proved a mirage; with freight rates reverting to more normal levels, the asset bubble burst, driving many new owners into the arms of their creditors and releasing a wave of over-priced tonnage into a market already unbalanced by the arrival of hundreds of 'standard' ships ordered for government account during the war, but largely delivered after it.

Tramp shipping markets began to return to some semblance of normality after 1922, and owners who had decided to rebuild their fleets began to invest what would for the more prudent have been significant financial reserves in what was now reasonably priced tonnage. Trading conditions, however, remained challenging throughout the 1920s, doing little more than matching pre-war levels from 1923 to 1927 and then slipping slightly below them in 1928-29. The collapse of world financial markets in late 1929 and the four-year long Great Depression which followed made even the 1920s look prosperous. British tramps made their way to long-term lay-up in estuaries around the U.K. coast and shipbuilding came to a near complete stop, with almost every yard closing, some for good. The curtains did not really begin to lift until 1934 and, even then, confidence remained fragile. Most surviving tramp companies began to invest again, but even with Government assistance through subsidised loans, fleet renewal remained cautious right up to the beginning of the Second World War in 1939.

The market-leading British tramp companies, which had developed substantial businesses throughout the cyclical swings of the pre-1914 era, had thus to face far greater and more diverse challenges in the 25 years which followed. Some either did not survive or were sold to new owners. Those that carried on successfully employed a range of different business models and fleet renewal and replacement strategies. This study considers the record of four leading tramp operators between 1914 and 1939: Maclay and McIntyre of Glasgow, Ropner of West Hartlepool, Runciman of Newcastle and Watts, Watts and Company of London, each of which faced the range of challenges enumerated above in different ways.

Four tramp fleets in 1914

Joseph Maclay and Walter McIntyre of Glasgow began business in 1885 with the acquisition of six ships, five of them second-hand. Thereafter the firm added new ships steadily but became a consistently aggressive participant in the second-hand market, buying vessels across a wide age spectrum and selling even the newest members of the fleet if the price was right. The partners moved into limited liability almost immediately, but used multiple single-ship companies, only beginning to consolidate the fleet into larger corporate entities in their third decade of operations. At the outbreak of the war, Maclay and McIntyre controlled one of the largest but most heterogeneous British tramp fleets, second-hand acquisitions accounting for 19 of its 48 vessels. Average vessel age was high at over 13 years, this being partially due to the presence of six ships built in the 1880s, three of these iron-hulled, compound-engine antiques from 1881-82. The

One of a number of Maclay and McIntyre acquisitions that were given names beginning 'M', *Meraggio* (2,418/1889) was built by Raylton Dixon and Company, Middlesbrough as *Hibernia* for Christopher Marwood, Whitby. Bought in 1906, Maclay and McIntyre registered her under one of their many single-ship companies, the Steam Ship Meraggio Co. Ltd. She was sold in 1914 to Greece as *Empros*, but was abandoned off Brest on 13th November 1916 following a collision with Ellerman's *City of Cairo* (7,882/1915). *[Roy Fenton collection]*

company had no single naming convention; while most new ships were given African place-names ending in 'A', others were given derivatives of women's names (*Janeta*, *Jeanara*, *Marthara* and *Magdala*), while some repeated names were imported into the fleet through acquisition (*Meraggio*, *Merannio* of 1891 and *Mersario* of 1906).

Robert Ropner, a German emigrant, had entered ship ownership in 1868 as a partner in the West Hartlepool firm of Appleby, Ropner and Company, before going solo in 1874 with a fleet of five. Already a man of some standing in the local business community, he was able to attract capital to fund rapid fleet expansion. In 1888 he achieved vertical integration by acquiring the Stockton shipyard of Mountjoy Pearse and Company, a builder which as Ropner and Son would supply all the firm's new vessels from the *Maltby* of 1889 until the early 1920s. At the same time, Ropner began giving his ships Yorkshire place-names ending in *-by*. These vessels would continue to be owned on the traditional 64th share basis until 1919, but in 1903 it was decided to set up a limited liability company to attract a different type of investor, the new creation being the Pool Shipping Co. Ltd., whose ships were given compound names ending *-pool*. The new company, whose ships were generally larger than their opposite numbers, was an immediate success, matching the number of 64th owned vessels within a decade. By 1914, the combined fleet was 55 strong, only two of which had been acquired second-hand, and was the largest tramping concern not only in Britain but in the world. Ropner tended to retain his vessels significantly longer than many of his peers, and six of this fleet were at least 20 years old. The average fleet age, however, was just over 11 years, due to the presence of 12 vessels built in 1910-14. In the middle of the fleet age-wise were no fewer than 19 Trunk deck steamers built between 1896 and 1908, products of Ropner's only partially successful attempt to match the Doxford Turret ship.

Walter Runciman, a former master mariner, had entered ship ownership at South Shields in 1885 with the purchase of one small, 20-year old steamer. He ordered his first new vessel in 1889, adopting the *-moor* nomenclature with which he became synonymous, and thereafter began to increase his fleet steadily, adding new ships in every year bar two between 1894 and 1914. Runciman's normal practice was to replace ships as they reached middle age, and by the second decade of the 20th century he had achieved a steady

Newby (2,168/1890) was an early product of the yard Ropner bought at Stockton-on-Tees. She was sold to Temple, Thomson and Clark in 1915, only to fall victim to *U 35* which sank her with gunfire on 26th September 1916 in the Mediterranean whilst on a voyage from Saint Rafael to Larne. *[The Bristol Series]*

Seen in the Humber Runciman's Doxford Turret *Jerseymoor* of 1901 was wrecked on Burbo Bank in the River Mersey when arriving with a cargo of wheat from Bombay on 23rd June 1915. *[Barnard and Straker/J. and M. Clarkson]*

programme of rolling fleet renewal. At the outbreak of the war he controlled a very modern fleet of 35 vessels with an average age of just over eight years. Most of these ships were owned by the Moor Line Ltd., but there were several other small ship-owning companies under management, including the Novocastrian Shipping Co. Ltd., which Runciman had taken over in 1907. While most ships were registered at London, company headquarters remained on the Tyne. Runciman had been one of the more enthusiastic buyers of Doxford Turret ships, and there were 11 of these vessels in the fleet in 1914 including the fleet's only second-hand purchase (the *Queenmoor* of 1903) and the last ship built to the design at Doxford's Pallion shipyard (the *Orangemoor* of 1911).

Watts, Watts and Company, the smallest of the four concerns in this study, was also by far the oldest; Edmund Hannay Watts, a native of Blyth, having first gone into business in partnership with William Milburn of Newcastle as Watts, Milburn and Company in 1857. Watts subsequently moved to London and, on the dissolution of the original partnership in 1879, carried on his ship management business first as Watts, Ward and Company, and then from 1895 as Watts, Watts and Company. Watts was one of the first tramp owners to move to limited liability, forming the Britain Steamship Co. Ltd. in 1884 to take over ownership of all the company's ships, which had hitherto been owned on the traditional 64th share basis. By 1914, the company was controlled by E.H. Watts' second son, the impressively named Fenwick Shadforth Watts. The 20-strong fleet had a normal size profile but was slightly above average age, the latter feature being largely the product of the hiatus in new vessel additions between 1905 and 1911. Only four ships were second-hand additions, of which the oldest, the 1887-built *Woolwich*, was also the most unusual, having started life as the T. and J. Harrison cargo-liner *Electrician*. The Watts had their own distinct nomenclature, calling most of their ships after London suburbs, but occasionally falling victim to a weakness for further-flung locales with military (*Aldershot* and *Sandhurst*), and sporting or royal (*Ascot*, *Henley* and *Windsor*) connections.

Watts' first *Ascot*, built in 1902 by Napier and Miller Ltd. at Glasgow. One of the oldest ships of the Britain Steamship Co. Ltd. in 1914, she steamed through the First World War and on until 1931 when she was broken up at Genoa. She had one serious accident, when a fire broke out in her cargo of oilcake she had loaded in the Black Sea in August 1927. The fire was detected off Bizerta, and when she arrived at Gibraltar had spread to three of her holds. To make matters worse, in thick fog she hit the Admiralty Mole whilst berthing, seriously damaging her bow and flooding the forepeak. The fire, which spread to the fourth hold, was not extinguished for over a week. Given her age, it is surprising that she lasted another four years. *[The Bristol Series]*

The impact of war, 1914-1918

The four companies together lost no fewer than 70 vessels to enemy action during the First World War (all but four of them to submarines or submarine-laid mines), together with another 11 to a variety of marine causes (including one vessel posted missing whose loss might have been due to war causes). Just three submarines, *U 35*, *U 38* and *U 39*, accounted for 18 of the losses between them, but this was not coincidental as these were the three most successful U-boats of the war, which together sank 519 ships totalling just under one and one quarter million gross tons. The two companies whose fleets were not significantly affected by wartime sales or purchases each lost roughly half of their vessels. Ropner, the largest operator, lost 24 ships to the enemy and a further four to marine causes. Losses were rarely spread evenly, and Ropner suffered a flurry of early casualties, including two veterans, the *Glenby* of 1900 and the *Kirkby* of 1891, part of a 10-vessel haul sunk by *U 38* in the St. George's Channel on 17th August 1915. The firm was unlucky to lose three of its ships to three different German commerce raiders in distant waters, but the most striking feature of its losses was the uneven spread of casualties across its two fleets, only two of the losses coming from the 14-strong Pool Shipping Company.

The smaller Runciman fleet suffered higher percentage losses: 18 to the enemy and three to shipwreck. The first two of these losses, the brand new *Spennymoor* and then the *Tullochmoor*, were sunk within hours of each other on 28th May 1915 in the western entrance to the English Channel by *U 41*.

Both Maclay and McIntyre and Watts lost 12 ships to the enemy and another three to marine accidents. At the beginning of the war, the Glasgow fleet had been more than twice the size of the London one, but the statistical burden of casualties was more even than first appears to be the case, as large scale Maclay and McIntyre vessel disposals were matched by equally significant second-hand acquisitions on the part of Watts.

War and marine losses, August 1914 – November 1918: Maclay and McIntyre

Vessel	Tons/Built	Lost	Cause	Location
MASCARA	4,957/1912	2.7.1915	Wrecked	White Sea near Danilov Island
MEADOWFIELD	2,750/1904	9.7.1915	U 20	St. George's Channel south west of Tuskar Rock
JEANARA	4,386/1907	10.7.1915	Wrecked	White Sea north west of Gorodetsky Light
MANGARA	1,784/1889	28.7.1915	UB 16	North Sea east of Aldeburgh, Suffolk
CAIRO	1,698/1882	13.8.1915	U 24	St. George's Channel south south west of Tuskar Rock
SAMARA	3,172/1906	19.8.1915	U 38	North Atlantic west of Bishop Rock
MASUNDA	4,952/1909	28.2.1916	U 35	Mediterranean south west of Cape Matapan
CRAIGENDORAN	2,783/1899	3.3.1917	UC 37	Mediterranean east of Cape Sigli, Algeria
VICTORIA	1,620/1887	29.4.1917	UB 21	North Sea north east of Scarborough
IRTHINGTON	2,845/1897	23.9.1917	UC 53	Mediterranean east north east of Capo Vaticano, Italy
MADURA	4,484/1901	18.10.1917	U 62	North Atlantic west south west of Bishop Rock
NYASSA	2,579/1897	24.11.1917	UB 57	English Channel east south east of the Lizard
MEREDDIO	3,069/1897	11.1.1918	U 84	Bay of Biscay west of Quiberon
KASSANGA	3,015/1899	20.3.1918	U 103	St. George's Channel south east of Arklow Light
INDUNA	4,426/1898	11.7.1918	Collision	South Atlantic north east of River Plate
RUTHERGLEN	4,214/1906	24.7.1918	UB 50	Mediterranean east south east of Port Mahon, Minorca
NYANZA	4,053/1897	29.9.1918	UB 95	North Channel north west of Corsewall Point Light

Maclay and McIntyre's final war loss was *Nyanza* in September 1918, en route from Cardiff to Archangel with coal. She had been built in 1897 for the Steam Ship Nyanza Co. Ltd. by Alexander Stephen and Sons, Linthouse, Glasgow. She was photographed at Penarth. *[Roy Fenton collection]*

Dromonby was one of three Ropner ships to be sunk by German commerce raiders, captured by *Möwe* on 13th January 1916 and scuttled with explosives whilst on a voyage from Cardiff to Cape Verde with coal. *[The Bristol Series]*

War and marine losses, August 1914 – November 1918: Ropner				
Vessel	**Tons/Built**	**Lost**	**Cause**	**Location**
HAWNBY	2,136/1895	10.9.1914	Wrecked	North Sea near Montrose
SELBY	2,137/1895	30.9.1914	Mined	North Sea south east of Newarp Light
WILLERBY	3,630/1912	20.2.1915	PRINZ EITEL-FRIEDRICH	South Atlantic north east of Pernambuco
OAKBY	1,976/1897	23.2.1915	U 8	English Channel east of Royal Sovereign Light
COLEBY	3,824/1907	27.3.1915	KRONPRINZ WILHELM	South Atlantic north east of Pernambuco
GADSBY	3,497/1899	1.7.1915	U 39	North Atlantic south south west of Wolf Rock
GLENBY	2,196/1900	17.8.1915	U 38	St. George's Channel west of the Smalls
KIRKBY	3,034/1891	17.8.1915	U 38	St. George's Channel west of Bardsey
SCAWBY	3,658/1911	6.10.1915	U 33	Mediterranean east of Malta
DROMONBY	3,627/1900	13.1.1916	MÖWE	North Atlantic west of Lisbon
ASHBY	1,947/1896	15.2.1916	Wrecked	English Channel off Ushant
THORNABY	1,730/1889	28.2.1916	UC 3 (mine)	North Sea north east of Shipwash Light
TRUNKBY	2,635/1896	27.5.1916	U 39	Mediterranean south of Port Mahon, Minorca
SALMONPOOL	4,905/1913	1.6.1916	U 39	Mediterranean north east of Cape Carbon, Algeria
WRAGBY	3,641/1901	4.1.1917	UC 37	North Atlantic west of Cape Spartel
MARTIN	1,904/1895	14.1.1917	UC 18	English Channel north of Ushant
BURNBY	3,655/1905	26.2.1917	U 39	Mediterranean north of Cape Falcon, Algeria
DALEBY	3,628/1900	29.4.1917	U 70	North Atlantic north west of the Fastnet
WESTONBY	3,795/1901	15.6.1917	U 82	North Atlantic south west of the Fastnet
BROOKBY	3,679/1905	19.6.1917	U 60	North Atlantic south of the Fastnet
THIRLBY	2,009/1898	2.7.1917	UC 31	North Atlantic north west of the Fastnet
TEESDALE	2,470/1904	2.8.1917	Foundered	North Sea north of Saltburn Pier
ROLLESBY	3,955/1906	15.9.1917	U 48	North Sea east north east of Muckle Flugga
ROMANBY	3,835/1908	23.12.1917	Collision	North Atlantic
MALTBY	3,977/1906	26.2.1918	UC 27	Mediterranean south west of Pantellaria
ROCKPOOL	4,502/1912	2.3.1918	U 94	North Atlantic north east of Eagle Island, Ireland
MOUNTBY	3,263/1898	10.6.1918	UC 49	English Channel east of the Lizard
BALDERSBY	3,613/1913	28.9.1918	UB 91	St. George's Channel east of Coding Light

Right: 19 of the 44 Trunk deck ships built at Stockton-on-Tees were for Ropner's own account. This is the last but one of these, *Coleby*, which was sunk by the German auxiliary cruiser *Kronprinz Wilhelm* in March 1915. *[Roy Fenton collection]*

Left: Runciman's oldest war losses were the 1894-built *Glenmoor* built by Priestman at Sunderland seen here in the Avon, and *Fernmoor* from Readhead at South Shields. *[The Bristol Series]*.

War and marine losses, August 1914 – November 1918: Runciman				
Vessel	**Tons/Built**	**Lost**	**Cause**	**Location**
BLAKEMOOR	3,752/1901	14.2.1915	Wrecked*	North Sea on Specton Sands, Yorkshire
SPENNYMOOR	3,992/1915	28.5.1915	U 41	English Channel south west of Start Point
TULLOCHMOOR	3,520/1899	28.5.1915	U 41	English Channel north of Ushant
JERSEYMOOR	3,746/1901	23.6.1915	Wrecked	River Mersey on Burbo Bank
INGLEMOOR	4,331/1912	1.7.1915	U 39	English Channel south west of the Lizard
LINKMOOR	4,306/1914	20.9.1915	U 35	Mediterranean west of Cape Matapan
GLENMOOR	3,075/1894	6.11.1915	U 38	Mediterranean north east of Cap de Fer, Tunisia
ROSEMOOR	4,303/1914	17.7.1916	U 39	Mediterranean north east of Algiers
GRANGEMOOR	3,198/1911	20.7.1916	U 39	Mediterranean north west of Algiers
HOPEMOOR	3,740/1911	14.2.1917	U 60	North Atlantic north west of the Skellings
DUNBARMOOR	3,651/1903	8.3.1917	U 44	North Atlantic west north west of the Fastnet
FERNMOOR	2,300/1894	17.4.1917	U 35	North Atlantic west of Gibraltar
NENTMOOR	3,535/1903	20.4.1917	U 35	North Atlantic west of Gibraltar
CLODMOOR	3,753/1902	3.5.1917	UB 40	English Channel south west of Newhaven
ELMMOOR	3,744/1910	23.5.1917	UC 67	Mediterranean east of Syracuse, Sicily
FORESTMOOR	2,844/1910	5.10.1917	UB 51	North Atlantic west of Cape Spartel
VENTMOOR	3,456/1900	14.2.1918	UC 37	Aegean south west of Skyros Light
USKMOOR	3,189/1912	5.3.1918	UB 80	English Channel south west of Prawle Point
MARSTONMOOR	2,744/1906	14.4.1918	U 107	North Atlantic north north east of Cape Wrath
WESTMOOR	4,329/1911	1.7.1918	U 91	North Atlantic north west of Casablanca
YORKMOOR	4,253/1912	16.7.1918	Wrecked	River Plate on Lobos Island
(* BLAKEMOOR abandoned to underwriters; subsequently repaired and sold to T.G. Berg, London for further trading)				

Right: The first ship lost to Runciman during the war was the Doxford Turret *Blakemoor*, which went aground at Specton Sands, Yorkshire on 14th February 1915 whilst on a ballast voyage from London to the Tyne. Although refloated, Runciman presumably was happy with the insurance payout, and in 1916 the underwriters sold her to the Berg Shipping Co. Ltd., Cardiff. In 1920 she was renamed *Wye Valley* and transferred to another company managed by T.C. Berg, the Wye Shipping Co. Ltd. But it did not prosper, and its last ship was sold in 1925, *Wye Valley* having already been sold in 1923 to Richards, Longstaff and Co., London to become *Yorkvalley*. She went for scrap in Italy during 1926.

Bottom: *Marstonmoor* was built by J. Blumer and Company, Newcastle for Runciman's Moor Line Ltd. in 1906. She was torpedoed and sunk on 14th April 1918 in position 59.34 north, 04.54 west after sailing from Milford Haven with mail, coal and general cargo for Murmansk, presumably to support forces trying to counter the Bolshevik revolution in Russia. *[Both; The Bristol Series/J. and M. Clarkson]*

One of Watt's 1916 acquisition was the *Reynolds* from Bolton Steam Shipping Co. Ltd., London which became *Chertsey*. Built by J.L. Thompson and Sons Ltd., Sunderland, she was sunk by torpedo and gunfire from UC 67 just north of Algiers on 26th April 1917 when bound for Alexandria with Tyne coal. The Mediterranean remained a dangerous place for British ships from mid-1915 to the end of the war. *[Roy Fenton collection]*

Watts embarked on a buying spree in 1916, but continuing losses in the remaining war years more than made up for the additions. *Talavera* was one of four remaining ships of the Scholefield Shipping Co. Ltd. of Newcastle bought in 1916. Like others in the Watts' fleet, she had been built by Ropners. Renamed *Taplow*, she left Huelva with copper ore for Port Talbot on 5th June 1917 and disappeared, presumably torpedoed. *[Roy Fenton collection]*

War and marine losses, August 1914 – November 1918: Watts, Watts				
Vessel	**Tons/Built**	**Lost**	**Cause**	**Location**
DULWICH	3,276/1893	15.2.1915	U 16	English Channel north north east of Cap D'Antifer
RICHMOND	3,214/1904	1.7.1915	U 39	North Atlantic south west of Wolf Rock
FINCHLEY	4,174/1912	20.8.1915	Wrecked	White Sea on Trek Island
WOOLWICH	2,936/1887	3.11.1915	U 35	Mediterranean south of Cape Sidero, Crete
CHERTSEY	3,264/1898	26.4.1917	UC 67	Mediterranean north of Algiers
LEWISHAM	2,810/1898	17.5.1917	U 46	North Atlantic west of Ireland
TAPLOW	2,891/1905	5.6.1917	Missing	Bay of Biscay
TOTTENHAM	3,106/1906	14.6.1917	U 35	Mediterranean south west of Planier Island
HIGHBURY	4,831/1912	14.6.1917	U 82	North Atlantic west south west of Bishop Rock
MOLESEY	3,218/1912	30.11.1917	UB 81	English Channel south west of Brighton Light
GREENWICH	2,938/1899	5.12.1917	UC 67	Mediterranean south of Planier Island
ROMFORD	3,035/1898	10.2.1918	UC 54 (mine)	Mediterranean east of Cape Carthage
HENLEY	3,249/1894	10.4.1918	UB 109	English Channel south west of the Lizard
ISLEWORTH	2,871/1896	30.4.1918	UC 17	English Channel south west of Ventnor
PETERSHAM	3,381/1899	5.5.1918	Collision	Bristol Channel north of Trevose Head
SANDHURST	3,034/1897	6.5.1918	UB 72	North Channel north west of Corsewall Point Light
CHATHAM	3,592/1904	21.5.1918	k.u.k. U 34	Mediterranean south west of Cape Matapan

Sedgepool of 1918 was a rare example of a new ship added to one of the four tramp fleets during the First World War. She was sunk by *U 99* west of the Hebrides on 19th October 1940 whilst carrying a cargo of Canadian wheat to Manchester. Three members of the crew were lost. *[Roy Fenton collection]*

The four companies together took delivery of only six new ships during the war. Three of these went to Runciman and one to Maclay and McIntyre in 1915, all but one of the former having been ordered before the war. Watts was not active at all, having built its last new ship in 1912. Ropner was unusual in adding two new vessels in 1917-18. The cost of these two vessels (both built by the company's own yard and thus presumably free of oversize builder mark-up) is indicative of the ongoing increase in prices. The *Swainby* of 1917 cost £73,428 compared to the £58,769 paid for a similar ship in 1913. Her successor, the *Sedgepool* of 1918, was larger by some 15%, but that alone came nowhere near accounting for a doubling of price to £149,520. Overall, there was little private sector new building during the last two years of the war, partially because of the very steep inflation in contract prices, and partially because a large part of yard capacity was taken up by the Government's standard ship construction programme. Even Ropner, whose two new vessels became in turn comfortably the largest ships to join the fleet, probably only undertook new building to take up spare capacity at its own shipyard.

The First World War years witnessed a much higher than usual turnover in ship ownership in both the tramp and liner sectors, this despite new Government legislation which prohibited sales to foreign owners. There were several factors at play here. Some ship owners sold up either because death (often in military service) disrupted plans for family ownership succession, or because the operational challenges of maintaining their business simply became too great. As the war wore on, the second-hand market gained fresh strength from progressive increases in asset values. This was a two-way process. Buyers, often relative newcomers to the industry, paid higher and higher prices for tonnage whose earning potential itself appeared to be multiplying under the stimulus of spiralling freight rates. This attracted sellers who were prepared to cash out and sell their ships at multiples of their book values, in some cases to leave the industry altogether, and in others in the expectation that only a portion of sales receipts would be required to re-enter the industry when normal trading conditions returned. One of the clearest results of these varied market forces was the concentration of the much-reduced British tramp fleet into the hands of significantly fewer owners. West Hartlepool, arguably the country's pre-eminent tramp shipping port, had hosted 44 shipping company head offices in 1914; a number which had fallen to just 10 after the war.

Three of the companies considered here, Maclay and McIntyre, Ropner and Runciman, made no wartime second-hand acquisitions. On the other side of the ledger, three made limited disposals. Ropner sold off two of the oldest vessels in its fleet, the *Newby* of 1890 and the *Slingsby* of 1892, both in 1915. Watts also sold two ships, one in 1915 and one in late 1918. The first of these, the *Aldershot* of 1897, was the oldest vessel in the fleet at the time of her sale, while the second, the *Windsor* of 1903, was a second-hand purchase which had only entered the fleet the year before her sale. Runciman disposed of three vessels later in the war, the *Kirriemoor* of 1897 in 1916 and two of his older Turret ships, the *Aviemoor* and *Bleamoor* of 1902, in 1917. While these vessels were significantly newer than those sold off by

The Turret *Aviemoor* was sold by Runciman to the Bombay and Persia Steam Navigation Co. Ltd. in 1916, being subsequently renamed *Naderi*. She was sold to Japan as *Ise Maru* in 1923 and survived a stranding in April 1940 at Shinyasaki, Aomori Prefecture but was broken up in 1941. *[The Bristol Series]*

Ropner, their sale fitted in with Runciman's pre-war disposal policy. Two companies, however, were extremely active participants in the second-hand market, Maclay and McIntyre as a seller, and Watts as a buyer.

Maclay and McIntyre had remained active investors in their polyglot fleet up until the beginning of 1915, buying two newish second-hand vessels in 1911, adding two new ships in 1912, and then single new vessels in 1913, 1914 and January 1915. At this distance in time and in the absence of company records it is difficult to know exactly why their outlook changed, but in the same month that the brand new *Nyassa* arrived from the Sunderland shipyard of Bartram and Sons, Maclay and McIntyre sold two other vessels, neither of them particularly old (the *Tugela* of 1900 and the *Mersario* of 1906). This was just the beginning, and before the end of the year, another eight ships had gone. Two, the *Saxon* of 1881 and the *Peveril* of 1882 were out-and-out museum pieces, but the rest were no worse than middle-aged. Seven more ships followed between February and April 1916, with total wartime disposals being brought up to 20 by one further sale in late 1916 and two in 1918.

Whatever else was involved, these sales were not driven by an across-the-board clean out of older tonnage; while every surviving ship built before 1900 was disposed of, so too were three of the four newest vessels in the fleet. While 13 of the vessels sold went to a variety of smaller British tramp operators, and one to an oil company for conversion to a tanker, the destinations of the other six were more interesting, being the product of efforts by foreign interests to get around the prohibition on selling British ships outside the U.K. Two of the earlier sales went to Brys and Gylsen Ltd., representatives of Belgian interests which in 1917 would take final form as Lloyd Royal Belge (Great Britain) Ltd. The first four sales in 1916, including

Watts's second-hand acquisitions, 1916-19

Vessel	Tons/Built	Seller	Location	Date	New Name
INCA	3,034/1897	C. T. Bowring & Co. Ltd.	London	8.1916	SANDHURST
REYNOLDS	3,264/1898	Bolton Steam Shipping Co. Ltd.	London	10.1916	CHERTSEY
TANTALLON	3,076/1898	Maclean Shipping Co. Ltd. (W. Maclean)	West H'pool	11.1916	DATCHET
TALAVERA	2,891/1896	Scholefield Shipping Co. Ltd.	Newcastle-on-Tyne	11.1916	TAPLOW
EVERSLEY	2,871/1896	Scholefield Shipping Co. Ltd.	Newcastle-on-Tyne	11.1916	ISLEWORTH
SALAMANCA	3,218/1912	Scholefield Shipping Co. Ltd.	Newcastle-on-Tyne	11.1916	MOLESEY (1)
LOVAINE	3,125/1898	Scholefield Shipping Co. Ltd.	Newcastle-on-Tyne	12.1916	MORTLAKE
CLINTON	3,381/1899	H. Samman & Co. Ltd.	Hull	12.1916	PETERSHAM (1)
LYNTON	3,232/1899	Johnston, Sproule & Co. Ltd.	Liverpool	1.1917	PUTNEY
ALSTON	3,955/1903	Webster & Barraclough Ltd.	West Hartlepool	11.1917	WINDSOR
CLIFTON	3,592/1904	Webster & Barraclough Ltd.	West Hartlepool	11.1917	CHATHAM
DUNBAR	3,672/1900	Dunedin Steamship Co. Ltd.	Leith	1.1918	CHERTSEY
ROKEBY	3,786/1899	Pyman Steamship Co. Ltd.	West Hartlepool	4.1918	MOLESEY (2)
BARTON	3,751/1899	Webster & Barraclough Ltd.	West Hartlepool	5.1918	HOUNSLOW
COMERIC	3,985/1898	Christian Salvesen & Co. Ltd.	Leith	6.1918	PETERSHAM (2)
BEDEBURN	3,449/1896	Kent Steamship Co. Ltd. (S. Walton)	London	7.1918	CHISWICK*
SOUTHVILLE	3,518/1904	Ville Steamship Co. Ltd. (Balls & Stansfield)	North Shields	9.1918	GREENWICH
EASTVILLE	3,545/1902	Ville Steamship Co. Ltd. (Balls & Stansfield)	North Shields	9.1918	CHATHAM
HAXBY	3,445/1892	Robert Ropner & Co. Ltd.	West Hartlepool	4.1919	FINCHLEY

*Renamed CHISWICK after loss of CHISWICK of 1904 on 2.1.1919

The Ropner-built Trunk deck steamer *Barton* was one of many wartime acquisitions by Watts, becoming *Hounslow* in May 1918. Sold in 1929 she was briefly renamed *Cliddesden* by the McAllum Steamship Co. Ltd. before moving on to the Greek Kulukundis family as *Theseus*. She was demolished at La Spezia in 1932. *Hounslow* was photographed entering Dunkirk in 1920 with a cargo of manganese ore from the Gulf of Suez. *[Roy Fenton collection]*

A product of Ropner's own yard at Stockton-on-Tees, *Haxby* was sold to Watts in 1919 to become *Finchley.* Already 27 years old, she lasted another seven years before being broken up at Gateshead by J.J. King and Sons. Note the unloading gantries in this photograph taken at Rotterdam whilst *Haxby* was working for Belgian Relief. *[Martin Lindenborn]*

all three of the modern ships, went to the Bay Steamship Co. Ltd., a British-registered company set up by the French Government to purchase tonnage it would not otherwise have been able to acquire. All these proxy sales took place in the first half of the war, before second-hand values underwent their steepest increases, but it is probable that the foreign buyers were prepared to offer premium prices to attain the required results. This notwithstanding, the question of why Maclay and McIntyre embarked on such a comprehensive programme of retrenchment, one which would combine with losses to reduce the fleet by three quarters, remains open. One explanation can be discarded; while Joseph Maclay was appointed Shipping Controller in 1917 with a brief that might well have persuaded him to lighten his business load, this took place well after most of the sales were completed.

Watts, Watts and Company were completely quiet in both the new building and second-hand markets in the opening years of the war. Indeed, the company's only activity between 1906 and 1916 had taken place in one spending spree in 1911-12 when it had added five new steamers and purchased a six-year-old vessel from Harris and Dixon of London. Early war losses were no worse than average, four ships being lost in 1915 (one to marine causes) and none in 1916. Towards the end of the latter year, however, the managers appear to have taken a positive view of shipping prospects. In August 1916, Watts made its first wartime second-hand acquisition, and after that the purse-strings loosened. Eight further ships were acquired in a spending spree between October 1916 and January 1917 and then, after a ten-month hiatus, nine more between November 1917 and September 1918 to bring the final asset acquisition count to 18. If the object was to expand the fleet rather than simply replace losses, events moved against the company. In the 13-month period between April 1917 and May 1918, Watts lost 13 ships, so that, taking account of earlier losses and the two vessels sold, the fleet emerged 19-strong, one down on the pre-war count.

While Maclay and Mcintyre had largely been selling in the first half of the war when second-hand prices were still relatively modest, Watts had been buying in the second half of the war when asset inflation was becoming a real issue. In two instances, Watts might have achieved reasonable prices because they were dealing with small companies selling out of the business rather than with harder-nosed asset traders. The four remaining ships of the Scholefield Shipping Co. Ltd. of Newcastle were purchased in 1916, while a year later the remaining ships owned by Webster and Barraclough of West Hartlepool were also acquired, the sale in this case being prompted by the death of Thomas Barraclough, the active partner in the firm. While these transactions might have eased the investment burden, it is difficult to believe that the overall effect on the company's balance sheet can have been positive. Of the ships acquired, 11 had been built in the 1890s, and six between 1900 and 1905, leaving only one vessel, built in 1912, in what might be considered the relatively modern category. The damage to the fleet's age profile was somewhat limited by late war losses to older ships, but the average age at the end of the war had risen to over 15½ years, a situation which would require early attention if the company was to be competitive far into the peacetime era.

Boom and bust, 1919-1922

Freight rates and second-hand vessel prices had already risen steeply in the last two years of the war, but the arrival of peace saw even further acceleration. Anticipation of a post-war shipping boom was widespread, and entrepreneurs prepared to pay grossly inflated prices for any available tonnage took little account of either inherently short-term market conditions such as port congestion or trade dislocation (often the product of Government requisition), or of the fact that heavy new building in 1916-19 meant that the world deep-seas fleet was actually larger than it had been in 1914. Speculation itself continued to drive the market upwards, with rates and prices both peaking in 1920 at levels over four times those of 1913. Collapse was inevitable, and when the bubble did burst the effects were severe. The index of freight rates compiled by 'The Economist', which took 1913 as the base year with a value of 100, peaked at 438.7 for 1920 and then imploded to 158.4 for 1921, 122.0 for 1922 and 109.7 for 1923. While profitable operation was perfectly possible for established fleets with strong balance sheets, there was no hope for most of the new arrivals, whose overvalued assets were heavily financed by loans and mortgages they could not possibly service.

In common with many other established operators, two of the firms in our study undertook only a handful of transactions in 1919-1920. Ropners sold off three vessels, two of them veterans built in the 1890s. The oldest of these, the *Haxby* of 1892, was purchased by Watts two months after the end of the war and renamed *Finchley*. Even by the standards of Watts' wartime acquisitions, this ship was ancient, and it can only be assumed that the price was very attractive. Neither company embarked on any other sales or purchases, the only other change in either fleet resulting from the shipwreck in January 1919 of Watts' *Chiswick* of 1904. In contrast, Maclay and McIntyre continued with the policy of retrenchment which appears to have been in place since early in the war. Wartime losses and sales had already reduced the fleet from 48 to 11 by the end of 1918, but the company did not stop there. Five more ships were sold between January and August 1919 to five different owners. There can be little doubt that these vessels will have fetched good prices and contributed to a build-up of reserves for eventual fleet replacement, but the net effect was to complete the reduction of one of the world's largest tramp fleets to something less than even an also-ran. Even the remaining fleet was not particularly young, with only one vessel, the *Kalimba* of 1914, having been built after 1909.

Built by R. Thompson and Sons, Sunderland for Maclay and McIntyre's Glasgow Navigation Co. Ltd., *Basuta* was sold to a Cardiff company in 1916. She was to become yet another war loss, torpedoed and sunk by *U 53* on 8th February 1918 whilst carrying coal from Newport to Blaye. She was photographed at Boston on 30th September 1910. *[William A. Schell]*

Maclay and McIntyre sales, 1915-19 (see page 23)

Vessel	Tons/Built	Buyer	Location	Date	New Name
TUGELA	3,308/1900	Brys & Gylsen Ltd. [Lloyd Royal Belge]	London	1.1915	ANGLIER
MERSARIO	3,847/1906	Reid Steamship Co. Ltd. (W.S. Reid)	London	1.1915	
SAXON	1,595/1881	Macbeth & Co.	Glasgow	4.1915	
ATBARA	2,730/1899	Red Cap Steamship Co. Ltd. (J. Good)	Hull	4.1915	RED CAP
DENABY	2,987/1900	West House S.S. Co. Ltd. (Lambert, Barnett)	Cardiff	5.1915	
DONGOLA	4,362/1898	Brys & Gylsen Ltd. [Lloyd Royal Belge]	London	6.1915	ERINIER
HYDRA	4,061/1902	Imperial Oil Co. Ltd.	London/ Sarnia, Ont.	6.1915	RETLAW
UGANDA	4,257/1905	La Plata Steamship Co. Ltd. (J. Barnett)	Liverpool	9.1915	
SAHARA	4,085/1897	Houlder, Middleton & Co. Ltd.	London	12.1915	
PEVERIL	1,687/1882	Charles A. Stewart & Co.	London	12.1915	
GOWANBURN	4,274/1905	Bay Steamship Co. Ltd. [French Gov.]	London	2.1916	BAYGOWAN
ANGOLA	4,962/1912	Bay Steamship Co. Ltd. [French Gov.]	London	2.1916	BAYGOLA
MASARUA	4,986/1913	Bay Steamship Co. Ltd. [French Gov.]	London	2.1916	BAYSARUA
NYASSA	4,937/1915	Bay Steamship Co. Ltd. [French Gov.]	London	3.1916	BAYNYASSA
KINSALE	2,412/1896	Tree S.S. Co. Ltd. (Howard-Jones & King)	Cardiff	3.1916	
BASUTA	2,876/1897	Italian Export Shipping Co. Ltd. (Barnett)	Cardiff	4.1916	
IVANHOE	2,282/1888	Franco-British Steamship Co. Ltd. (Olivier)	London	4.1916	CITY OF REIMS
MERANNIO	2,390/1891	R. Temple-Thompson & P. Clark	London	12.1916	
GENERAL GORDON	2,994/1899	English Shpg. Co. Ltd. (Letricheux & David)	Swansea	8.1918	HURLINESS
YARBOROUGH	3,077/1900	Letricheux Line Ltd. (Letricheux & David)	Swansea	10.1918	
EVERILDA	3,076/1897	Ella Sayers S.S. Co. Ltd. (Fisher, Renwick)	Newcastle	11.1918	
OCEANA	4,846/1906	Nautilus Steam Shipping Co. Ltd. (Ritson)	Sunderland	1.1919	MAPLE BRANCH
NEWLANDS	3,012/1902	Italian Export Shipping Co. Ltd. (Barnett)	Cardiff	2.1919	
DOMIRA	3,113/1905	Preston Steam Nav. Co. Ltd. (Becker & Co.)	London	5.1919	
MARTHARA	3,910/1905	Lyndon Shipping Co. Ltd. (Cottle, Roberts)	Cardiff	6.1919	
KASSALA	3,825/1897	Merlin Spg. Co. Ltd. (Roberts, Price, Phillips)	Cardiff	8.1919	

While the shrinkage of the Maclay and Mcintyre fleet was dramatic, Runciman was to complete something even more spectacular. The Runciman fleet had suffered the worst percentage losses of the war, 21 combined war and marine casualties accounting for 60% of the 1914 fleet, and three new buildings being balanced out by three vessel sales. The fleet was reduced further when the *Exmoor* of 1912 was wrecked in early 1919, but Runciman still controlled a well-balanced fleet of 13, averaging 10 years of age, with only one vessel, the *Hazelmoor* of 1894, being obviously overdue for replacement. The war itself had seen some large-scale fleet disposals in the tramp sector, most notably the sale of all but one of the Glasgow fleet of Burrell and Son to a variety of buyers in 1916, and that of the Hain Steamship Co. Ltd. to the P & O/British India Group. The post-war boom, however, witnessed the arrival of a new group of buyers eager to participate in the anticipated peacetime shipping boom, and willing to pay premium prices to facilitate rapid entry. One of the most aggressive of these new arrivals was Edgar Edwards of Cardiff, who had started to make individual second-hand purchases during the second half of the war. The last of these single acquisitions had been made in May and July 1919, the prices being paid for two medium-sized steamers built in 1907, the *Queen Elizabeth* for £130,000 and the *Maylands* for £122,500, indicating just how inflated prices had become. Edwards was apparently driven by a desire to make his Western Counties Shipping Company the largest fleet owned in South Wales and sought out large block transactions. In November 1919 Walter Runciman agreed to sell the entire Moor Line fleet for £1,804,000, an average of £138,769 per vessel, or just under £22 per deadweight ton. While it would subsequently become clear that this was a ruinous price, this was not apparent at the time; indeed, an independent valuation undertaken in the wake of the transaction set a value of £1,885,000 on the thirteen ships.

Runciman was paid in cash, and it says a lot about the investment climate that Edwards succeeded in issuing shares and debentures to repay the short-term bank loan of £1,620,000 he had taken out to finance the transaction. Moor Line shareholders received a very generous return for their shares, while Runciman was left with a large war chest to finance eventual re-building, something he was almost certainly always intent on. The Runciman ships began to join Western Counties in early 1920, in each case adopting a name ending in *-Mead* in line with existing company policy. Except for *Jerseymoor*, which was renamed *Westmead*, the changes followed the path of least resistance, simply substituting the suffix *-Mead* for *-Moor*. Edwards was not finished, however, and in February 1920, before most of the Runciman ships had joined his fleet, he negotiated another extravagant purchase with a Tyneside tramp owner. On this occasion, he agreed to pay £1,825,000 for the 11 ships controlled by Sir Arthur Sutherland. Here he could not meet the entire purchase price in cash, even after selling on three of the ships, and the balance was covered by a mortgage in favour of Sutherland. Subsequently, another mortgage, this time for £1 million, was arranged with the finance house B.S.T. Ltd., largely it would seem to underpin working capital.

Edwards' over-leveraged behemoth sailed through 1920 but falling freight rates in 1921 soon found it wanting. Money could not be found to cover fleet insurance premiums when they became due, and when the debenture holders pushed through changes to the mortgage trust deed to allow fresh finance, Sutherland took the view that his rights as mortgagee had been interfered with and seized his former vessels, quickly selling them off. The debenture holders then commenced their own action against the company, completing the destruction of Western Counties, and a winding up order

Valuation of Runciman fleet for sale to the Western Counties Shipping Company, 1919

Vessel	Built	D.W.T.	Valuation	Value/ D.W.T.
HAZELMOOR	1894	5,100	£80,000	£15.14s
INCHMOOR	1900	5,800	£115,000	£19.17s
LOWMOOR	1902	6,225	£130,000	£20.18s
QUEENMOOR	1903	6,270	£115,000	£18.7s
PEARLMOOR	1905	7,070	£140,000	£19.16s
CASTLEMOOR	1906	6,395	£150,000	£23.9s
DALEMOOR	1909	7,100	£150,000	£21.3s
ZURICHMOOR	1910	6,410	£155,000	£24.4s
ORANGEMOOR	1911	7,100	£160,000	£22.11s
JEDMOOR	1913	5,550	£155,000	£27.18s
KELSOMOOR	1914	5,550	£160,000	£28.14s
ARRANMOOR	1915	5,575	£165,000	£29.12s
JERSEYMOOR	1915	7,850	£220,000	£28.5s
13 ships		**81,795**	**£1,885,000**	**£23.9s**

Runciman sales to and purchases from the Western Counties Shipping Company, 1920-22

Vessel	Tons/Built	Re-named	Re-sold	Re-named	Disposal	Fate
HAZELMOOR	3,096/1894	HAZELMEAD			[CTL 1920]	
INCHMOOR	3,445/1900	INCHMEAD	Spain	JOSE		
LOWMOOR	3,976/1902	LOWMEAD	U.K.	NICHOLASTON		
QUEENMOOR	3,753/1903	QUEENMEAD	Denmark	KNUD		
PEARLMOOR	4,119/1905	PEARLMEAD	Germany	ANNELIESE		
CASTLEMOOR	3,732/1906	CASTLEMEAD	Runciman	GLENMOOR	1927	Sold
DALEMOOR	4,124/1909	DALEMEAD	Germany	RUTH		
ZURICHMOOR	3,778/1910	ZURICHMEAD	Runciman	HALLMOOR	1931	Wrecked
ORANGEMOOR	4,134/1911	ORANGEMEAD	Norway	BOGEN		
JEDMOOR	3,175/1913	JEDMEAD	Runciman	LINKMOOR	1930	Wrecked
KELSOMOOR	3,174/1914	KELSOMEAD	Runciman	KELSOMOOR	1937	Sold
ARRANMOOR	4,008/1915	ARRANMEAD	Runciman	MIDDLEMOOR	1936	Sold
JERSEYMOOR	5,662/1915	WESTMEAD	Runciman	JERSEYMOOR	1927	Sold
[MAYLANDS]	3,854/1907	MAYMEAD	Runciman	ISLEMOOR	1927	Sold
[QUEEN ELIZABETH]	4,225/1907	VALEMEAD	Runciman	NEWTONMOOR	1926	Sold

Reproducible photographs of ships with Western Counties names have proved elusive and we must be content with this Mersey shot of the former *Kelsomead* of 1914, which reverted to *Kelsomoor* on return to Runciman in 1922.

The Blumer-built steamer remained with Runciman until 1937, when sold to Chinese owners as *Hai Yu*. She quickly gravitated to the Wheelock, Marden fleet as *Gemlock*, but stranded on 2nd March 1939, subsequently being declared a constructive total loss. However, Wheelock, Marden bought her back from the underwriters and had her repaired, and she evidently made her way west as she is reported to have been damaged in the Mediterranean in 1945. This time it spelt the end, and in July 1946 she was scuttled in the Mediterranean with 'obsolete ammunition', which may or may not have included shells containing poison gas. *[B. and A. Feilden/J. and M. Clarkson]*

was finally granted by the Court on 25th April 1922. The sale of the remaining fleet realized only £240,685, and while the debenture holders got back 6s. 8d. in the £, the entire ordinary share capital of £2.25 million was wiped out.

By the time B.S.T. Ltd., the remaining mortgagee, put what was left of the Western Counties fleet up for sale, the Moor Line had already embarked on a programme of new construction, the first products of which were launched by Doxford on the Wear and Northumberland Shipbuilding on the Tyne between January and March 1922. The opportunity to accelerate fleet re-building at fire-sale prices, however, was too good to pass up, and the Moor Line purchased no fewer than eight ex-Western Counties ships. It is not clear whether Runciman had a free choice across the whole portfolio or was restricted by the activities of the other buyer, F.V. Eberhart and Co. Ltd. of London, who were themselves only a middleman. In any event all the certificates of sales bore the same date, and Runciman came away with six of his old ships, including the four most modern, and two 1907-built vessels, the *Maymead* (ex-*Maylands*) which was renamed *Islemoor* and the *Valemead* (ex-*Queen Elizabeth*) which became *Newtonmoor*. For two ships the renaming process was simply reversed, the *Kelsomead* reverting to *Kelsomoor* and the *Westmead* to her original name *Jerseymoor*. The other ships all received new names, the former *Castlemoor* returning as *Glenmoor*, the *Zurichmoor* as *Hallmoor*, the *Jedmoor* as *Linkmoor* and the *Arranmoor* as *Middlemoor*, in at least some cases because their original *Moor* name had been allocated to new construction.

Rebuilding 1922-1929

Very few established tramp operators placed orders for new vessels in the immediate post-war period. A substantial portion of berth space was still occupied completing contracts for standard ships placed by the Shipping Controller in 1917-1918, and liner companies, which were driven by a stronger imperative to replace losses quickly, helped ensure that prices remained very high across the shipbuilding industry. The first of the four firms in this study to begin building was Runciman, which was re-starting from scratch after the sale of its fleet to Western Counties two years before. The Moor Line was in a strong financial position after its profitable adventure with Edgar Edwards, and fleet replacement was pushed forward at an impressive pace. By September 1922, the re-born fleet was already 14-strong. Eight of these ships were purchases from the Western Counties mortgagees, half of which were under ten years old, while the remaining vessels were new deliveries, three 420-footers from William Doxford, and three slightly smaller ships from Northumberland Shipbuilding.

Runciman's new building programme maintained its momentum over the next three years, with a total of 11 more ships arriving in 1923-25. Unlike the earlier deliveries, there was a multiplicity of designs. While Northumberland produced one more sister of their 1922 design, the South Shields yard of John Readhead and Sons delivered four medium-sized vessels, each varying in dimensions from its predecessor. Runciman also appears to have decided to experiment with smaller ships, two 2,700-ton vessels arriving from Blyth Shipbuilding and Drydocks in 1924, and two 1,900-ton near-coasters from John Crown of Sunderland in the winter of 1924-25. The former pair was of the Arch-deck design, a model commonly associated with the coal trade, but there is evidence that they were employed on medium-distance tramping routes. The smaller pair may well have been ordered with a specific trade in mind, but whatever the case do not appear to have been a success and lasted only a couple of years. The most significant arrivals, however, were the *Vinemoor* and *Westmoor*, delivered by William Doxford in September 1924. These were motor ships, of which Doxford was to become a significant builder in succeeding years. Doxford's engineers had been working on Diesel technology for the best part of the decade, and their approach paid off: their reliable engine succeeding where other early ventures such as the Maclagan had failed.

Runciman new building, 1922-1928						
Vessel	**Tons**	**Dimensions**	**Engine**	**Delivery**	**Builder**	**Location**
BLYTHMOOR	6,582	420 x 54 x 34	T.3-cyl	3.1922	Wm. Doxford	Sunderland
DALEMOOR	5,796	400 x 53 x 33	T.3-cyl	4.1922	Northumberland	Howdon-on-Tyne
ALNMOOR	6,573	420 x 54 x 34	T.3-cyl	5.1922	Wm. Doxford	Sunderland
EASTMOOR	5,811	400 x 53 x 33	T.3-cyl	6.1922	Northumberland	Howdon-on-Tyne
CASTLEMOOR	6,574	420 x 54 x 34	T.3-cyl	8.1922	Wm. Doxford	Sunderland
FERNMOOR	5,812	400 x 53 x 33	T.3-cyl	9.1922	Northumberland	Howdon-on-Tyne
ORANGEMOOR	5,775	400 x 53 x 33	T.3-cyl	3.1923	Northumberland	Howdon-on-Tyne
PEARLMOOR	6,049	400 x 52 x 34	T.3-cyl	4.1923	John Readhead	South Shields
QUEENMOOR	4,862	405 x 54 x 27	T.3-cyl	1.1924	John Readhead	South Shields
TULLOCHMOOR	2,740	320 x 43 x 24	T.3-cyl	9.1924	Blyth Shipbuilding & D.D.	Blyth
VINEMOOR	4,369	375 x 53 x 26	2S CSA oil	9.1924	Wm. Doxford	Sunderland
WESTMOOR	4,369	375 x 53 x 26	2S CSA oil	9.1924	Wm. Doxford	Sunderland
USKMOOR	2,743	320 x 43 x 24	T.3-cyl	11.1924	Blyth Shipbuilding & D.D.	Blyth
ROYALMOOR	1,907	268 x 38 x 18	T.3-cyl.	11.1924	John Crown	Sunderland
SILVERMOOR	1,906	268 x 38 x 18	T.3-cyl.	3.1925	John Crown	Sunderland
YORKMOOR	4,457	381 x 52 x 27	T.3-cyl.	1.1925	John Readhead	South Shields
ZURICHMOOR	4,455	372 x 55 x 26	T.3-cyl.	8.1925	John Readhead	South Shields
GLENMOOR	4,393	375 x 53 x 26	2S CSA oil	4.1928	Wm. Doxford	Sunderland
INNESMOOR	4,392	375 x 53 x 26	2S CSA oil	5.1928	Wm. Doxford	Sunderland
JEDMOOR	4,392	375 x 53 x 26	2S CSA oil	6.1928	Wm. Doxford	Sunderland
NORTHMOOR	4,392	375 x 53 x 26	2S CSA oil	11.1928	Wm. Doxford	Sunderland

In 1924 Runciman took delivery of two Arch-deck steamers from the Blyth Shipbuilding and Dry Dock Co. Ltd. The design was particularly suited to colliers, and the *Tullochmoor* and *Uskmoor*, considerably smaller than their Runciman fleet mates, were used in the Continental Europe, Mediterranean and White Sea trades. *Tullochmoor* had an even longer career than *Westmoor*, although sold in 1936 to German owners as *Birgitte*. Taken as a prize at Hamburg in 1945 she became *Empire Soar* briefly, before being allocated as war reparations to Greece. A succession of names under Greek and later Panamanian flags followed: *Preveza*, *Danapris*, *Armonia*, and *Charlie*, before she was broken up at Hong Kong in 1960. *[J. and M. Clarkson]*

The Runciman motor ships were conventional as far as hull and superstructure design were concerned, and were also something of an experiment. Leaving aside the smaller steamers, they were followed by two conventional steamships from Readhead. Thereafter the company took a three-year holiday from new building, no doubt carrying out a systematic comparison of steam and diesel technology. There can be little doubt that the new motor ships passed this test with flying colours, as the company's next order for new ships, placed in 1927-28, was for four sister ships to the 1924 Doxford pair. These acquisitions were balanced by rationalization elsewhere in the fleet. The three oldest ships picked up from the wreckage of Western Counties, the *Glenmoor* of 1906 and the *Islemoor* and *Newtonmoor* of 1907, were sold in 1926-27, having apparently done their job in launching the re-building campaign. The newest of the former Edwards ships, the 12-year-old *Jerseymoor*, was also sold, in this case presumably for an attractive price.

Westmoor was one of two Doxford motorships delivered to Runciman in 1924, although their profile, with a hatch between bridge and superstructure, could be mistaken for that of a steamer. *Westmoor* had a particularly long career, sold in 1947 to become *Akri Hill* for a single-ship company managed by Counties Ship Management Co. Ltd. They sold her to Italy as *Montegiove* in 1950 and she subsequently helped rebuild the German tramp fleet by becoming *Westsee* in 1951. She was delivered to breakers at Bremerhaven in May 1958. *[Roy Fenton collection]*

Finally, the small John Crown-built pair, the *Royalmoor* and *Silvermoor*, were sold to a Chilean company after only two to three years in service, having apparently failed to impress in whatever role they were employed. Overall, Runciman could look back on an extremely successful six-year period of rebuilding, which had left the company with a fleet of 23 vessels with an average age of 5¾ years, only four of which (the remaining ex-Western Counties veterans) were candidates for early replacement. Whatever the risk involved in the complete fleet disposal of 1919-20, it had been handsomely rewarded.

While Ropner did not take delivery of its first new ship until the spring of 1923, one important measure of corporate re-structuring was undertaken in 1919. Half the fleet had still been owned on the outdated 64th share basis, and these 13 ships were now taken over by a new company, the Ropner Shipping Co. Ltd., established with an issued capital of £1.3 million. The new entity's late arrival placed it at a disadvantage compared to its well-established partner, the Pool Shipping Co. Ltd. The latter, as a limited company, had been able to build up significant reserves on its balance sheet, not just to fund future construction, but also to underwrite dividend pay-outs when trading results were poor. The new company enjoyed no such luxury, profits having been distributed as they were earned on 64th share-owned vessels. The result was not only that the Pool Shipping Co. was able to maintain a higher and more consistent dividend pay-out record than its newer partner, but also that it could underwrite more new-building, 19 new ships emerging with *-pool* names between 1923 and 1929 compared to 12 with the *-by* suffix.

New building commenced in a small way in 1923 when Ropner took over a ship on the stocks at its own yard after the prospective owner went bankrupt. Thereafter new construction got underway on a massive scale, Ropner proving willing to order large numbers of ships of identical specifications even when building was spread over several yards. The first group was composed of 12 sister ships built between 1924 and 1927. Apart from the leading vessel, the *Salmonpool*, built by Irvine's of West Hartlepool, construction was shared between two firms. Ropner's own yard completed four, the last of which, the *Willowpool* delivered in May 1925, would be the final ship built by the company for its own account, the yard closing in the same year. The remaining seven ships were built by William Gray of West Hartlepool who would be Ropner's main supplier for the next two decades. A second group of 11 sisters commenced with the delivery of the *Rockpool* in late 1927. These were supplemented by a smaller group of five in 1928-29, and two vessels which might well have been bought off the stocks. William Gray remained the largest builder, accounting for 11 ships, with Cowpen Dry Docks and Shipbuilding of Blyth contributing four, Smith's Dock of Middlesbrough two, and Sir James Laing of Sunderland one.

While there was some variation in hull dimensions across the 30 ships built between 1923 and 1929, there was less of substance in basic design. Ropner had moved to the long bridge deck configuration several years before the war, and the company stayed true to this design throughout the 1920s. While the new vessels were larger, there was little to distinguish them from the last pre-war ships, although the hull model did begin to improve with the second large group of steamers which married increased length with finer lines. The company also remained true to the triple-expansion steam engine. In 1928, William Ropner opined rather stuffily that 'The initial cost of a motor ship is much greater than that of a steamship of similar size, and it has yet to be shown by actual experience that the expenses of the engine department of putting a motor ship through her periodical surveys when she attains a ripe old age (say 16 – 20 years), will in any way compare with that of a steam vessel…' Whatever the merits of this statement (and it is only fair to say that Ropner was still in the majority as an advocate of coal and steam),

Roxby was Ropner's first post-war new building, although taken over on the stocks when the company that ordered her went out of business. She was photographed by the United States Coastguard, probably at New York, on 12th July 1942. On 7th November 1942 she was torpedoed by *U 613* whilst outward bound from Cardiff for Halifax with coal. Of the 46 crew and gunners on board, only 12 survived. *[USCG/Roy Fenton collection]*

Ropner new building, 1922-1929

Vessel	Tons	Dimensions	Engine	Delivery	Builder	Location
ROXBY	4,252	378 x 53 x 25	T.3-cyl.	4.1923	Ropner	Stockton
SALMONPOOL	4,803	390 x 56 x 26	T.3-cyl.	3.1924	Irvine's	West Hartlepool
BRIDGEPOOL	4,845	390 x 56 x 26	T.3-cyl.	5.1924	Ropner	Stockton
REEDPOOL	4,838	390 x 56 x 26	T.3-cyl.	9.1924	Ropner	Stockton
DRAKEPOOL	4,838	390 x 56 x 26	T.3-cyl.	11.1924	Ropner	Stockton
RUDBY	4,846	390 x 56 x 26	T.3-cyl.	11.1924	William Gray	West Hartlepool
WILLOWPOOL	4,815	390 x 56 x 26	T.3-cyl.	5.1925	Ropner	Stockton
AINDERBY	4,860	390 x 56 x 26	T.3-cyl.	6.1925	William Gray	West Hartlepool
FIRBY	4,868	390 x 56 x 26	T.3-cyl.	6.1926	William Gray	West Hartlepool
OTTERPOOL	4,867	390 x 56 x 26	T.3-cyl.	7.1926	William Gray	West Hartlepool
WARLABY	4,876	390 x 56 x 26	T.3-cyl.	2.1927	William Gray	West Hartlepool
TROUTPOOL	4,886	390 x 56 x 26	T.3-cyl.	5.1927	William Gray	West Hartlepool
ROMANBY	4,887	390 x 56 x 26	T.3-cyl.	6.1927	William Gray	West Hartlepool
ROCKPOOL	4,889	405 x 54 x 27	T.3-cyl.	11.1927	William Gray	West Hartlepool
ULLAPOOL	4,891	405 x 54 x 27	T.3-cyl.	12.1927	William Gray	West Hartlepool
ASHBY	4,871	405 x 54 x 27	T.3-cyl.	12.1927	Cowpen Dry Docks	Blyth
MANSEPOOL	4,894	405 x 54 x 27	T.3-cyl.	1.1928	William Gray	West Hartlepool
THIRLBY	4,889	405 x 54 x 27	T.3-cyl.	2.1928	William Gray	West Hartlepool
GULLPOOL	4,870	405 x 54 x 27	T.3-cyl.	2.1928	Cowpen Dry Docks	Blyth
HINDPOOL	4,897	405 x 54 x 27	T.3-cyl.	5.1928	William Gray	West Hartlepool
CARPERBY	4,890	405 x 54 x 27	T.3-cyl.	6.1928	William Gray	West Hartlepool
KIRKPOOL	4,840	405 x 54 x 27	T.3-cyl.	6.1928	Sir James Laing	Sunderland
STONEPOOL	4,803	405 x 54 x 27	T.3-cyl.	7.1928	Smith's Dock	Middlesbrough
LACKENBY	5,112	412 x 54 x 27	T.3-cyl.	7.1928	William Gray	West Hartlepool
CRAGPOOL	5,127	420 x 54 x 27	T.3-cyl.	7.1928	Cowpen Dry Docks	Blyth
RUSHPOOL	5,125	420 x 54 x 27	T.3-cyl.	9.1928	Cowpen Dry Docks	Blyth
BOULDERPOOL	4,803	405 x 54 x 27	T.3-cyl.	10.1928	Smith's Dock	Middlesbrough
HERONSPOOL	5,202	421 x 54 x 27	T.3-cyl.	4.1929	William Gray	West Hartlepool
HAXBY	5,207	421 x 54 x 27	T.3-cyl.	5.1929	William Gray	West Hartlepool
SWIFTPOOL	5,205	421 x 54 x 27	T.3-cyl.	7.1929	William Gray	West Hartlepool
YEARBY	5,666	435 x 56 x 28	T.3-cyl.	12.1929	William Gray	West Hartlepool

the company did introduce superheat with the *Heronspool* of 1929 and went on to retro-fit it to 15 earlier ships, in the process greatly improving fleet efficiency.

While all this building was taking place, 10 older vessels left the fleet, seven by sale and three, the *Wandby* of 1899, the *Troutpool* of 1903, and the *Somersby* of 1913, in a mini-wave of marine casualties in the early 1920s. The net effect was to leave Ropner with a fleet of 45 ships totalling 216,000 gross tons with an average age of eight years, the latter figure inflated slightly by the company's policy of running ships well past the 20-year-old mark, which had left five pre-1910 veterans still in service. While the number of vessels owned was 10 short of the 1914 figure, total tonnage was up by 30,000 and average age was down by three years. Further new ships were on order, and the company could look back on a re-building effort which few other operators could match.

Having been steady sellers of tonnage from 1915 through 1919, it is scarcely surprising that Maclay and McIntyre made no early moves to rebuild its fleet. The four oldest members of the remaining six-strong fleet had been built in 1905-06 and were past middle age, but there was no immediate imperative to replace any of these ships. The senior shareholders might well have been considering whether they should leave the industry altogether, but the fact that no further

Ropner's Stockton shipyard closed in 1925; perhaps surprisingly as Ropners were in the middle of a major fleet renewal programme. *Swiftpool* of 1929 was ordered from William Gray and Co. Ltd., West Hartlepool. Almost inevitably, she too became a war loss, torpedoed by *U 372* on 5th August 1941 whilst carrying 8,000 tons of ore from Pepel for Middlesbrough. With such a cargo, she would have sunk quickly, and *Swiftpool* took 42 of the 49 on board with her. *[B. and A. Feilden/J. and M. Clarkson]*

sales were made as second-hand prices surged further upwards in 1920 makes it more likely that they were biding their time before investing in new tonnage. Re-building finally did begin with the delivery of the *Domira* in July 1924, the first of two sisters from William Gray which, at 352 feet long, were a bit on the small side compared to the 400-footers the company had been ordering before the war. These ships were joined by the opportunistic acquisition of an incomplete vessel with an attenuated past. The *Californier* had been laid down in 1920 at Whiteinch on the Clyde by Lloyd Royal Belge (Great Britain) Ltd., a yard set up with British Government approval on a site originally occupied by John Reid and Co. to build ships for the Belgian Government's British flag shipping company of the same name. To all intents and purposes a Type A War Standard ship, she had been left incomplete on the stocks when the Belgian venture was wound up in 1921, the yard itself passing first to the Australasian Steam Navigation Co. before being taken over by Barclay, Curle. Maclay and McIntyre purchased the ship in 1924 and she was launched as *Invella* in June.

Fleet renewal throughout the second half of the decade was steady rather than dramatic. Alexander Stephen's Linthouse yard delivered one ship in 1925, while D. and W. Henderson built three sisters at their Meadowside yard in Partick over a period of 2½ years between 1926 and 1928. The new building programme was completed in 1929 with the arrival of two slightly larger sisters, one each from Stephen and Barclay, Curle. The company achieved something close to an integrated naming policy re-using a mixture of African place names and derivates of women's names, all ending with an 'A'. The arrival of the last of the new buildings was also the signal for the disposal of the three oldest vessels in the fleet, one of which, the *Janeta*, passed her name straight on to a new vessel. The decade came to a slightly sour end with the loss through shipwreck of the *Domira* of 1924. This left Maclay and McIntyre with a relatively modern fleet of 11 vessels with an average age of 7½ years, only two of which were candidates for early retirement. This represented a significant step forward from the situation in 1920, but it was clear by this time that the managers had long since firmed up on their wartime decision to scale back their fleet.

Watts' Britain Steamship Co. Ltd. had followed a completely different path from most established tramp operators, buying second-hand tonnage aggressively in the latter half of the war. These acquisitions had ended in early 1919, and the company made no asset acquisitions or disposals whatsoever until 1924. When activity did resume in the latter year it rapidly became clear that Watts were sticking to the business model they had started employing in 1916. Second-hand purchases re-started with a bang in 1924, when no fewer than 10 ships were purchased in just eight months. A further four were bought in 1925, eight in 1926, two in 1927, one in 1928, and two in 1929, bringing the entire spending spree to a total of 27. At one level, these acquisitions made more sense than those of 1916-18, as second-hand prices had fallen significantly. On the other, Watts was not picking up high quality assets: only five of the vessels purchased had been built after 1910, while the remainder all dated back beyond 1907, with eight of these having already passed 20 years of age at the time of purchase. The company stretched its net much wider than it had during the war. Most of the vendors were other British tramp operators, some of whom were probably distressed sellers. Two ships, however, came from large British shipping groups and three from abroad, two from Belgium and one from Denmark. Some of the acquisitions

Maclay and McIntyre new building, 1924-1929

Vessel	Tons	Dimensions	Engine	Delivery	Builder	Location
DOMIRA	3,852	352 x 50 x 25	T.3-cyl.	7.1924	William Gray	West Hartlepool
INVELLA	5.026	400 x 52 x 29	T.3-cyl.	8.1824	Barclay, Curle	Glasgow
INGOLA	3,846	352 x 50 x 25	T.3-cyl.	2.1925	William Gray	West Hartlepool
INDUNA	5,086	402 x 52 x 28	T.3-cyl.	5.1925	Alexander Stephen	Glasgow
MARTHARA	4,999	403 x 52 x 27	T.3-cyl.	1.1926	D. & W. Henderson	Glasgow
UGANDA	4,966	403 x 52 x 27	T.3-cyl.	10.1927	D. & W. Henderson	Glasgow
NYANZA	4,974	403 x 52 x 27	T.3-cyl.	6.1928	D. & W. Henderson	Glasgow
MASUNDA	5,250	403 x 55 x 29	T.3-cyl.	6.1929	Alexander Stephen	Glasgow
JANETA	5,312	403 x 55 x 29	T.3-cyl.	11.1929	Barclay, Curle	Glasgow

A fine view of the 1927-built *Uganda* in the Mersey. Maclay and McIntyre registered her under the Steam Ship Livingstonia Co. Ltd. She was torpedoed and sunk by *U 38* on 19th October 1940 whilst on a voyage from Montreal to Milford Haven with a cargo of steel and lumber in convoy HX.79. Maclay and McIntyre's *Loch Lomond* of 1934 was sunk by *U100* in the same convoy battle. *[B. and A. Feilden/J. and M. Clarkson]*

had very complicated pasts. The *Cookham*, purchased in 1925, had already sailed under five other names, *Garscube*, *Craigmohr*, *Neilrose, Heathside* and *Arncliffe*, while the second *Remenham* had flown both French and Belgian colours, and the *Chislehurst* had started under those of the Hapsburg Empire, subsequently flying both U.S. commercial and naval colours and those of the new Republic of Hungary. At a more whimsical level, the sheer scale of acquisitions clearly taxed the London suburb naming model, with the net being cast wide enough to catch obscure, distant Thames Valley villages such as *Remenham* and *Medmenham*, and towns well outside any normal definition of Greater London such as *Maidenhead* and *Wokingham*.

While a certain degree of speculation is required here, Watts was obviously now pursuing a radically different business model from that with which the company had entered the war. This most likely had two main elements. In the first case, the lower capital costs of second-hand vessels would require relatively modest allowances for depreciation and interest, and reasonable scope for profitable operation

Watts second-hand acquisitions, 1924-28

Vessel	Tons/Built	Seller and location	Date	Renamed
ROCHDALE	3,718/1906	Rochdale Steamship Co Ltd. (C. Radcliffe), Cardiff	4.1924	AMERSHAM
SINGAPORE	4,268/1906	Westminster Sg. Co. Ltd. (Eggar, Forrester & Parker), London	5.1924	CHESHAM
LEXINGTON	4,088/1906	Furness, Withy & Co. Ltd., Liverpool	5.1924	DENHAM
GILWEN PARK	3,708/1906	Gilwen Shipping Co. Ltd. (Harrison, Sons & Co. Ltd.), Cardiff	7.1924	EGHAM
RIVER TRENT	3,584/1906	D.R. Llewellyn, Merrett & Price Ltd., Cardiff	7.1924	WOKINGHAM
PRESIDENT BUNGE	3,742/1905	Cie. Royale Belgo-Argentine (Armement Deppe), Belgium	8.1924	TWYFORD
MONKSHAVEN	3,360/1911	Federated Coal & Shipping Co. Ltd., Cardiff	9.1924	REMENHAM (1)
BURNHOLME	3,474/1904	Rowland & Marwood's S.S. Co. Ltd. (Headlam), Whitby	9.1924	MEDMENHAM
NEWQUAY	4,191/1914	Red Cap S.S. Co. Ltd. (J. Good & Sons Ltd.), Hull	10.1924	MAIDENHEAD
WALLACE	3,930/1905	Lewis S.S. Co. Ltd. (T. Lewis), Cardiff	11.1924	WOOBURN
DARNLEY	4,020/1907	Romney S.S. Co. Ltd. (Fawcett, Coverdale & Co.), London	8.1925	LALEHAM (1)
APSLEY	3,655/1906	Romney S.S. Co. Ltd. (Fawcett, Coverdale & Co.), London	10.1925	TOTTENHAM
ARNCLIFFE	3,583/1906	Care & Marquand Shipping Co. Ltd., Cardiff	11.1925	COOKHAM
DUBLIN	3,245/1905	D/S A/S Patria (O. Oveson), Denmark	11.1925	FULHAM
ANTIOPE	3,004/1904	New Egypt & Levant S.S. Co. Ltd. (T. Bowen Rees & Co.), London	2.1926	MORTLAKE
TAPTON	3,569/1904	Batheaston Trading Co. Ltd. (C.H. Wade & Co.), Cardiff	4.1926	PUTNEY
WESTRA	4,772/1912	Morgan & Cadogan Ltd., Cardiff	8.1926	FINCHLEY
LLANGORSE	4,703/1904	Llangorse S.S. Co. Ltd. (E.T. Radcliffe & Co.), Cardiff	10.1926	LALEHAM (2)
KATANGA	3,317/1901	South Georgia Co. Ltd. (Christian Salvesen & Co.), Leith	11.1926	NEWNHAM
OVERDALE	3,606/1903	South Georgia Co. Ltd. (Christian Salvesen & Co.), Leith	11.1926	WINSLOW
ARLON	3,155/1903	Cie. Transatlantique Belge (Armement Deppe), Belgium	11.1926	REMENHAM (2)
DUNOLLY	3,281/1901	Scottish Navigation Co. Ltd. (Glen & Co.), Glasgow	11.1926	HIGHGATE
ROQUELLE	4,363/1918	Imperial Direct Line Ltd. (Elder Dempster & Co. Ltd.), Liverpool	10.1927	DATCHET
GLOFIELD	4,395/1906	Globe Shipping Co. Ltd. (Humphries (Cardiff) Ltd.), Cardiff	12.1927	HAMPSTEAD
FENWELL	3,843/1912	Fen S.S. Co. Ltd. (P. Samuel), London	11.1928	CHISLEHURST
BOHEME	4,497/1911	Soc. Anon. di Nav. Marco U. Martinolich, Italy	1.1929	NORBITON
LINGFIELD	4,082/1910	Woodfield S.S. Co. Ltd. (Woods, Tylor & Brown), London	8.1929	CHATHAM

With what was picturesquely known as a 'teapot bow', *Mortlake* was built as *Cragside* for Pyman Brothers, who favoured this rather eccentric design. As *Antiope* she was bought by Watts in 1926, and is seen here in lay-up on the River Dart in 1932 alongside J. and C. Harrison's *Lamington* (3,539/1907). In 1933 *Mortlake* went to Latvian owners as *Valdona*, and was subsequently caught up in the Second World War in the Baltic. Taken as a prize by Germany in 1941, she carried a number of names, culminating in *Baltenland* as which she was sunk by the Russian submarine *K56* off Stolpmunde on Christmas Day 1944. *[World Ship Society Ltd.]*

in challenging trading conditions, although the upside would be limited by the fall-off in fuel efficiency and the higher maintenance costs which would come with age. In the second case, none of the vessels involved represented a long-term investment or were part of a strategic fleet renewal plan, with the result that the company could capitalize on any selling opportunity that arose to realize even a moderate capital gain. Watts did begin to sell off some of its oldest purchases in 1926, disposing of seven ships by the end of 1928. Six of these were very old vessels acquired before 1920, most of which had done a decade's service since acquisition. Only one of these ships went to the breakers, so the company might have realized some modest capital gains. The final sale, that of the 15-year-old *Remenham* to Japanese buyers only two years after purchase, appears more likely to have been an opportunistic transaction delivering a higher return. The disposal programme moved up a gear in 1929 when a total of eight ships were sold, six to Greek owners. Half of this group was made up of the remaining wartime acquisitions, 30-year-old veterans which had all been in company colours for 11 years. The remainder were slightly newer 1920s acquisitions, the sales of which are more likely to have realized worthwhile profits.

After dealing exclusively in the second-hand market for over a decade, Watts finally ordered new tonnage in late 1927. In a total break with the past, the company placed an order with a Scottish builder, Caledon Shipbuilding and Engineering of Dundee, for three new vessels. These ships were delivered between August and November 1928, becoming the first new buildings to join the fleet since 1912. To underline the break with the recent past, management also adjusted vessel nomenclature, beginning a convention of giving sister ships names beginning with the same letter, in this case *Watford*, *Wanstead* and *Wendover*, even at the expense of reaching beyond the London boundaries to towns

Watts new building, 1928

Vessel	Tons	Dimensions	Engine	Delivery	Builder	Location
WATFORD	5,421	406 x 54 x 28	T.3-cyl.	8.1928	Caledon	Dundee
WANSTEAD	5,423	406 x 54 x 28	T.3-cyl.	9.1928	Caledon	Dundee
WENDOVER	5,419	406 x 54 x 28	T.3-cyl.	11.1928	Caledon	Dundee

Watts vessel disposals, 1926-1929

Vessel	Tons/Built	Acquired	Age at acquisition	Disposal	Age when sold	Years of service	Disposal	Where
MORTLAKE	4,125/98	12.1916	18	1.1926	28	10	Sold	Greece
FINCHLEY	3,444/92	4.1919	27	2.1926	34	7	Scrapped	
PUTNEY	3,232/99	1.1917	18	3.1926	27	9	Sold	Italy
REMENHAM	3,368/11	9.1924	13	11.1926	15	2	Sold	Japan
HAMPSTEAD	3,447/96	6.1905	9	5.1927	31	22	Sold	Greece
DATCHET	3,076/98	11.1916	18	5.1927	29	11	Sold	Greece
CHISWICK	3,449/96	7.1918	22	11.1928	32	10	Sold	Latvia
PETERSHAM	3,798/98	6.1918	20	1.1929	31	11	Sold	U.K.
CHATHAM	3,545/02	9.1918	16	2.1929	27	11	Sold	Greece
HOUNSLOW	3,751/99	6.1918	19	3.1929	30	11	Sold	U.K.
CHERTSEY	3,672/00	1.1918	18	4.1929	29	11	Sold	Greece
NEWNHAM	3,316/01	11.1926	25	8.1929	28	3	Sold	Greece
HIGHGATE	3,281/01	11.1926	25	8.1929	28	4	Sold	Greece
AMERSHAM	3,718/06	4.1924	18	9.1929	23	5	Sold	Greece
PUTNEY	3,569/04	4.1926	22	10.1929	25	3	Sold	Greece

Petersham was over 30 years old when sold by Watts in 1929. She had been built by Russell and Co. Ltd. in 1898 as *Comeric* for Andrew Weir, and after a brief sojourn with Christain Salvesen was expensively bought and renamed *Petersham* in June 1918. Like *Hounslow*, she passed briefly through the hands of the McAllum Steamship Co. Ltd. who just had time to rename her *Ashenden* before offloading her to Latvian owners as *Margarete*. In June 1933 she collided with the Portuguese steamer *Luso* (6,207/1912) off the Dutch coast, an encounter which left the old girl fit only for F. Rijsdijk's breakers' yard at Hendrik-ido-Ambacht. *[E.N. Taylor/Roy Fenton collection]*

None of Watts 'W' class from Caledon survived the Second World War. *Watford* had the shortest career, wrecked at Cape Percy near Glace Bay, Nova Scotia on 10th September 1932 bound from Montreal to Sydney, Nova Scotia in ballast. *[World Ship Photo Library]*

in the wider south east. These ships featured large hatches and a comprehensive suite of winches and derricks, including one with a 25-ton lifting capacity. Their design also featured a significantly higher standard of crew accommodation than was common in the industry, an innovation which would be developed further in future vessels.

Watts' vessel ownership peaked in 1928 at 39 vessels totalling 157,000 tons, roughly twice the size of the fleet in 1914. Average vessel age, however, was 21¼ years, making mass early disposals inevitable. The latter process was already underway and gathered momentum with the eight-ship disposal programme of 1929. While the company had finally begun to order new tonnage, this could not replace time-expired capacity on anything approaching a one-to-one basis. If Watts was intent on maintaining a large fleet, it would have to remain an active buyer of second-hand vessels. There are two pieces of evidence to suggest that the managers were intent on spreading their wings.

The first suggestion of diversification was the incorporation in February 1929 of the Watts Shipping Co. Ltd. with a nominal capital of £300,000, of which £104,000 was initially issued, £100,000 of it to the parent Britain Steamship Co. Ltd. This was attended by the transfer to the new venture of four vessels, the *Highgate* of 1901, the *Winslow* of 1903 and the *Hampstead* of 1906, all of which had originally been purchased in 1926-27, and the *Norbiton* of 1911 which had just been acquired. The transfer price was set at £80,000, and although this was simply a paper transaction, the objective might have been to establish a special corporate entity to trade on the second-hand market. In the first year of operation, the new company sold its oldest ship, the *Highgate,* which stood on the books at £12,302, at a loss of £732, and purchased the newer and larger *Chatham* for what must have been the largest part of the total capital expenditure for the year of £37,000, the largest part of the difference being funded by a loan from the management company.

The second step into new territory was the takeover of the management of the seven-strong fleet of the Dominion Shipping Co. Ltd. of Montreal, Quebec. The latter was just one part of a large vertically integrated concern which controlled a group of coal and iron ore mines, and steel plants in Canada's Atlantic provinces. The ships were employed primarily in moving coal from the Maritimes to the St. Lawrence and carrying iron ore from Newfoundland to blast furnaces in Nova Scotia. The obvious attraction to Watts was the opportunity to deploy some of its own ships on Dominion business, an arrangement which would long outlast the management agreement itself.

Unusually, *Norbiton* was bought by Watts from a continental company, although she had been built in 1911 by Doxfords, her original owners as *Boheme* being M.U. Martinolich of Lusinpiclo, then part of the Austro-Hungarian empire, but shortly to become Italian. She was transferred to the Watts managed Alexandria Navigation Co. S.A.E. to move British coal to Egypt and return (after a good clean up, one hopes) with cotton. Renamed *Star of Alexandria*, she briefly returned to Watts' ownership in 1933 before going to Italian breakers. *[Ships in Focus]*

Facing the Great Depression 1929-1933

When dealing with the impact of the Great Depression of 1929-33, it is very important not to fall into the trap of hindsight. There was little advance signal of the cataclysm which would be triggered by the Wall Street crash on Black Tuesday, 29th October 1929. All four companies in this study had been investing in new tonnage in 1928-29, and both Ropner and Watts had new ships scheduled for delivery in 1930. Freight markets did not collapse immediately, but rates commenced a steady decline which would not bottom out until 1934. Every tramp owner was forced to lay up tonnage, often for many months on end. Similarly, each owner had to re-think its assumptions on vessel economic viability and to consider squeezing at least some return on the less viable investments from the rock-bottom second-hand and scrap markets.

Two companies, Ropner and Runciman, entered the depression with large well-found fleets. Neither achieved miracles; in the former case, for example, the Pool Shipping Company paid its last dividend in 1930 and the Ropner Shipping Company its last in 1931, neither paying another until 1936. Both had to endure its share of lay-ups, but neither was forced to undertake a fire sale of assets. Having already pruned the oldest ships in its post-war inventory, Ropner disposed of only two vessels between 1929 and 1933. These were both Trunk-deck steamers built in 1905-07, but four other ships of the same design and vintage remained with the fleet. Runciman made no disposals at all from his relatively young fleet, but suffered fleet shrinkage from other causes, its two oldest ships, the *Hallmoor* of 1910 and the *Linkmoor* of 1913 being wrecked in 1930-31. Both companies suffered further wastage from marine causes in 1933-34. In a rare double tragedy, Ropner lost two elderly vessels, the *Saxilby* of 1914 and the *Millpool* of 1906, which foundered with all hands in early winter Atlantic storms in November 1933 and October 1934 respectively. Runciman lost two more modern ships, the *Fernmoor* of 1922 and the *Queenmoor* of 1924, in the same time frame, but in both cases to shipwreck with no loss of life.

The much smaller fleet of Maclay and McIntyre had sold off its three oldest ships in 1929 and went on to dispose of its two other pre-1910 veterans in 1932-34, leaving only the *Kalimba* of 1914 to trade with the eight 1920s era ships in its small but modern fleet. There was, however, no such

The Readhead-built *Queenmoor* of 1924 was wrecked on 7th September 1934 on Chelsea Point, South Africa whilst on a voyage from Kotka to East London with a cargo of timber. *[J. and M. Clarkson]*

manageable scenario for Watts, whose very large collection of 25- to 30-year-old veterans must have struggled to find business even at break-even levels. Whatever the assumptions underpinning the Watts business model, these would have been swept away by the depression. The result was something akin to a fire sale of assets, many out of long-term lay-up, and most, almost certainly at, or only marginally above, break-up value. Six ships were sold in 1930, nine 1931, and five each in 1932 and 1933, the clean-out being completed by five sales in 1934-35. Of the 30 vessels sold, seven had been built for the company between 1901 and 1912 and had delivered more than two decades of service. The remaining 23 had all been acquired second-hand, all but one of them between 1924 and 1929. These ships had been in company ownership for an average of six years and given that many would have spent a fair portion of this time laid up, Watts may well have been forced to swallow capital losses on their sale. Neither Maclay and McIntyre nor Runciman would build or acquire any vessels between 1930 and 1933. Both Ropner and Watts, however, had new ships on the stocks when markets crashed. Ropner took delivery of a pair of sisters from William Gray in 1930. A single ship followed from the same builder in 1932, but she was constructed to a different design with, as we shall see, a specific trade in mind.

Watts also took delivery of three new vessels, extending its new custom by giving the ships names beginning with the same letter, in this case 'D', but without having to stretch its geographical focus in the way it had with the 'W' class. These ships were considerably more compact than their immediate predecessors and featured a range of innovations such as champfered-off plate ends to reduce water drag and curved bridge and superstructure frontage to reduce windage.

Each company made two second-hand acquisitions, although under rather different circumstances. In April 1931 Ropner bought two 20-year-old steamers from the Dominion Shipping Co. Ltd., renamed them *Coalby* and *Canby* and time-chartered them back to the same company. This was part of a larger strategic move, Ropner also time-chartering the new *Domby* which had been specially designed for the trade. This is an interesting case of two companies' business policies crossing if not colliding, as Watts was still the manager of the Dominion fleet at the time of the Ropner buy-in. The London company would give up management in 1932 but would continue to take an active part in the trade. Neither of the veterans Ropner had purchased to facilitate entry had a lengthy subsequent career, *Canby* being wrecked in 1934 and *Coalby* going to a British Scrap and Build buyer in 1936.

Ropner new building, 1930-33

Vessel	Tons	Dimensions	Engine	Delivery	Builder	Location
DEERPOOL	5,167	421 x 54 x 27	T.3-cyl.	8.1930	William Gray	West Hartlepool
SOMERSBY	5,168	421 x 54 x 27	T.3-cyl.	10.1930	William Gray	West Hartlepool
DOMBY	5,582	421 x 56 x 28	T.3-cyl.	3.1932	William Gray	West Hartlepool

Watts vessel disposals, 1930-1935

Vessel	Tons/Built	Acquired	Age when acquired	Disposal	Age on disposal	Years of service	Disposal	Buyers
LALEHAM	4,784/04	10.1926	22	7.1930	26	4	Sold	Greece
HAMPSTEAD	4,395/06	1.1928	22	8.1930	24	2	Sold	Greece
TOTTENHAM	3,655/06	10.1925	19	9.1930	24	5	Sold	Latvia
WOKINGHAM	3,584/06	7.1924	18	12.1930	24	6	Sold	Latvia
WINSLOW	3,573/03	11.1926	25	12.1930	29	4	Sold	Egypt
ILFORD	4,213/01	9.1901	new	2.1931	30	30	Scrapped	
BECKENHAM	4,566/01	7.1901	new	8.1931	30	30	Scrapped	
ASCOT	4,334/02	5.1902	new	8.1931	29	29	Scrapped	
CHESHAM	4,295/06	5.1924	18	8.1931	25	7	Sold	Romania
DENHAM	4,086/06	5.1924	18	8.1931	25	7	Scrapped	
EGHAM	3,708/06	7.1924	18	8.1931	25	7	Sold	Estonia
CHATHAM	4,082/10	8.1929	19	9.1931	21	2	Sold	Egypt
NORBITON	4,497/11	1.1929	18	10.1931	20	2	Sold	Egypt
EPSOM	4,556/01	12.1901	new	12.1931	30	30	Sold	Italy
REMENHAM	3,155/03	11.1926	23	3.1932	29	6	Sold	Estonia
COOKHAM	3,583/06	11.1925	19	6.1932	26	7	Scrapped	
WILLESDEN	4,881/05	12.1905	new	11.1932	27	27	Sold	India
TWYFORD	3,742/05	8.1924	19	12.1932	27	8	Sold	Estonia
WOOBURN	3,930/05	11.1924	19	12.1932	27	8	Scrapped	
MEDMENHAM	3,474/04	9.1924	20	6.1933	29	9	Scrapped	
GREENWICH	3,518/04	9.1918	14	7.1933	29	15	Scrapped	
CHISLEHURST	3,859/12	11.1928	16	8.1933	21	5	Sold	China
MORTLAKE	3,037/04	2.1926	22	12.1933	29	7	Sold	Latvia
DATCHET	3,610/18	10.1927	9	12.1933	15	6	Sold	Greece
FULHAM	3,245/05	11.1925	20	2.1934	29	9	Sold	U.K.
TWICKENHAM	4,891/12	6.1912	new	2.1935	23	23	Sold	U.K.
BLACKHEATH	4,868/11	5.1911	new	5.1935	24	24	Sold	Germany
FINCHLEY	4,773/12	8.1926	14	7.1935	23	9	Sold	Germany
MAIDENHEAD	4,191/14	10.1924	10	12.1935	21	11	Sold	Greece

Ropner second-hand acquisitions, 1931					
Vessel	**Tons/Built**	**Seller**	**Location**	**Date**	**Renamed**
WABANA	4,804/1911	Wabana S.S. Co. Ltd. [Dominion Coal Co. Ltd.]	Montreal	4.1931	CANBY
KAMOURSKA	4,903/1911	Kamourska Shipping Co. Ltd. [Dominion Coal Co. Ltd.]	Montreal	4.1931	COALBY

Above: *Domby* of 1932 temporarily broke the mould of Ropner's long-bridge-deck steamers, although a number more were to follow. She had a satisfyingly long career, and after sale in 1951 carried the names *Cibou* (British), *Caledonia II* and *Peter* (both Finnish), and *Kettara V* (Lebanese). She was broken up in Japan during 1960. *[Ships in Focus]*

Middle right: The 19-year-old, very long bridge deck steamer *Lingfield* was bought by Watts in 1929, but as *Chatham* she may well simply have been repainted and put straight into lay-up in Hull, as seen here. In 1931 she was renamed *Star of Cairo* (lower right) for the Watts-managed Alexandria Navigation Co. Ltd. S.A.E. In 1936 she moved on to another London owner who renamed her *Aylsham* before selling her to owners in Stettin. As *Gerrit Fritzen* she was wrecked on Schiermonnikoog Island on 25th November 1939.

Star of Cairo is seen turning in Gladstone Dock, Liverpool ready to go through the passage towards Hornby Dock.*[Middle: Barnard and Straker/J. and M. Clarkson, bottom: B. and A. Feilden/J. and M. Clarkson]*

Watts for their part purchased two second-hand vessels in 1933. One, the 1925-built *Antinous*, was renamed *Willesden*, the choice of a 'W' name reinforcing the belief that she was a replacement for the *Watford* which had been wrecked while engaged in the Canadian coal trade the year before. The other purchase, the 20-year-old *Neotsfield*, can only have been an opportunistic short-term acquisition and would not play any long-term role in the fleet. One further acquisition, the small Arch-deck collier *Ruckinge*, would follow in 1936, but will be considered in the following section. Watts also undertook a second outside management venture. The company built on an existing coal contract with the Egyptian State Railway and contacts with a range of other local investors to set up the Alexandria Navigation Co. (which traded under the name Red Rose Line) to carry British coal out to Egypt and Egyptian cotton back to the U.K. Watts sold two ships to the new venture, the *Chatham* of 1910 becoming the *Star of Cairo* and the *Norbiton* of 1911 the *Star of Alexandria*. These vessels flew the Egyptian flag, and further investment in the fleet came from other sources, although Watts would revive a management connection with one of the principals, Ladislas Pathy, after the Second World War.

Watts new building, 1930-33

Vessel	Tons	Dimensions	Engine	Delivery	Builder	Location
DARTFORD	4,075	366 x 52 x 25	T.3-cyl.	10.1930	Smith's Dock	Stockton
DEPTFORD	4,040	366 x 52 x 25	T.3-cyl.	1.1931	Smith's Dock	Stockton
DULWICH	4,040	366 x 52 x 25	T.3-cyl.	3.1931	Smith's Dock	Stockton

Watts second-hand acquisitions, 1933-36

Vessel	Tons/Built	Seller	Location	Date sold	Renamed
NEOTSFIELD	4,793/1913	Bell Line Ltd. (J. Bell & Co. Ltd.)	Hull	1.1933	PUTNEY
ANTINOUS	4,563/1925	New Egypt & Levant S.S. Co. Ltd. (T. Bowen Rees & Co.),	London	7.1933	WILLESDEN
RUCKINGE	1,742/1925	Constants (South Wales) Ltd.	Cardiff	12.1936	MORTLAKE

Dartford alongside Millennium Mills in Royal Victoria Dock, 7th June 1933 showing her anachronistic counter stern. All three of Watts' 'D's became war losses. *Dartford* survived one convoy to north Russia in early 1942, but on 12th June that year was torpedoed by *U 124* in the North Atlantic whilst on a voyage from the Tyne to Sydney, Nova Scotia in ballast. Despite being in a convoy, ONS 100, 30 of her crew were lost. *[R.A. Snook/F.W. Hawks]*

Deptford completed in 1931 still looked smart in this photograph dated 17th June 1937. She was torpedoed and sunk by *U 38* on 13th December 1939 off Honningsvaag, Norway having loaded iron ore at Narvik. *[Nautical Photo Agency]*

Bought in 1933, *Willesden* was a 1925 product of Workman, Clark and Co. Ltd. She was to have a number of 'adventures' during her Watts' career. On 17th October 1933 she ran aground east of Yaruilgach Lighthouse in the Crimea whilst carrying Black Sea grain to the United Kingdom but was refloated none the worse ten days later.

More serious were two collisions on 8th May 1937. At 12.50 am in dense fog she first came into contact with the Italian steamer *Gianfranco* (8,181/1915) off Dover. She was badly holed and sent out an SOS message, which was responded to by Albyn Line's *Thistleglen* (4,750/1924) who came to pick up the crew. Unfortunately, at 07.59 am *Willesden* contrived to hit her erstwhile rescuer, although the latter was not badly damaged. At 12.35 pm *Willesden* was beached between Dungeness and Rye with the help of the Dover tug *Lady Brassey* (362/1913). Refloated two days later, *Willesden* was taken to Dover from where, a week later, she sailed for the Tyne for repair.

Her next adventure was her last. Bound from New York to Egypt on 1st April 1942 she was confronted by the German auxiliary *Thor*, formerly *Santa Cruz* (3,862/1938) in the South Atlantic. *Thor* used her seaplane to disable *Willesden's* radio, and although the latter is reputed to have put up a 'gallant fight', *Thor's* 5.9-inch shells killed five of her crew whilst the remaining 42 ended up as prisoners-of-war in Japan. *[Roy Fenton collection]*

Back to business, 1934-39

Like the world economy in general, the shipping industry was slow to recover from the Great Depression. Freight rates and volumes crept up slowly, with pre-crisis levels only being reached in 1937-38. In most cases, owners attempted only modest levels of fleet renewal, depending largely on vessels which had come from the builders in the 1920s. Many governments sought to help their mercantile marines recover, in Britain this assistance taking the form of the Scrap and Build scheme, a programme which offered subsidized finance for new tonnage when the owner sent twice as much old tonnage to the breakers yard. None of the four companies in our study received Scrap and Build financing, although several of Watts veterans were purchased by other owners to fill their scrap quotas.

Maclay and McIntyre resumed fleet renewal in 1934 with the delivery of three broadly similar vessels from three different Clyde builders. These arrivals were marked by the introduction of a new nomenclature featuring the names of Scottish lochs. The final pre-war veteran, the *Kalimba* of 1914, was sold in 1936, and the company completed its rebuilding campaign in the following year when J.L. Thompson and Co. Ltd. of Sunderland delivered the *Loch Dee* and *Loch Don*. These latter were products of the Wearside firm's 'economy ship' programme and were pre-sisters to the *Dorington Court*, one of the forerunners of the mass-produced Second World War standard ships. Maclay and McIntyre arrived in 1939 with a modern, well-balanced fleet of 12 vessels with an average age of only 8½ years. While no longer one of British tramping's largest owners, it had steered a steadier course than most through the troubled inter-war years and was undoubtedly one of the best established medium-sized operators.

Ropner had maintained its record of running its vessels well into their third decade throughout the first half of the decade, but the return of some life to the shipping market from 1934 on was the signal for a clear out of the pre-war veterans. Eight elderly vessels were disposed off between 1934 and 1938, including the last two Trunk-deck steamers, the *Stagpool* and *Teespool*, both of which reached their 30th birthday before going to the breakers. This left only one pre-war vessel, the *Pikepool* of 1910, in the fleet, the other veterans being the *Swainby* and *Sedgepool* of 1917-18. The disposals themselves did not result in any fleet shrinkage, as they were more than compensated for by six new buildings and three modern second-hand acquisitions.

Photographed at Cape Town in the 1940s, *Loch Dee* was one of a pair of Thompson's version of the 'economy' steamers delivered in 1937 to Maclay and McIntyre who registered her to the Steam Ship Induna Co. Ltd. For a steamer she enjoyed a comparatively long life, being sold in 1955 to Greek owners who put her under the currently-fashionable flag of Costa Rica as *Cape Ora*. She arrived at Hong Kong to be demolished in November 1959. *[Ships in Focus]*

Maclay and McIntyre new building, 1934-38						
Vessel	**Tons**	**Dimensions**	**Engine**	**Delivery**	**Builder**	**Location**
LOCH MADDY	4,996	415 x 56 x 26	T.3-cyl.	9.1934	Lithgows	Port Glasgow
LOCH LOMOND	5,452	414 x 56 x 28	T.3-cyl.	9.1934	D. & W. Henderson	Glasgow
LOCH RANZA	4,958	415 x 56 x 26	T.3-cyl.	9.1934	Alexander Stephen	Glasgow
LOCH DEE	5,252	420. X 59 x 26	T.3-cyl.	5.1937	J.L. Thompson	Sunderland
LOCH DON	5,249	420. X 59 x 26	T.3-cyl.	6.1937	J.L. Thompson	Sunderland

Ropner had achieved large-scale fleet replacement from 1924 to 1932 through repeat batch orders for traditional long bridge tramps powered by triple-expansion engines, the only significant concessions to modernization being the introduction of a slightly finer hull form and superheat in boilers in the late 1920s. When the economic clouds finally began to lift in the mid-1930s, management finally set its adherence to the triple-expansion steam engine aside and ordered two pairs of vessels fitted with alternative forms of propulsion. Long-time supplier William Gray delivered the *Clearpool* and *Hawby*, each powered by two of the firm's steam turbines, which were double reduction geared to a single shaft. The other pair of vessels, the *Moorby* and *Wearpool*, came from the Pallion shipyard of William Doxford and were members of that yard's stable of 'economy' motor ships, driven by the same reliable three-cylinder Diesel which had been fitted to Runciman's pioneering craft in the previous decade. The Gray turbine ships retained the established long-bridge deck and split superstructure profile, but the Doxford pair were shelter deckers with a single composite midships structure.

There can be little doubt that Ropner would have planned an extended comparative evaluation of steam turbine and Diesel propulsion before plotting the course of future fleet renewal, but circumstances were to blur the outcome of any such experiments. The short recovery in freight rates faltered badly late in the decade and, with war clouds looming, most companies put building plans on hold. Ropner added only two further new ships, both equipped with triple-expansion engines. The first of these, the *Alderpool*, was

Ropner new building, 1934-38						
Vessel	**Tons**	**Dimensions**	**Engine**	**Delivery**	**Builder**	**Location**
CLEARPOOL	5,404	428 x 55 x 27	2 stm.trb.	11.1935	William Gray	West Hartlepool
MOORBY	4,992	424 x 54 x 26	2SCSA oil.	4.1936	William Doxford	Sunderland
HAWNBY	5,404	428 x 55 x 27	2 stm.trb	7.1936	William Gray	West Hartlepool
WEARPOOL	4,982	424 x 54 x 26	2SCSA oil	8.1936	William Doxford	Sunderland
ALDERPOOL	4,313	382 x 53 x 25	T.3-cyl.	8.1936	William Pickersgill	Sunderland
DANBY	4,258	386 x 53 x 25	T.3-cyl.	6.1937	William Gray	West Hartlepool

Ropner second-hand acquisitions, 1931					
Vessel	**Tons/Built**	**Seller**	**Location**	**Date**	**Renamed**
KITTY TAYLOR	4,640/1929	Eros Steamships Ltd. (Lambert Bros. Ltd.)	London	9.1934	DALEBY
IRON CHIEF	4,560/1930	Essex Oak Ltd. (Meldrum & Swinson)	London	6.1935	STAGPOOL
EASTVILLE	3,709/1925	Balls & Stansfield Ltd.	Newcastle	5.1937	EASTPOOL

A fine view of the Doxford 'Economy' *Wearpool* on the River Scheldt. She was to be another long-lived vessel, and after sale by Ropner in 1954 became successively the Swedish *Adelsö*, the Greek *Lefkipos* and *Dimitros* before being broken up at La Spezia in 1979. *[World Ship Society Ltd.]*

Photographed in the Mersey, *Daleby* was purchased in 1934 by Ropner as *Kitty Taylor*, built in 1929 by Armstrong, Whitworth and Co. Ltd., Newcastle. Although intended to be a permanent addition to the fleet, the Kriegsmarine had other ideas, and she was sunk by *U 89* on 4th November 1942 in the North Atlantic whilst on a voyage from Halifax to London with grain, tanks and vehicle parts. *[B. and A. Feilden/J. and M. Clarkson]*

unusual, having been launched by a Sunderland builder in 1930 for an owner which then went bankrupt and then awaiting a buyer for six years before Ropner had her completed. The other ship, the *Danby*, was a single-deck steamer, slightly smaller than normal for the fleet which may also have arrived due to some form of order default.

Ropner did not normally buy second-hand tonnage, the acquisition of the two Dominion colliers in 1931 being driven by a special corporate imperative. In 1934-37, however, the company did purchase three relatively modern ships from other owners, almost certainly taking advantage of individual opportunities to replace retiring vessels at moderate cost.The first two of these vessels, the *Kitty Taylor*, purchased from Lambert Brothers, and the *Iron Chief*, re-sold by Meldrum and Swinson after purchase from an Australian owner, were renamed *Daleby* and *Stagpool* respectively and became permanent additions to the fleet. The third, the smaller and older *Eastville*, survived only ten months as *Eastpool* before being sold to a Turkish company. This brought the total net additions to the feet in 1934-38 to eight, exactly matching the number of vessels sold.

Ropner had achieved an impressive feat of fleet renewal over the inter-war period. Although the fleet numbered 45 in 1939 compared to 55 in 1914, this was compensated for by increased vessel size, total gross tonnage having increased from 186,000 tons to 223,000 tons. Average fleet age had remained the same at 11½ years, and only three pre-1923 vessels would have been candidates for early replacement had war not intervened.

Runciman was the least active participant in post-Depression fleet renewal. Four ships were sold off in 1936-37. Two of these were the last remnants of the Western Counties adventure, the *Kelsomoor* of 1914 and the *Middlemoor* of 1915, each of which had contributed 14 to 15 years of service after their return to the fleet. The other

Stagpool, bought in 1935, must have proved a good investment for Ropner. Surviving the war (and seen here at Cape Town, still in drab wartime colours, but with guns and floats removed), she was sold to Tsavliris group in 1951 at what would have been a good price. She remained with this London Greek group, initially as *Granny Suzanne* under British registry, and later as *Carmen* under the Costa Rican flag until 1963. On 23rd June that year she collided with the Turkish *Sadikzade* (7,434/1945) in the English Channel and sank whilst on a voyage from Takoradi to Burntisland. *[C.R.V. Solomon]*

Runciman new building, 1934-38						
Vessel	Tons	Dimensions	Engine	Delivery	Builder	Location
KIRRIEMOOR	4,970	412 x 54 x 26	2SCSA oil	5.1935	William Doxford	Sunderland
FERNMOOR	4,972	412 x 54 x 26	2SCSA oil	5.1935	William Doxford	Sunderland

One of two Doxford 'Economy' type motor ships, *Fernmoor* gave Runcimans almost two decades of service before stranding on the coast of Palawan in the Philippines on 5th February 1954 during a voyage from Kosseir in Egypt to Japan with a cargo of phosphate. Although quickly refloated she sank the next day. *[Ships in Focus]*

departures were the *Uskmoor* and *Tullochmoor* of 1924, significantly smaller than the normal fleet profile at 320 feet long/2,740 gross tons, and perhaps no longer required for a specific trade. These departures were balanced only by the arrival of two new ships, a pair of motor ships from William Doxford, the *Kirriemoor* and the *Fernmoor*, significantly larger developments of the vessels delivered by the firm in the 1920s. The net result of these movements was to leave the company with a fleet of 17 ships of 88,000 tons, a significant reduction on the 35 ships/127,000 tons fleet of 1914. As new building had been skewed towards the 1920s, fleet age at 13¼ years was becoming an issue, although this was balanced by the presence of eight motor ships. Although the Moor Line itself might have slipped downwards in the rankings of large tramp companies, this was partially a product of the managing family spreading its interests more widely than many others, most notably into national politics and a separate London-based shipping venture.

After the wild round of second-hand acquisitions and sales which had dominated the inter-war years, Watts ended the 1930s on a relatively quiet note. The last two 1920s second-hand additions, the *Finchley* of 1912 and the *Maidenhead* of 1914, were sold in the closing months of 1935. They were followed in May 1936 by the 23-year-old *Putney*, acquired in a fit of regressive behaviour three years earlier. One final second-hand ship moved in and out of the fleet in 1936-37, the 1,740-ton collier *Ruckinge* lasting only six months as *Mortlake* before re-sale. The main investment drive was directed towards a third group of three new vessels, this time given place names (only one of them a London suburb) beginning with the letter 'B'. Watts returned to Caledon of Dundee for the new ships, whose design cemented the firm's growing reputation for innovation, not least in the provision of greatly superior crew accommodation. The ships themselves arrived one year at a time, the last in September 1938. Watts thus approached the second war with a modern fleet of nine vessels, eight of which had been designed to its own specifications. Having staged a huge experiment in the second-hand market, the company had come around full circle to a position not dissimilar to that from which it had entered the First World War.

Watts new building, 1934-38						
Vessel	Tons	Dimensions	Engine	Delivery	Builder	Location
BLACKHEATH	4,637	409 x 57 x 25	T.3-cyl.	7.1936	Caledon Shipbuilding	Dundee
BECKENHAM	4,636	409 x 57 x 25	T.3-cyl.	10.1937	Caledon Shipbuilding	Dundee
BEACONSFIELD	4,635	409 x 57 x 25	T.3-cyl.	9.1938	Caledon Shipbuilding	Dundee

Beckenham has a distinctly unusual superstructure in this photograph, although earlier shots show her identical to sisters *Blackheath* and *Beaconsfield*. This may have resulted from rebuilding after one of her several casualties. On 26th March 1943 she was mined in the Mediterranean. In 1946 she went aground off Brazil, and was towed back to South Shields for repairs. It was third time unlucky for *Beckenham* and on 7th October 1953 on a voyage from Igarka to London with timber she went aground in the Kara Sea near Cape Ratmanova, broke in two and quickly became a constructive total loss. *[J. and M. Clarkson]*

Seen on the Mersey on 1st July 1939, *Beaconsfield* had the most satisfactory career of the three Caledon-built 'Bs'. After sale to Hong Kong in 1958 she steamed on as *Twinhorse* until 1964 when, leaky and old, she went to breakers at Hiao, Japan who began demolishing her in April. *[John McRoberts/J. and M. Clarkson]*

A retrospect

Maclay and McIntyre, Ropner, Runciman and Watts had all achieved a great deal between 1918 and 1939. War losses had hit every company heavily, at their worst accounting for more than half of peacetime strength. Renewal and re-building was undertaken against a backdrop of generally challenging trading conditions, including a highly destructive post-war asset bubble and the deepest depression ever experienced by the modern world. The fact that all four companies had survived as significant ship operators was itself an achievement. Many of their competitors did not. The reconstruction of the Ropner fleet stands out not least because of its sheer scale, while Runciman staged a handsome recovery on the back of a very bold initial decision to sell out. For whatever reason, Maclay and McIntyre had decided to downscale their business as early as 1915-16, and the compact fleet they controlled in 1939 was as modern as any. Watts took a completely different path from the others, and its large-scale entry into the second-hand market might have come partially unstuck because of the Great Depression. Their return to new building, however, produced some of the most advanced vessels in the industry, even if the fleet was mid-sized at best.

Comparative fleet size and age, 1914-1939

Company	Date	Vessels	Tonnage	Average size	Average age
Maclay and McIntyre	1.8.1914	48	169,378	3,529	13.7
	31.12.1918	11	46,343	4,213	12.5
	31.12.1920	6	27,637	4,606	12.3
	31.12.1928	13	60,386	4,645	10.7
	1.9.1939	12	60,367	5,031	8.8
Ropner	1.8.1914	55	186,276	3,387	11.4
	31.12.1918	27	104,360	3,865	12.6
	31.12.1920	24	93,867	3,911	13.6
	31.12.1928	42	198,648	4,730	7.2
	1.9.1939	45	223,132	4,958	11.4
Runciman	1.8.1914	35	127,355	3,639	8.3
	31.12.1918	14	54,505	3,893	10.2
	31.12.1920	0	0		
	31.12.1928	23	108,646	4,724	5.7
	1.9..1939	17	88,321	5,195	13.3
Watts	1.8.1914	20	74,809	3,740	12.4
	31.12.1918	19	74,202	3,905	15.7
	31.12.1920	19	74,401	3,916	19.0
	31.12.1928	39	157,463	4,038	21.2
	1.9.1939	9	41,807	4,645	7.4

EVERY PICTURE TELLS A STORY

If the story is ever written of the evolution of ship's cargo gear, and how it influenced cargo ship design, we may learn why *Daghild* (7,978/1916) had such an enormous array of kingposts: at least seven major sets plus what looks like a series of smaller posts set between them. Given her ownership in the 1920s by a Canadian coal company, it might be concluded that the transverse-framed ship was a very large collier, but 'Lloyd's Register' lists her as having a 'tween deck, which made her less suitable for loading coal.

She was launched in August 1916 for A/S Daghild, managed in Norway by John P. Pedersen and Son. At this stage of the First World War the Government was not going to allow such a large cargo carrier to be delivered to a neutral, and she was duly registered in the ownership of John H. Glover, London. This was probably on behalf of the Shipping Controller, with whom the principals of Glover Brothers were working closely, and she was later transferred to the Shipping Controller with Jenkins Brothers, Cardiff as managers. Return to her rightful owner was delayed until late in 1922, but in the following June she was re-registered in the ownership of the Daghild Canadian Steamship Co. Ltd., Halifax, Nova Scotia. The owners were associated with the Dominion Coal Co. Ltd. of Sydney, Cape Breton, and they and Pedersen were listed as joint managers. In February 1934 she was bought by the Tenax Steamship Co. Ltd. (Muir, Young Ltd., managers), London still as *Daghild*. She had recently visited the U.K. and Norway, but after her sale mainly worked in Canadian waters. In 1937 she went to Germany as *Katharina Dorothea Fritzen*. In 1938 she was recorded as trading between Continental Europe, the Baltic and the River Plate, most likely with coal out and grain home. Details of her fate are confined to the terse statement '4.6.1942: Mined and sunk off Borkum'.

The photograph was taken on the Mersey in 1935, and prompts the question what was she doing there. A note on the back of a print says 'taken in the rain', so it was possible that Basil Feilden had made a trip especially to see her, suggesting her visit was rare, if not unique. *[B. and A. Feilden/J. and M. Clarkson]*

Searching hard for photographers to illustrate Ian Wilson's article on early steam participants in the Belfast coal trade, one of the editors was delighted to discover this photograph of John Bacon's *Plantagenet* (696/1883). However, his joy was quickly dispelled when researching her history, as the *Plantagenet* mentioned by Ian as being built in 1869 was wrecked on the coast of Spain on 14th October 1880 whilst on a voyage from Newport to Barcelona with coal. A quick check revealed that owners John Bacon of Liverpool had a second *Plantagenet*, built and engined in 1883 by Allsup and Sons of Preston. Although the ship in the photograph looked a real antique, it would much more likely be the second of the name, and so not appropriate for Ian's article.

However, it was still of interest, firstly as it was likely to be unique in showing *Plantagenet*, a photograph of which does not appear in Robins' and MacRonald's recent, well illustrated 'Powell, Bacon and Hough: Formation of Coast Lines Limited'. Secondly, it must have been taken at Bristol before 21st March 1897 when the ship was wrecked at Black Head, near the Lizard whilst on a voyage from St. Valery to Runcorn with a cargo of flints. Referring to our article on the York Collection in 'Record' 63, this may well be the earliest definite date for a photo in the collection. Sure, this includes even older ships than *Plantagenet*, but all of these outlived her and could have been photographed later.

MARACAIBO TO MANCHESTER

In 1956 and 1957 Esso Petroleum placed in service on the British coast four tankers built in the USA for use on Lake Maracaibo. Memories, good and bad, of British seafarers who served on these ships formed part of a major feature on Maracaibo tankers in the estimable 'South Coast Packet', journal of the South Coast Branch of the World Ship Society for August 2013. This in turn sparked a vivid early memory for one of the editors who, whilst routinely trespassing on the banks of the Manchester Ship Canal as a schoolboy in the 1950s, saw one of these tankers waddling up to Manchester. This short illustrated feature draws on just some of the material in 'South Coast Packet', with the blessing of its industrious editor Trevor Cox.

The Maracaibo tankers in brief

The story of the tankers begins with the exploitation of the crude oil below this Venezuelan lake in 1914. Lake Maracaibo itself, and the bar at its seaward entrance, were not deep enough for ocean-going tankers, hence a shuttle service was instituted using shallow-draughted tankers. They carried crude to the Dutch islands of Aruba and Curaçao where there were facilities to tranship it to larger tankers and, increasingly, refineries. The best-known fleet was that of Lago Shipping Co. Ltd., built mainly by Harland and Wolff, and initially managed by Andrew Weir of Bank Line. This eventually numbered 21 tankers running to Aruba, where at San Nicolas there were transhipment facilities and later a refinery.

However, there were other oil companies exploiting Maracaibo crude. In 1915 and 1916 Royal Dutch Shell built a refinery at Willemstad on Curaçao, and their subsidiary Curaçaosche Petroleum Maatschappij began a tug and lighter service to supply it with crude. In 1928 Standard Oil of New Jersey, better known under its later name Esso, bought into the existing Creole Petroleum Corporation and later came to own a refinery at Aruba. Determined to increase its involvement in the rich Maracaibo oilfield, Standard Oil acquired the British Lago Shipping Co. Ltd. in 1932 and in 1937 took over its management from Andrew Weir, adding further shallow-draught tankers.

Negotiating the bar at the entrance to Lake Maracaibo, and then the narrow channel to the oil loading berths, was a severe test of seamanship, as there was often just 18 inches of clearance beneath the tanker's keel and the bar could produce some serious waves. Eventually the entrance to the lake and the channel to the loading berths began to be dredged and by 1939 could accept tankers with a draft of 17 feet, so that the Maracaibo tankers were progressively replaced with larger vessels. The facilities at Aruba and Curaçao and the tankers serving them were obvious targets for U-boats during the Second World War and, to replace losses, the Creole Petroleum Corporation ordered ten tankers from yards at Duluth and Sparrow's Point, Maryland. After the war, dredging of the bar and the lake channel was intensified so that ocean-going tankers could load at terminals within the lake, making the shallow-draught tankers redundant.

Above: A sister to the four tankers which came to Britain, the Venezuelan-flag *Esso Guiria* (3,401/1943) working on Lake Maracaibo. She had been built at Duluth as *Guiria*, was renamed *Esso Guiria* in 1948, and was broken up at Hamburg in 1962. *[World Ship Society print collection]*

Left: *Esso Chelsea*, the first of the group to be registered in the United Kingdom, typically deep-laden on the Thames. These tankers had so little freeboard that pilots could simply hop over their rails from the pilot boat. *[Roy Fenton collection]*

Panama to London

In the 1950s Esso moved four of their war-built and Panama-registered Maracaibo tankers to the United Kingdom, principally to carry heavy oil from their refinery on the Solent at Fawley and their depot at Purfleet to oil-fired power stations on the Thames, at Portishead and elsewhere. The process began in 1955 when, in September, Esso requested the Board of Trade to approve the names *Esso Chelsea* and *Esso Fulham* for the *Amacuro* and *Trujillo*. The ships were sent to the Tyne to be refitted and adapted for British conditions and regulations. It is possible that this work was protracted, as the two tankers were not registered until work was completed in November 1956. By then Esso had decided to send over *Caripito* and *Guarico* and in August 1956 the Board of Trade sanctioned their renaming as *Esso Lambeth* and *Esso Wandsworth*, respectively. A similar delay ensued until they were registered in March and June 1957. Refitting was done by Brigham and Cowan Ltd. at South Shields and by Palmers (Hebburn) Co. Ltd. at Hebburn.

ESSO CHELSEA 1956-1969
O.N. 187494 4,352g 2,110n 5,572d.
366.1 x 60.3 x 15.1 feet.
Two 3-cyl. (16, 26 and 43 x 27 inches) by Vulcan Iron Works, Wilkes-Barre, Pennsylvania, USA driving twin screws; each 1,000 IHP, 7½ knots.
7.4.1945: Launched by Bethlehem-Sparrow's Point Shipyard Inc., Sparrow's Point, Maryland, USA (Yard No. 4441) for the Creole Petroleum Corporation, Panama as AMACURO.
5.1945: Completed.
19.11.1956: Registered at London (Port No. 175/1956) in the ownership of the Esso Petroleum Co. Ltd., London as ESSO CHELSEA.
30.6.1969: Arrived at Bruges to be broken up by Brugse Scheepssloperij.
2.7.1969: Register closed.

ESSO FULHAM 1956-1970
O.N. 187495 4,352g 2,110n 5,572d.
366.1 x 60.3 x 15.1 feet.
Two 3-cyl. (16, 26 and 43 x 27 inches) by Vulcan Iron Works, Wilkes-Barre, Pennsylvania, USA driving twin screws; each 1,000 IHP, 7½ knots.
21.4.1945: Launched by Bethlehem-Sparrow's Point Shipyard Inc., Sparrow's Point, Maryland, USA (Yard No. 4442) for the Creole Petroleum Corporation, Panama as TRUJILLO.
6.1945: Completed.
19.11.1956: Registered at London (Port No. 176/1956) in the ownership of the Esso Petroleum Co. Ltd., London as ESSO FULHAM.
10.6.1970: Arrived at Bilbao in tow of AZNAR JOSE LUIS to be broken up by Revalorizacion de Materiales S.A.
11.6.1970: Register closed.
15.6.1970: Demolition began.

ESSO LAMBETH 1957-1965
O.N. 187549 4,352g 2,110n 5,400d.
366.1 x 60.3 x 15.1 feet.
Two 3-cyl. (16, 26 and 43 x 27 inches) by Vulcan Iron Works, Wilkes-Barre, Pennsylvania, USA driving twin screws; each 1,000 IHP, 7½ knots.
19.12.1942: Launched by the Barnes-Duluth Shipbuilding Company, Duluth,

Esso Chelsea once more, this time photographed near Cardiff, judging by the tug's funnel colours (top). *[Roy Fenton collection]*
Esso Fulham (middle). *[J. and M. Clarkson]*
Esso Fulham leaving the Thames for the breakers 5th May 1970 (bottom). *[J. and M. Clarkson]*

Esso Lambeth. [FotoFlite incorporating Skyfotos]

Minnesota, USA (Yard No. 13) for the Creole Petroleum Corporation, Panama as CARIPITO.
9.1943: Completed.
18.3.1957: Registered at London (Port Number 37/1957) in the ownership of the Esso Petroleum Co. Ltd., London as ESSO LAMBETH.
19.6.1962: In collision in Gravesend Reach, River Thames with the motor vessel SCOTTISH TRADER (11,563/1962) whilst entering Tilbury with a cargo of fuel oil. Beached off Gravesend, patched and taken to Tilbury for permanent repairs.
27.9.1965: Arrived Hamburg to be broken up by Eisen und Metall A.G.
7.10.1965: Register closed.

Esso Wandsworth. [Roy Fenton collection]

ESSO WANDSWORTH 1957-1965
O.N. 187594 4,352g 2,110n 5,549d.
366.1 x 60.3 x 15.1 feet.
Two 3-cyl. (16, 26 and 43 x 27 inches) by Vulcan Iron Works, Wilkes-Barre, Pennsylvania, USA driving twin screws; each 1,000 IHP, 7½ knots.
20.5.1943: Launched by the Barnes-Duluth Shipbuilding Company, Duluth, Minnesota, USA (Yard No. 17) for the Creole Petroleum Corporation, Panama as GUARICO.
10.1943: Completed.
25.6.1957: Registered at London (Port Number 92/1957) in the ownership of the Esso Petroleum Co. Ltd., London as ESSO WANDSWORTH.
23.9.1965: Damaged in collision with Dutch motor vessel MOERDYK (11,127/1965) near the Ovens Buoy in Lower Hope Reach, Thames, in fog, whilst on a voyage from Thames Haven to Dartford with a cargo of fuel oil. Beached with tug assistance upstream of the buoy.
26.9.1965: Refloated and towed to Purfleet for discharge of her remaining cargo, 400 tons of which had been lost. Later taken to Commercial Wharf. Gravesend.
12.10.1965: During work to cut away the damaged structure, sparks from a cutting torch are believed to have ignited fumes from oil residues, causing an explosion and fire. Dry-docked at Tilbury, it was found that damage was so extensive that she was declared a constructive total loss.
11.12.1965: Delivered at Grays, Essex to be broken up by T.W. Ward Ltd.
8.6.1966: Register closed.

Esso Wandsworth in tow of *Sun XVII* in October 1965. The collision damage can be seen on her port bow. *[J. and M. Clarkson]*

Driving the 'dingbats'

With their shallow draught and slow speed these tankers gained an unenviable reputation for being difficult to manoeuvre. They appeared to have earned the nickname 'dingbats' when a pilot remarked that their speed was like a 'dingbat out of hell', while a Manchester Ship Canal Pilot once reported the ship 'was built like a grapefruit'.

A mate on an Everard tanker recalled 'overtaking one in the River Thames which seemed to take sudden shears. I was talking to the mate of her one day and he was explaining she was a hell of a ship to steer'. A former second mate of *Esso Fulham* who later went into pilotage said 'Thank god I never had to pilot one'. A former helmsman described them as 'Terrible steering ships, pilots hated them as we the A.B.s did'.

A navigator noted 'The *Esso Chelsea* had a maximum speed of about 8 or 9 knots and I remember the interesting navigational requirement of having to offset the course across the mouth of The Wash by something like 30 degrees to counteract the rapid tidal ebb'. A slightly tongue-in-cheek comment sums up their slow speed, especially in bad weather 'I also remember one rough trip from Milford Haven to Dingle on the Mersey - I think we passed the South Stack light three times in eight hours'.

A fourth engineer joined *Esso Wandsworth* for the first time at Milford Haven in 1964. 'I vividly remember a group of us standing on the jetty as she came alongside, and the first question was 'which b****y way round is she?' Since the bow and stern looked similar and her steering was a little uncertain - she hit the jetty.'

He also remembers how 'in the engine room everything was driven by steam reciprocating engines and D.C. motors, and the twin triple-expansion engines had no rev counters, so responding to telegraph instructions was a matter of uneducated guesswork. On 'full away' we used to try to match the speeds of the engines by standing between them and trying to match the rate of movement of the high pressure con rods, and we rarely got it right so the bridge would assist us by telling us what steering angle they had to maintain to go more or less straight, following which we would carry out adjustments (or not as we thought fit). The one thing I really remember, apart from the twin scotch boilers that would blow rivets at regular intervals and blow back from the furnace fronts if they took exception to you, was the 'fridge system that worked on chlorine gas. Every now and again the 'fridge pumps would start to attempt pumping liquid chlorine, and that caused a massive overload in the D.C. pump motors. The result was a dimming of the engine room lamps and, if we didn't get to the pumps quickly enough, an enormous bang as the fuse blew and blasted the back panels off the switchboard.'

Being designed for the relatively calm waters of Lake Maracaibo the tankers were not best suited for work around the British coast, especially in winter. One former seaman reported that 'The period of roll was four seconds, whether two degrees either side, or 22 degrees'. Another claimed, 'she could roll like a pig when minded to. The ship's laundry room was on the other side of the companionway to the engine room door, and when she rolled to a certain angle the washing machine would shoot out of the laundry room and into the engine room.' A former officer added 'It was the only ship where you had to stow the chart rubbers to stop them falling off the chart table'. On one occasion *Esso Wandsworth* had to take fuel oil across to Cherbourg to bunker *Queen Mary* as conditions were too severe to risk her entering Southampton. 'That's when we really found out how a dingbat could roll. The period of roll didn't come into it - it got close to the revs per minute!'

Despite these comments, the ships did engender a degree of affection. *Esso Lambeth* was a 'great little ship, and yes, a brilliant feeder'. A former deck officer recalls being 'very upset on being moved to a dingbat from *Esso Lancashire* (49,397/1962)... but it only took a couple of days to realise what a great life it was on the dingbats: London River, load at Thameshaven or Purfleet, discharge at the power stations. Occasionally to Fawley to load and a deep-sea trip to Plymouth'. Another said 'Certainly not exactly palatial, but the standard of feeding, as throughout Esso, was superb, and I know what I would rather have'. A second mate who was in *Esso Fulham* adds 'These were good times and although it was hard work it was also rewarding. Experience gained rock dodging and ship handling which if you were a junior officer on larger tonnage would just never happen. Good ships - good times.' The quotes are published on the shipsnostalgia.com website.

Whatever their strange traits, the four tankers fulfilled an important role in the 1950s at a time when British power stations were turning from coal and requiring huge deliveries of heavy fuel oil. They helped begin the enormous increase in the average size of coastal tankers, leading to the situation where ships which would have been regarded as ocean-going monsters in 1956 are now routinely employed coasting.

ABERDEEN LINERS WERE IN FOR THE LONG HAUL

Peter Myers

Dreadnought (150/1907) was built by Hall, Russell and her long career as a liner ended when she was broken up in 1956. *[Aberdeen City Libraries]*

Ythan Braes (270/1917) came from the John Duthie Torry Shipbuilding Co. Ltd., Aberdeen and was previously named *Margaret Morrice* and *Grace Wetherly*. *[Aberdeen City Libraries]*

Aberdeen was not only once Scotland's premier trawling port but also its biggest port for the great line fishing with four-fifths of the country's annual great line catch landed there. During the rapid growth of the steam trawling industry in the late 19th century, many fishermen from the coastal villages near the city bought steam vessels, known as liners, for line fishing. Most liners were owned by individual fishermen, whose income came from the vessel's earnings which fluctuated depending on the size of the catch and what it fetched at the market.

Baskets filled with lines were assembled at the port's Old Torry Pier, waiting to be stowed aboard the liners. Each coiled line carried a snood every 21 feet and which had a hook to catch halibut, skate, torsk and ling. The lines were made from the finest Italian hemp and 'barked' with a preservative called cutch. They were hand-baited at sea with squid or herring before being shot; the liners usually caught the herring using their own nets. Line-caught fish tended to be larger and in better condition than fish caught by the trawl net.

Fortunes of the liners

The liners were outnumbered by steam trawlers but still formed a significant part of Aberdeen's fishing fleet. In 1911 there were 217 steam trawlers and 53 liners at the port with the latter fishing mainly in home waters with varying fortunes as I learned from a log dating from 1910-11 and kept by John Baxter, skipper of the *Morning Star* (120/1895) and built by Alexander Hall and Co. Ltd. of Aberdeen. On 21st June 1910, the liner had a good haul of large halibut after shooting 17 lines 36 miles north of Foula, Shetland before heading south to a position off Strathy Point, on the north coast of Sutherland, where they shot 29 lines but 'got practically no fish at all' despite the 'splendid weather'.

Winter weather could affect fishing performance as happened on 22nd February 1911 when all 16 lines were hauled at 3 am just as 'the wind went away to the S.W. & blew very strong. We battened everything down & put the lines below, & set away for home full speed. Every other two or three minutes she had to be stopped at sea, the wind having increased greatly since we last hauled. Knocked in one of the front windows'. The *Morning Star* (A 773) returned safely to Aberdeen where her catch made £132 at the market.

In Shetland waters she was leaving Lerwick on 2nd March when 'we struck a rock with our bilge keel. We were going full speed at the time and she happened to slide over it. The *Cruden Bay* was going ahead of us & he struck too'. On their return to Aberdeen the *Morning Star* was one of 15 line boats at the market and made £93 while the *Cruden Bay* (125/1899) made £89.

The *Morning Star* was windbound at Aberdeen on 14th March but Skipper Baxter noted that '*Caledonia* (144/1898) was the only line boat at the fish market today. He has about 45 Scores fish. He knocked overboard one of his crew when hauling, but managed to get him aboard again.'

The nature of the seabed could also be detrimental to a liner's fishing performance as happened on 6th April when, after shooting 30 lines, they found 'Red stones on the lead. Not the proper bottom at all.' Six days later 'the *Vigilant* came and spoke to us when we had 5 (lines) to haul. He hadn't shot a hook all day, looking for bottom to shoot their lines on.' When they returned to Aberdeen the *Vigilant* (139/1902) made only £20 while the *Morning Star* earned £63 at the market.

The liners could be vulnerable to the occasional mishap at sea as when the *Star of Victory* (235/1917) ran aground in Sinclair's Bay, near Keiss, Caithness on 25th October 1939. Her skipper tried to free his ship using a kedge anchor, first forward and then aft, but she remained fast. The next day a gale was blowing and heavy seas battered the casualty. The Wick lifeboat *City of Edinburgh* came to her aid and, despite the conditions, Coxswain William More brought his boat alongside and rescued the vessel's crew of 10. A few days later a salvage team of seven went aboard the *Star of Victory* but a sudden fresh wind blew up and they were taken off by the Wick lifeboat. The vessel remained fast and became a total loss.

The ill-fated *Star of Victory* had been among the liners which voyaged to Greenland in the summer of 1939 to shoot their lines for the great halibut. Earnings fluctuated, but big catches brought high financial rewards as it did for the Middlesbrough-built *Chassiron* (258/1913) in July that year after a trip to Greenland. The liner, which was owned jointly by her skipper, Alexander Milne, and James Mackie, landed 40 score of halibut, 70 score of cod and 10 score of skate which fetched almost £1,200 at Aberdeen fish market. Her earnings helped to dispel claims that poor prices were being paid for fish at the port. Two other liners, the *Charles Doran* (273/1917) and *Mount Keen* (258/1936), had headed for Grimsby in expectation of higher rewards but their catches fetched poorer prices than those earned by the *Chassiron*.

Fifteen years earlier, the former Castle class Admiralty trawler *John Gillman* (235/1917), commanded by Skipper Buchan, landed 90 score of halibut at Aberdeen in 1924. The halibut were, on average, more than six feet and, because of the fish market's floor-space demands, landing of the catch was spread over two days. The *John Gillman* (A 230) was owned at the time by Richard W. Lewis and Sons Ltd. which, like several other Aberdeen fishing vessel owners, was remarkably self-sufficient in having engineering, carpentry, boiler making and coal-importing interests. The *John Gillman* later switched to trawling out of Aberdeen and was the subject of a General Post Office Film Unit's drama-documentary entitled 'North Sea' which was released in 1938 and is available on DVD. The former naval trawler had also been in the limelight in the First World War when she sank the German submarine *UB 30* with depth charges off the Tyne on 13th August 1918.

A world-record shot of halibut was landed at Aberdeen on 24th April 1950 by the steam liner *Ellena* (257/1921), skippered by John Taylor, while fishing off Iceland. The catch, which took seven hours to discharge, weighed only three hundredweight short of 58 tons and was sold for £7,783. The vessel also landed 60 hundredweight of other fish species which earned about £100. Skipper Taylor jointly owned the *Ellena* with Aberdeen trawler owner Alex Hay.

Some steam drifters at Peterhead switched to great line fishing about the middle of March at the end of the winter herring fishing season in the 1920s. The *North Briton* (97/1894), owned by James G.A. Stephen, was notably successful at the line fishing in 1924, and her catches of halibut fetched good prices at Aberdeen.

Liner skippers

The liner *Lord Talbot* (325/1917) was commanded by Tom Watson who, like many of the great line skippers, came from the East Neuk of Fife. He became known as 'Yankee Tom' after he and his crew rescued George and Blanche Hutchinson and their daughters, Kathryn and Janet, an American family nicknamed the Flying Hutchinsons, on 13th September 1932. They and the four crew members were attempting a west-east air crossing in a Sikorsky S-38 amphibian, but were forced to ditch off Greenland. Skipper Watson told a news agency that they found the wrecked aircraft in Ikersuak Fjord while searching among the ice floes. The *Lord Talbot* was joined in the search by two other Aberdeen liners, the *Mount Ard* (255/1931) and *Star of Victory*. The three vessels steamed on parallel courses for 55 miles before the crew of the *Lord Talbot* spotted a distress flare. They carefully negotiated a passage through an icefield before establishing radio contact at night with the Hutchinsons who said they and the crew were safe and well. Their rescue was delayed until daylight because of a strong swell, and the liner's small boat was used to bring them to safety. The *Lord Talbot* steamed home with the rescued party to Aberdeen, where Skipper Watson's employers sacked him for spending time rescuing the aviators rather than fishing. There was a public outcry at his treatment and he was reinstated.

Lord Talbot arrives at Aberdeen on 22nd September 1932 after her epic rescue of the Flying Hutchinsons off Greenland. *[Planet News Ltd.]*

Mount Ard (255/1931) was built by John Lewis and Sons Ltd., Aberdeen in 1931 and went great line fishing off Greenland in her early years. *[Aberdeen City Libraries]*

Kinaldie sails from Aberdeen in the 1950s. She is fitted out as a trawler but had been a liner in the 1930s when she was owned by the Leiper family. *[Aberdeen City Libraries]*

Doonie Braes (1946) was originally the Royal Navy's *MFV 1534* and replaced a steam liner of the same name which was wrecked off Orkney in 1955. *[Aberdeen City Libraries]*

Among other liner skippers in the 1930s was James Strachan, from Cairnbulg, Aberdeenshire, who took command of the liner *Ben Rossal* (260/1929) in 1933. She was built by Hall, Russell and Co. Ltd., Aberdeen for Richard Irvin and Sons Ltd. whose vessels fished out of Aberdeen and North Shields. Skipper Strachan left Irvin in 1956 and pursued the great lining with his own boat, *Strachans* (78/1956). He retired from the sea in 1965 but his three sons, Albert, Alexander and James, continued to operate the 1956-built *Strachans* out of Fraserburgh.

Many skippers had first gone to sea at an early age including Robert Bruce who began life as a fisherman when he was 13. He was in his early 20s when he became skipper of the liner *Kinaldie* (197/1914), owned by the Leiper family who were the most prominent of Aberdeen's line fishing vessel owners. After the Second World War he took command of another steam liner, *Doonie Braes* (213/1918), which he also owned. She had the misfortune to run aground near the Old Man of Hoy, Orkney on 20th April 1955 while returning from northern waters with a catch of 135 hundredweight of halibut. Skipper Bruce had hoped it was possible to tow the *Doonie Braes* off, but she had filled up with water and hopes of salvaging her were abandoned. Her skipper soon returned to sea in the *Grasby* (113/1946), a former Admiralty-type motor fishing vessel, which was renamed *Doonie Braes*.

George Leiper, who was born in 1914, was another prominent line skipper from Aberdeen and first went to sea in 1932. He recalled some of his experiences in the BBC2 TV documentary series, 'The Call of the Sea', broadcast in 1997. On his first ship they lived in the forecastle which had carbide gas lighting. When he asked where the lavatory was he was told it was down in the stokehold but he couldn't stand the heat there. He asked where else he could relieve himself and was told to 'put your backside over the rail and do it there'. He said: 'I had to grab two iron bars while seated over the stern of the ship to do my business.'

Catching the geni

By 1939 George was already a skipper and commanded the liner *General Botha* (244/1916). At Aberdeen she embarked London journalist Eldon

Moore, who wrote an article, 'Geni: the Story of the Halibut Fishery', which appeared in 'The Listener' magazine on 19th October 1939. It is a vivid account and evokes a way of life that has now vanished. Moore wrote that the line was anchored 600 feet down and after one line had been joined to the next they eventually covered nine miles of the ocean bed. He described the hauling in of the line which was done by a small steam winch. A man stood by the winch and 'grabs each snood as it comes up, and unhooks the fish on the end of it. Other men are redding the lines – getting them into perfect order for the next day's shooting. Others are gutting and cleaning fish, cutting some for bait. Everybody is busy, including the skipper, who takes turn and turn about at each job, like all the other fishermen.'

There was great excitement when they caught their first geni: 'Everybody dropped whatever he was doing, grabbed one of the nine-foot gaffs, and dashed to the side by the winch. The winch chattered like a demon as it raced free. Down in the water I could see some great body threshing the sea to foam. Then the long sharp gaffs came down, and four strong men strained and heaved to the roll of the vessel. Over the side came the biggest fish I had ever seen, fighting madly. He had to be stunned first, then killed by a jab through his gills into the top of his spine, before he was unhooked'

The geni was highly prized by fishermen in 1939 as it fetched £4 to £5 at the market while the halibut oil extracted from their livers realised about £60 a gallon. The halibut was also highly profitable for some of the big restaurants – one had bought a whole one for £5 and it brought in £112 after it had been served in portions to customers.

Moore praised the Aberdeen fishermen whom he had lived with for a month and wrote that he 'couldn't wish for finer company' and had looked after his safety and comfort 'like a corps of nurses'. He added that they were 'a folk apart, cut off from their families and their kind for over three hundred days a year. For most of that time they are working on deck in Arctic gales and blizzards. They get out of it, too, just what luck gives them. They earn no wages, but are shareholders in the enterprise.'

General Botha featured in a magazine article in 1939 about great line fishing after a journalist wrote about his trip on her to the Arctic Circle. *[Aberdeen City Libraries]*

Fishermen redding or preparing the lines on the *General Botha* in the late 1930s. *[Aberdeen Art Gallery and Museums]*

Mount Keen of 1936 when she was fitted out for great lining. *[Aberdeen Art Gallery and Museums]*

Notable great liners

The liners were readily identifiable by the absence of trawl gallows and winch. However, the *Mount Keen* (258/1936) was built by John Lewis and Sons Ltd. of Aberdeen as a dual-purpose fishing vessel. She pursued trawling in winter while in summer the after gallows were removed and she was adapted for great line fishing. Her bow and stern were reinforced for the ice conditions which she would experience around Greenland.

George Leiper was skipper of the *Mount Keen* (A 411) between circa 1948 and 1955 when she switched to trawling. George made many trips on her to Iceland and Greenland while fishing for the great halibut, and he told the author that for the long trip she carried 160 tons of coal in her bunkers and the fish-room while 20 to 30 tons in bags were stowed on deck. Her average daily fuel consumption at full speed during the trip was seven to eight tons. The *Mount Keen* was reported in the press as Aberdeen's last coal-fired steam trawler when she left the port for the final time on 19th February 1963 to be broken up at Montrose.

There were about 40 great liners fishing out of Aberdeen in 1950, but their numbers declined steadily. Among the few diesel-engined liners was the *Loch Brora* (191/1958), built by Livingston and Company, Peterhead for Malcolm Smith Ltd. Her skipper in the 1970s was George Barclay of Anstruther, Fife, one of Britain's leading line fishermen. A catch of 660 kit (825 hundredweight) of fish from a 21-day trip to the Rockall grounds by the *Loch Brora* (A 198) sold for a record £12,005 at Aberdeen in the autumn of 1973 while in early November 1974 she returned to her home port after a 20-day trip to Faroe and her 501 hundredweight catch fetched £9,364 at the market.

Another Peterhead-built motor vessel was the *Glenstruan* (183/1958) which was completed at Alex. J. Mitchell's yard for Peter and J. Johnstone Ltd. of Aberdeen. Skipper George Morrice commanded her on her maiden trip to fish for halibut off Iceland and Greenland, and which was filmed by the Esso Petroleum Co. Ltd.'s film unit. The documentary was entitled 'Hook, Line and Sinker' and is available on DVD, giving a fascinating insight into great line fishing. The *Glenstruan* (A.200) was later converted to trawling.

A further great liner to come from Livingston's yard at Peterhead

Mount Keen switched to trawling in 1955 and is seen passing Hall, Russell's shipyard while outbound from Aberdeen, circa 1959. *[World Ship Society Ltd.]*

Loch Brora of 1958 fished out of Aberdeen as a liner until February 1976 when she was towed to the Medway to be scrapped. *[Aberdeen City Libraries]*

Glenstruan manoeuvres in the Albert Basin, Aberdeen, circa 1960. A documentary film was made of her maiden trip as a liner to Iceland and Greenland in 1958. *[Aberdeen City Libraries]*

was the *Jarlshof* (206/1963) which was completed for Buchan Trawlers Ltd., who were forced to return her to the White Fish Authority because of a shortage of great line fishermen. She made only two trips before she was laid-up at Peterhead, where she was converted to a trawler and renamed *Ardenlea* by the Aberdeen firm Craig Stores.

The wooden-hulled *Radiation* (139/1957) was Aberdeen's top-performing great liner in the 1970s. She was owned jointly by Alex Gardner, of Cellardyke, Fife and Peter and J. Johnstone Ltd. of Aberdeen. The 97-foot *Radiation* (A 115) was built by Smith and Hutton Ltd. of Anstruther and launched on 31st January 1957. She was constructed of larch on oak with an Oregon pine deck and her Mirrlees oil engine gave her a speed of 9.5 knots. The *Radiation* sailed from Aberdeen on 25th May 1957 on her maiden fishing trip when she headed to the grounds around Rockall. Her other favoured grounds were off the south and west of Iceland. The liner carried 42 lines which were each 400 fathoms in length.

The *Radiation* grossed a record £109,000 in 1973 and the feat was marked by the presentation of a silver salver to Skipper Gardner from the Radiation Fishing Co. Ltd., her registered owners. Gardner's son, John, who also sailed aboard the vessel, also received a presentation. Robert Patrick of Anstruther took over as skipper and joint owner of the *Radiation* in January 1975 and was joined in the new enterprise by George Muir and Derek Chater, mate and engineer respectively of his previous command, the *Twinkling Star*.

Another Fife line fisherman was John Muir, who was skipper and owner of the *Ocean Dawn* (131/1956). She had been built by Richards Ironworks Ltd., Lowestoft for Bloomfields Ltd., Great Yarmouth and was one of 21 motor drifter/trawlers built by the yard between 1949 and 1960. Skipper Muir bought her in 1969 and she was registered at Anstruther with the Kirkcaldy registration of KY 371, although her catches were landed at Aberdeen. The 91-foot *Ocean Dawn* had a crew of nine and averaged trips of 21 to 24 days, mainly to the Faroe and Bailey grounds. She was involved in a bizarre accident in September 1979 when she sank after becoming caught under a pier when the tide came in at Aberdeen. She was later raised and repaired.

Radiation fished as a liner from 1957 until 1980. There were several unsuccessful attempts to preserve her before she was sunk as a sheltered dive site in Scapa Flow, Orkney. *[World Ship Society Ltd.]*

Ardenlea lies at Commercial Quay, Aberdeen after she had been converted back to great lining. Her fishing registration was later changed from A 805 to KY 194. *[Aberdeen Journals Ltd.]*

Ocean Dawn was built as a drifter/trawler in 1956 and is seen at Lowestoft on 31st January 1968, the year before she came north to Scotland. *[J. and M. Clarkson]*

Ocean Dawn returns to Aberdeen after a fishing trip in July 1975. She is believed to be still afloat as a houseboat on the south coast of England. *[J. and M. Clarkson]*

Ocean Dawn after she sank at Aberdeen harbour on 10th September 1979. She was later raised and resumed fishing. *[Aberdeen Journals Ltd.]*

End of great lining

The invention of auto-lining gear removed the drudgery of traditional hand-baiting methods. In January 1979, J. Marr (Aberdeen) Ltd. announced it would install Norwegian-made Mustard auto-lining gear on the trawler *Glen Clova* (168/1976) and she later worked the Rockall and Faroe grounds under the command of George Barclay before being sold to new owners in Nova Scotia from where she continued auto-line fishing. Great lining with automatic gear was seen at the time as a viable alternative to bottom trawling, which faced difficult times because of contracting fishing areas and dwindling stocks. Three other Scottish vessels had been converted to auto-line fishing in joint ventures with the Highlands and Islands Development Board to supply its fish-drying plant at Breasclete on the Isle of Lewis.

The *Radiation*'s owners replaced her in 1980 with the *Ardenlea* which reverted to great lining and became one of the few liners allowed to fish in Faroese waters after Scottish trawlers had been excluded. However, Aberdeen's line fishing tradition was drawing to a close and the *Ocean Dawn* was the port's last great line fishing vessel when owner John Muir decided to retire at the age of 62 and sell her in March 1984 to be converted to an offshore standby vessel at Lowestoft. Right to the end she had been landing 30 to 50 boxes of halibut on good trips, as well as tusk, ling and cod.

Glen Clova off Aberdeen on 10th May 1979 after she had been converted from trawling to auto-lining. *[J. and M. Clarkson]*

A DOZEN COOL BEAUTIES

Tony Breach

The Second World War was a difficult time for merchant shipping generally and in particular for the reefers in the banana trades. Bananas were considered to be a luxury item and, in Northern Europe in particular, it was decided that more substantial foodstuffs were needed in order to feed the military as well as munitions workers. In the Atlantic theatre the importation of the fruit declined significantly leaving much of it to rot in the plantations, with the United Fruit Company estimating that 75,000 tons per month was lost in their Central American plantations. Available reefers were put into trans-Atlantic service bringing meat and other food products from both North and South America to Northern Europe as well as to troops stationed abroad. When the United States became involved, several of their larger, passenger-carrying reefers were taken into naval service as personnel and perishable supplies carriers. Some smaller ships remained in normal fruit delivery services, and the United Fruit Company was able to keep 16 ships carrying bananas. One interesting departure from banana shipments was when United Fruit contracted with the Defence Supplies Corporation offering to plant 20,000 acres of a crop of Abaca, also known as Manila Hemp (*Musa textilis*) without profit. This crop was shipped to North American ports where it was turned into Manila ropes which were much needed by the military as the Philippines, the major growing area, was under control of the Japanese.

The accompanying table gives my best estimate of the number of banana carriers lost in the Atlantic Theatre. However, there will be others from North European countries including Belgium, Netherlands and especially Norway.

Country	Sunk	Scuttled
France	12	4
UK (Fyffes)	14	
UK (Jamaica Banana)	2 (incl. 1 by collision)	
Denmark	4	1
USA	12	
Germany	10	
Italy	6	
Total	60	5

Following the end of hostilities in 1945 it took some time for the world to come to terms with the damage that had been caused in every respect and which delayed the return to 'normalcy'. In this respect I recall a photograph my mother had of myself at age about three, a war babe from 1944, stuffing a banana into my mouth titled 'His first banana'. However, rebuilding of the banana fleet was soon begun and it appears that there were naval architects who had ideas in respect of beauty, efficiency, simplicity and modem construction methods. One very interesting issue with these post-war reefers was that so many of them were delivered as motor ships. I have chosen 12 of what I consider to be the best-looking reefers built over a period of 22 years and hope readers will enjoy the photographs..

Editor's notes: in the details given of ships' careers the usual convention has been followed of not specifying the flag when it is the same as the domicile of the owner. Both length overall (l.o.a.) and length between perpendiculars (l.b.p.) are noted. Photographs are from the author's collection.

TARANTELLA

With its shipyards intact, Sweden was quickly off the mark with delivering reefers post war. However, *Joh. Gorthon* remained a one-off in the Gorthon fleet, which mostly comprised small general cargo ships and tankers. In contrast, as *Tarantella* (seen opposite) she was among many others in the fleet of Salenrederierna.

TARANTELLA
IMO 5172523 3,816g 4,170d.
121.21 l.o.a./111.25 l.b.p. x 16.16 x 7.12 metres.
Refrigerated capacity: 223,150 cubic feet.
Passengers: 12.
8-cyl. 2SCSA M.A.N.-type oil engine by builders; 5,250 BHP, 17.5 knots.
16.9.1946: Launched by Kockums Mekaniska Verkstads A/B, Malmo, Sweden (Yard No. 290) for Rederei A/B Gylfe (Stig O. Gorthon), Helsingborg, Sweden as JOH. GORTHON.
14.5.1947: Delivered.
1.1964: Sold to Salenrederierna A/B, Stockholm, Sweden for SEK 4,250,000 and renamed TARANTELLA.
11.1967: Sold to Sinli Navigation Corporation S.A., Panama and renamed SINCHION REEFER.
1972: Sold to Tung Yung Iron and Steel Works for demolition at Kaohsiung.
28.12.1972: Work commenced and completed 16.1.1973.

FORT RICHEPANSE

Fort Richepanse is the only member of this group built in a British yard, and then for a continental owner. With French shipyards still recovering from damage suffered during the occupation, her owners had little choice but to build abroad if they wanted to resume the carriage of West Indian bananas to France. Orders for two of the group were placed in Scotland and just one, *Fort Richelieu* (5,081/1951) with a home yard, Chantiers et Atelier de Provence at Port de Bouc. Most likely a French designer was responsible for the trio, with their particularly long bridge decks. The third member of the trio, *Fort Dauphin* (5,232/1949), was also built at Linthouse. It is intriguing that both the Scottish ships ended up being converted to ferries.

FORT RICHEPANSE
IMO 5118228 5,083g 4,035d.
122.47 l.o.a./117.00 l.b.p. x 16.00 x 5.49 metres.
Refrigerated capacity 196,656 cubic feet. Passengers: 12.
Two 8-cyl. 2SCSA Sulzer-type oil engines by the builders driving twin screws; total 8,000 BHP, 16.5 knots.
16.12.1948: Launched by Alexander Stephen and Sons Ltd., Linthouse, Glasgow (Yard No. 619) for Compagnie General Transatlantique, Havre, France as FORT RICHEPANSE.
2.7.1949: Delivered.
1965: Sold to Plate Shipping Co. S.A. (Rodriguez Group), Piraeus, Greece and renamed MARONIA.
1972: Sold to Compagnia Sarda di Navigazione Marittima S.A., Olbia, Italy and converted to a stern loading ro-ro ferry for Mediterranean service and renamed GOLFO DEGLIANGELI.
1980: Laid up at Genoa.
2.1985: Towed to La Spezia for demolition by Cantieri Navali del Golfo.
1.4.1985: Work began.

FRANCHINA FASSIO

Although this is an arbitrary sample, the German shipbuilding and engineering industry certainly score high, either building or at least designing the engines for over half and building a quarter of the hulls.

FRANCHINA FASSIO.
IMO 5119337 3,486g 3,029d.
115.37 l.o.a./104.58 l.b.p. x 15.45 x 6.29 metres.
Refrigerated capacity: 180,035 cubic feet.
7-cyl. 2SCSA oil engine by Maschinenbau Augsburg-Nürnburg, Augsburg, Germany; 4,670 BHP, 16.5 knots.
6.1953: Launched by H.C. Stülcken Sohn, Hamburg, Germany (Yard No. 820) for Villain e Fassio Societa Italiana di Navigazione Mercantile per Azioni, Genoa, Italy as FRANCHINA FASSIO.
10.1953: Delivered.
1957: Transferred to Villain e Fassio e Compagnia Internazionale di Genova Societa Riunite di Nav. S.p.A., Genoa.
1970: Sold to Société Naval Caennaise (Anct. G. Lamy et Compagnie), Caen, France and renamed DANAE.
1971: Badly damaged by fire when undergoing maintenance at Rouen.
1974: Sold to Ahmed Mohamed Baarbour and Ahmed Mohamed Baghlaf, Jeddah, Saudi Arabia and renamed BLUE OCEAN.
10.1.1981: Demolition commenced by A. Rehman and Co., Gadani Beach.

AHRENSBURG

German reefers were often cross-traders, rarely visiting their home ports, and *Ahrensburg* began her career working between South and North America. She was later chartered to Willy Bruns, under whose colours she did actually trade to the banana terminal in Hamburg. During her career she had just two principal owners, despite the number of inter-company transfers whilst with a Taiwanese group.

AHRENSBURG
IMO 5005988 3,062g 3,383d.
126.02 l.o.a./115.02 l.b.p. x 15.65 x 6.09 metres.
Refrigerated capacity: 217,678 cubic feet. Passengers: 12.
8-cyl. 2SCSA M.A.N.-type oil engine by the builders; 5,140 BHP, 17.0 knots.
15.11.1955: Launched by Kieler Howaldtswerke A.G., Kiel, Germany (Yard No. 1035) for Fruchtreederei Harald Schuldt und Co., Hamburg, Germany as AHRENSBURG.
22.1.1956: Delivered.
1966: Sold to Chung Lien Navigation Co. S.A., Panama (Great Pacific Navigation Co.Ltd., Taipei, Taiwan) and renamed CHEN CHENG.
1968: Transferred to Ho Thai Navigation Co. Ltd. (Great Pacific Navigation Co. Ltd.), Taipei.
1973: Transferred to Universal Seaways Co. (Private) Ltd., Singapore (Great Pacific Navigation Co. Ltd., Taipei) and renamed BLUE FRUIT under the Panama flag.
1977: Transferred back to Chung Lien Navigation Co. S.A., Panama (Great Pacific Navigation Co.Ltd., Taipei) and renamed BRIGHT FRUIT.
1983: Renamed ASIAN AMIGO and sold to Gi Yuen Steel Enterprise Co. Ltd., Kaohsiung where she arrived 9.6.1983.
20.6.1983: Demolition commenced.

CRUX

As *Cap Domingo*, *Crux* was built for service with Hamburg-Südamerikanische Dampfschiffahrts and their Columbus Line, but was nominally owned by Rudolf A. Oetker, the group's owner. She was followed from the Kiel yard by sister *Cap Corrientes* (4,505/1958) and somewhat later by a slight variation on the design, *Cap Valiente* (4,113/1960), both being placed in Hamburg-Süd ownership.

CRUX
IMO 5060574 2,974g 3,200d.
126.12 l.o.a./115.02 l.b.p. x 15.63 x 6.09 metres.
Refrigerated capacity 210,651 cubic feet. Passengers: 5.
9-cyl. 2SCSA M.A.N.-type oil engine by the builders; 6,000 BHP, 17.0 knots.
18.2.1958: Launched by Kieler Howaldtswerke A.G., Kiel, Germany (Yard No.1071) for Rudolf A. Oetker, Hamburg, Germany as CAP DOMINGO.
28.4.1958: Delivered.
3.10.1959: Heavily damaged in collision with Liberian-flagged tanker TRITON (10,603/1945) off Buenos Aires and subsequently towed by Dutch tug WITTE ZEE to Kiel where she was dry docked and repaired by her builders.
9.3.1970: Sold to Det Bergenske D/S (A/S Ludwig Mowinckels Rederi, manager), Bergen, Norway and renamed CRUX.
1973: Sold to Mediteranska Plovidba d.d., Korcula, Yugoslavia and renamed MARKO POLO.
4.10.1984: Laid up at Split.
1985: Sold to Brodospas for demolition.
17.5.1985: Work commenced.

LENEVERETT

The United States-owned Everett Steamship Corporation was set up at Shanghai in 1917, and gradually spread around South East Asia, so that by the 1970s, when it owned *Leneverett*, Everett was running ships under flags of convenience from an office in Yokohama. *Leneverett* was the final name for *Balsa*, built for Torvald Klaveness who had a mixed fleet in the early 1960s, with tankers and ore/oil carriers alongside the four reefers of his I/S Freezer. These included a sister to *Balsa* from the same builders, the *Baleares* (2,822/1959). After sale of *Balsa* to Willy Bruns as *Brunsberg* she spent a period on time-charter to Geest Line. Her sister, *Brunstal* ex *Baleares*, was illustrated on the River Ribble during a Geest charter in 'Record' 50, page 87.

LENEVERETT
IMO 5034977 2,824g 2,984d.
114.92 l.o.a./102.11 l.b.p. x 16.06 x 6.16 metres.
Refrigerated capacity: 217,708 cubic feet. Passengers: 6.
8-cyl. 2SCSA oil engine by Maschinenbau Augsberg-Nürnburg, Augsburg, Germany; 5,200 BHP, 17.0 knots.
1.4.1960: Launched by N.V. Verschure & Co. Scheepsvaart & Machinefabriek, Amsterdam, Netherlands (Yard No. Co. 378) for I/S Freezer (Torvald Klaveness), Oslo, Norway as BALSA.
9.1960: Delivered.
1966: Sold to Partenreederei m.s. 'Brunsberg' (W. Bruns und Co. (K-R), Hamburg, Germany and renamed BRUNSBERG.
1970: Sold to Everett-Orient Line Inc., Yokohama, Japan and renamed LENEVERETT under the Liberian flag.
8.8.1980: Arrived at Kaohsiung for demolition Chi Young Steel Enterprise Co. Ltd
15.8.1980: Work commenced.

JERRYEVERETT

The Swedish-built *Coral Sea* is illustrated under her final name, owners Everett-Orient Line adopting the unusual approach to nomenclature of running two personal names together. *Coral Sea* was the second of a trio built for this Swedish owner, she was preceded by *Pearl Sea* (6,287/1960) delivered in May 1960, and followed in November 1961 by *Crystal Sea* (6,425/1961).

JERRYEVERETT
IMO 5079525. 6,290g 6,130n. Later remeasured as an open shelter decker at 4,932g.
133.41 l.o.a./123.58 l.b.p. x 17.68 metres.
Refrigerated capacity: 254,980 cubic feet.
8-cyl. 2SCSA M.A.N.-type oil engine by the builders; 6,960 BHP, 18.0 knots.
1960: Launched by Kokkums Mekaniska Verkstad A/B, Malmo, Sweden (Yard No. 465) for Trelleborgs Ångfartygs A/B, Trelleborg, Sweden as CORAL SEA.
10.1960: Delivered.
1968: Transferred to Malmros Rederi A/B, Trelleborg.
1969: Sold to Everett-Orient Line Inc., Yokohama for USD 1,600,000 and renamed JERRYEVERETT under the Liberian flag.
11.5.1982: In collision with the Japanese motor cement carrier RYOEI MARU (498/1972) in fog off Himeshima, Japan. Six members of the crew of the Japanese vessel were lost.
26.3.1984: Arrived Busan, South Korea for demolition by Dong Ah Enterprise.
10.4.1984: Work began.
20.5.1984: Work completed.

PLOD

No comment is necessary on the inappropriateness of the name bestowed on the 18½-knot *Pentelikon* when she was sold to Yugoslavia, especially as the sale involved a year's back charter to Laeisz. Her original owner has a ship owning history over almost two centuries, and was once famous for its 'Flying P' line of large sailing ships. The tradition of giving names beginning with the letter P has been perpetuated through its period of reefer operating to the present day when it runs a large fleet comprising mainly container ships and vehicle carriers. *Pentelikon* was the first Laeisz reefer to be involved in the banana trade between Ecuador and Japan. In the photo *Plod* wears Lauritzen's funnel colours.

PLOD
IMO 5274230 4,747g 4,299d.
134.58 l.o.a./121.93 l.b.p. x 16.06 x 6.53 metres.
Refrigerated capacity: 254,576 cubic feet. Passengers: 4.
8-cyl. 2SCSA oil engine by Maschinenbau Augsburg-Nürnburg, Augsburg, Germany; 7,250 BHP, 18.5 knots.
25.8.1960: Launched by Deutsche Werft, Hamburg, Germany (Yard No.779) for F. Laeisz (K-R), Hamburg, Germany as PENTELIKON.
6.12.1960: Delivered.
1972: Transferred to Singapore flag.
1974: Sold to Mediteranska Plovidba.d.d., Korcula, Yugoslavia and renamed PLOD.
18.5.1986: Arrived at Gadani Beach for demolition by Rajab Ali and Company.
28.5.1986: Work began.

VOCE

Again in the colours of the state-owned Yugoslav reefer company is the former *Dragor Maersk*. She is a reminder that the mighty fleet of container ships and tankers now operated by A.P. Møller was once much more diverse. Like many of their ships of this period, she was built at the company's own ship yard in Odense. Something of a one-off, she was built for time charter to Salenrederierna of Stockholm.

VOCE
IMO 5093557 4,722g 5,550d.
132.63 l.o.a./121.92 l.b.p. x 17.68 x 7.85 metres.
Refrigerated capacity: 252,175 cubic feet. Passengers: 4.
9-cyl. 2SCSA oil engine by Burmeister & Wain's Maskin og Skibsbyggeri, Copenhagen, Denmark;
8,100 BHP, 19.0 knots.
2.7.1960: Launched by Odense Staalskibsvaerft A/S, Odense, Denmark (Yard No. 156) for A/S D/S Svendborg, D/S af 1912 A/S and A.P. Møller, Copenhagen, Denmark as DRAGOR MAERSK.
1.1961: Delivered.
1975: Sold to Mediteranska Plovidba, Korcula, Yugoslavia and renamed VOCE.
29.9.1988: Arrived at Chittagong for demolition by Steel Enterprise Ltd. who began work next day at Bhatiary.

VICTORIA REEFER

Espadon is French for swordfish. *Lethe*, bestowed by her new Swiss-based owner in 1977, is the Greek goddess of forgetfulness and oblivion and from whom the word lethargic derives, and is hardly a name to give a 17-knot reefer. *Espadon* had two near-sisters, *Tarpon* (4,903/1960), also built at Nantes but in a different yard, and the Dutch-built *Barracuda* (4,797/1960). Initially at least they ran from West Africa to French Mediterranean ports. The name of her final, Spanish-based owner suggests that as *Victoria Reefer* she finished her life as a fish reefer, although in her photograph she looks remarkably smart for this trade.

VICTORIA REEFER.
IMO 5106433 4,905g 3,707d.
115.27 l.o.a./106.36 l.b.p. x 16.03 x 6.103 metres.
Refrigerated capacity: 234,420 cubic feet.
Two 12-cyl. 4SCSA Pielstick Vee-type oil engines by Société Générale de Constructions Mecaniques, Le Courneve, France geared to a single shaft; 8,520 BHP total, 17.0 knots.
4.1.1962: Launched by Ateliers et Chantiers de Nantes (Bretagne-Loire), Nantes, France (Yard No. 665) for Société Générale de Transports Maritime, Marseilles, France as ESPADON.
7.1962: Completed and delivered.
1964: Owners restyled Compagnie Fabre, Société Générale de Transports Maritime, Marseille.
1977: Sold to Lethe Shipping Company, Monrovia, Liberia (Victor A. Sloutskis, Geneva, Switzerland) and renamed LETHE.
1979: Sold to Opaline Bay Shipping Co. S.A., Panama (Bay Shipping Co., Ltd., Geneva) and renamed OPALINE BAY.
1982: Sold to Compania de Vapores Kempe S.A., Panama (Mahonia Shipping Corporation, Monrovia) and renamed MOFREEZE.
1987: Sold to Comercio Internacional de Atun S.A. (COINASA), Panama (Pesquerias Hispano Africanas S.A., Bermeo, Spain) and renamed VICTORIA REEFER.
30.6.2004: Arrived at Alang to be broken up.
9.7.2004: Work began.

GOLAR FRUIT

This sample suggests reefers come in pairs, but the Norwegian-U.S. owners of *Golar Fruit* ordered four ships to the same design, others being *Golar Freeze* (6,709/1968) *Golar Frost* (7,173/1968) and *Golar Nel* (4,902/1968) from three different Norwegian yards, plus a couple of slightly different sizes. As can be seen from her funnel colours, *Golar Fruit* was chartered by Salenrederiena. The mismatch between her final name and that of her owning company looks like one is a misprint, but the names are attested by two reliable registers.

GOLAR FRUIT
IMO 6504929 5,687g 6,090d.
128.05 l.o.a./118.88 l.b.p. x 17.10 x 7.78 metres.
Refrigerated capacity: 258,529 cubic feet.
7-cyl. 2SCSA Sulzer 7RD68-type oil engine by Maschinenbau Bukaur-Wolf A.G., Kiel, Germany; 8,400 BHP, 19.0 knots.
12.12.1964: Launched by A/S Framnaes Mekaniska Verksted, Sandefjord, Norway, (Yard No. 168) for Golarfruit Inc., Monrovia, Liberia (Gotaas Larsen Inc., New York and Oslo) as GOLAR FRUIT.
3.1965: Delivered.
1977: Sold to Ionian Spirit Marine Inc. (Soutos [Hellas] Maritime Corporation), Piraeus, Greece and renamed SAMOS SEA. .
1987: Sold to Genesis Products Ltd., Kingstown, St. Vincent and renamed KATUCHKA.
1988: Renamed ARISTEA.
1989: Sold to Auber Shipping Corporation, Kingstown, St. Vincent (Kappa Maritime Ltd., London) and renamed AMBER STAR.
1991: Sold for scrap at US$175 per light deadweight ton.
28.6.1991: Arrived Gadani Beach for demolition by Chiltan (Private), Ltd. Work began next day.

SERGEY LAZO

Considering the size of its fleet, the USSR had a relatively small number of conventional reefer ships, although these were greatly outnumbered by its fish reefers. Whilst Poland provided the largest number - B365, B347 and B443 types – a smaller number were built in Denmark, Greece and Italy. The last named contributed a class of five delivered between 1967 and 1969: *Chapayev* (4,059/1967), *Kotovskiy* (4,079/1968), *Parkhomenko* (4,059/1968), *Sergey Lazo* (4,059/1968, illustrated and described here) and *Nikolay Shchors* (4,059/1969). They were fairly conventional, with four holds arranged in pairs either side of the superstructure, each served by three-ton derricks, but had a particularly tall superstructure, its height exaggerated by a large funnel. All were registered in Odessa, and on the break up of the Soviet Union they became the property of the Ukraine.

SERGEY LAZO
IMO 6802125 4,059g 4,490d.
121.88 l.o.a./110.01 l.b.p. x 17.05 x 7.5 metres.
Refrigerated capacity: 203,837 cubic feet.
7-cyl. 2SCSA Fiat A680.7L-type oil engine by Fiat S.G.M., Turin, Italy; 7,600 BHP, 19.0 knots.
1968: Delivered by Cantiere Navali Breda, Venice, Italy (Yard No. 255) to USSR-Black Sea Shipping Company, 'BLASCO', Odessa, Ukraine as SERGEY LAZO.
1991: Following the Ukrainian Declaration of Independence, owners restyled as Ukreefer, Odessa.
1998: Sold and renamed LIZA under the Cambodian flag.
4.5.1998: Arrived Alang for demolition.

SOURCES AND ACKNOWLEDGEMENTS

We thank all who gave permission for their photographs to be used, and for help in finding photographs we are particularly grateful to Jim McFaul and David Whiteside of the World Ship Photo Library; to Ian Farquhar, F.W. Hawks, Peter Newall (deceased), William Schell, George Scott; David Hodge and to Bob Todd of the National Maritime Museum, and other museums and institutions listed.

Research sources have included the *Registers* of William Schell and Tony Starke, 'Lloyd's Register', 'Lloyd's Confidential Index', 'Lloyd's Shipping Index', 'Lloyd's War Losses', 'Mercantile Navy Lists', 'Marine News', 'Sea Breezes' and 'Shipbuilding and Shipping Record'. Use of the facilities of the World Ship Society, the Guildhall Library, the National Archives and Lloyd's Register of Shipping and the help of Dr Malcolm Cooper and Professor Hugh Murphy are gratefully acknowledged. Particular thanks also to Heather Fenton for editorial and indexing work, and to Marion Clarkson for accountancy services.

Paddling in the North West
Sources used included Duckworth and Langmuir's 'West Coast Steamers' and 'Railway and Other Steamers'; Alistair Deayton's 'Directory of Clyde Paddle Steamers', Bram Hallam's article and brief fleet list of Manchester Ship Canal tugs in 'Sea Breezes' XLII (1968) pages 361 to 374; H. Campbell McMurray's superb 'Old Order, New Thing'; T.B. Maund's 'Mersey Ferries: Volume 1 –Woodside to Eastham'; Duncan Haws three-volume 'Merchant Fleets: Britain's Railway Steamers' John de S. Winser's 'B.E.F. Ships: before, at and after Dunkirk' and John Shepherd's 'The Liverpool and North Wales Steamship Company'.

Steel sailers to steam coasters
As lamented elsewhere in this issue, iron and steel shipbuilding in Cumberland has been more or less ignored by researchers. Some local antiquarians including Desmond G. Sythes and Daniel Hay have done work on Williamson's ships, mostly based on accounts in local newspapers, and including much in the way of anecdote. The Archives department of Cumbria County Council were most helpful in supplying copies of this work. The single most useful source was the Williamson yard list produced and published by the World Ship Society, which lists every ship with launch dates and allowed analyses to be made of overall output and launches per year. Ships's histories are from the usual sources: 'Lloyd's Register', the 'Mercantile Navy List', all checked in registration documents held in the National Archive at Kew. Some photographs were kindly provided by the Cumbria Archive Service.

Margaronis family shipowning
Malcolm consulted a book by Antony N. Charocopus entitled 'Pandelis Margaronis: His Life and Achievements', published in 2000.

Aberdeen Liners
Newspaper cuttings from the 'Press and Journal' and 'Evening Express' held at the library of Aberdeen Journals Ltd.; archive copies of 'Fishing News' held at Aberdeen Central Library; lists of Aberdeen-built fishing vessels and their histories compiled by the late Wilfred M. Dodds; George F. Ritchie, 'The Real Price of Fish, Aberdeen Steam Trawler Losses 1887-1961' (Hutton Press Ltd., 1991).

PADDLING IN THE NORTH WEST

Although paddle steamers are mostly associated with the Clyde estuary and English South Coast ports, they were actually quite widespread, and here we feature paddlers which worked in the North West.

A superb Feilden photograph depicts the *Jubilee Queen* (399/1897), which had a short and rather unsuccessful career with the Mersey and Blackpool Steamship Co. Ltd. She had been built at Southampton by Day, Summers and Company as *Duchess of Kent* for a railway service between Portsmouth and Ryde. The service continued into Southern Railway days but was interrupted by her three years' requisition as a minesweeper during the First World War. In 1933 she was sold to the New Medway Steam Packet Co. Ltd. to become *Clacton Queen*, but in 1935 moved to the Mersey to operate excursions from Liverpool and New Brighton to Southport, Blackpool and Fleetwood as *Jubilee Queen*. Although she appears very smart in the photograph she was by then getting long in the tooth, and the service did not thrive. In August 1936 she was tried between Barrow-in-Furness and Blackpool, but was too deep to berth at the seaside town at all states of the tide, and in September she was laid up. T.W. Ward broke her up at Preston in 1937, work beginning in June. *[B. and A. Feilden/J. and M. Clarkson]*

Another fine Feilden photograph taken at Llandudno shows *Lady Orme* (252/1888) (right). Built by J. McArthur and Company at Paisley as *Fusilier*, she was in David MacBrayne's fleet until 1934, operating both on the west coast and to the Hebrides, and from time-to-time on the Clyde itself. After a few months operating on the Forth, she was bought in December 1934 by the Cambrian Shipping Co. Ltd. and renamed to work out of Llandudno, operating cruises to the Menai Straits. She passed through several ownerships over the next four years, including one who gave her the rather ugly name *Crestawave*. Laid up after the 1938 season, she was scrapped in 1939. *[B. and A. Feilden/J. and M. Clarkson]*

The double-ended paddle steamer *Sapphire* (223/1898) hurries up river past the Albert Dock, en route for Eastham with passengers enjoying the view from the top deck (top). J. Jones of Liverpool built her and two somewhat smaller paddlers (both 171/1897), *Pearl* (middle, looking empty) and *Ruby* (bottom). Owners were the Eastham Ferry, Pleasure Gardens and Hotel Co. Ltd., and their purpose was simply to take punters to the owner's premises. The ferries also became popular with Liverpool's leisure cyclists who used it to shorten the pedalling distance to Chester and North Wales. All three vessels were scrapped in 1929, when the ferry service ended, the pleasure gardens having become run down and hence attracting fewer and fewer visitors. However, part of the pier at Eastham and the Eastham Ferry Hotel survive, and both facilities have given much pleasure to your editors over the years. *[Roy Fenton collection; B. and A. Feilden/J. and M. Clarkson]*

The Bickerstaffe family of Blackpool began services out of the seaside town in 1879 with the immodestly named *Bickerstaffe* (197/1879) (upper and middle), and in 1894 floated the Blackpool Passenger Steamboat Co. Ltd. to which she was transferred.

In the picture bottom left we see *Bickerstaffe* outside the Preston dock entrance. She has either come up river too soon before the gates could be opened or at the end of the previous tide and too late to get through before the gates were closed. Bottom right we see her going to her end-of-season lay-up berth circa 1928. *[All: J. and M. Clarkson]*

Bickerstaffe was quickly joined by the considerably larger *Queen of the North* (590/1895) (top) which like *Bickerstaffe* had been built at Birkenhead by Laird Brothers. The newer ship's work included excursions to the Isle of Man. Called up for minesweeping work in 1916, she was mined and sunk off Orfordness on 20th July 1917, leaving *Bickerstaffe* to soldier on alone until broken up at Garston in 1928, when the family's services ceased. *[J. and M. Clarkson]*

The old *Marquis of Bute* (196/1868) (middle) ended her days working out of Preston for the Ribble Passenger Transport Co. Ltd. Built by Barclay, Curle and Company, her first years were, unsurprisingly, spent on the Clyde. In 1904 she moved across to Ireland spending three years working between Belfast and Bangor and on Carlingford Lough. She began work in Preston in February 1907 but was scrapped in 1908, making this photographic record of her with a full load on the Ribble valuable. Despite cruising from Preston (usually to Blackpool) not being especially popular, the Ribble Passenger company survived until September 1925. *[J. and M. Clarkson]*

In contrast to other ships in this feature which came second-hand to the north west, *Lady Evelyn* (230/1900) (bottom) was built specially for service in the region, and only later worked elsewhere. The Furness Railway had her built by Scott of Kinghorn when they wished to develop sailings from Fleetwood to Barrow-in-Furness to encourage holidaymakers to visit the Lake District. She was so successful that in 1905 she had to be substantially lengthened.

Following wartime service as a minesweeper, she was returned to the railway company in 1919, but was almost immediately sold to a Bristol Channel operator. She passed to P. and A. Campbell who renamed her *Brighton Belle* in 1922 for service on the south coast. The Admiralty again requisitioned her for minesweeping in 1939, and in May 1940 sent her to Dunkirk. Returning with 350 rescued troops, she struck a submerged wreck off the Downs and quickly sank. *[Roy Fenton collection]*

The finest paddler of the Liverpool and North Wales Company was *La Marguerite* (1,554/1894). She was built for operation by Palace Steamers Ltd. between the Thames and France, but their inability to make her pay meant she was taken over by her builders, Fairfield Shipbuilding and Engineering Co Ltd. In 1904 she was transferred to the North Wales company in which Fairfield had a financial interest and became highly popular running from Liverpool to Llandudno and on to Menai Bridge. At 342 feet she is reputed to be the largest ship ever to enter the Menai Straits, and some measure of her capacity is her ability to carry 1,800 soldiers when trooping from Southampton to France during the First World War.

Post-war, she helped out on the Liverpool to Douglas route in 1919, but was back in North Wales for the 1920 summer season. Becoming progressively less reliable, at the end of the 1925 season she went to be broken up at Briton Ferry in South Wales. *[B. and A. Feilden/J. and M. Clarkson]*

Snowdon (338/1892) (middle) was built for the tug-owning Dodd family, who were already using their tugs on Sundays to offer excursions from the Mersey to Llandudno, their basic accommodation being compensated for by low fares and plentiful beer. However, the Dodds realised that rival steamers of the Liverpool and North Wales Steamship Company were doing better at attracting well-heeled excursionists, and it was decided to order the well-appointed *Snowdon* from Laird Brothers in Birkenhead. On Sundays she sailed from Liverpool to Menai Bridge and on weekdays worked between Llandudno and Caernarvon. She proved sufficiently successful that in 1899 amalgamation was agreed between her owning company, the Snowdon Passenger Steamship Co. Ltd., and the Liverpool and North Wales concern.

Snowdon was requisitioned for minesweeping in November 1915, first at Harwich and later Belfast. After a refit on the Clyde she returned to North Wales services in 1920. She is seen arriving in the Menai Straits probably during her last decade. In the 1930 and 1931 seasons she cruised from Blackpool, at the end of which she went to breakers at Port Glasgow. *[B. and A. Feilden/J. and M. Clarkson]*

Prince George (24/1891) provides a rare view of a Conway river paddle steamer; at least, the editors are not aware of other photographs (bottom). Owners were the St. George Steamship Co. Ltd. of Conway, a relative of the St. George Steam Packet Company, an important early operator of Irish Sea services who once intended to operate from Deganwy near the mouth of the Conway to Ireland. The paddle box carries the legend 'Deganwy, Conway and Trefrw', but despite her very modest length of 72 feet, she did cross Liverpool Bay and was recorded at least once at Preston.

Prince George was built of steel at the Amlwch yard of William Thomas and Sons, and launched on 8th March 1890, although not entering service until the 1891 season. She was not broken up until 1947. *[J. and M. Clarkson collection]*

The Isle of Man Steam Packet Co. Ltd. operated paddle steamers as late as 1929. A selection of their later examples begins with the second *Snaefell* (849/1876) at Douglas in 1904, waiting to be towed away to the Netherlands for demolition (top). She had been built of iron by Caird and Company at Greenock.

The third *Mona's Isle* (1,556/1882) was photographed at Morecambe on 3rd September 1919 awaiting breaking up (middle). She had arrived there two days previously, having been purchased by the Admiralty in 1915 to lay anti-submarine nets during the First World War. However, her work was more varied than that, and included working as a base ship for the salvage of a Dutch steamer that had beeen torpedoed off southern Ireland whilst carrying a cargo of gold bullion.

The second *Mona's Queen* (1,559/1885) arrives at Fleetwood (bottom). She was the very last paddler running to the island, and possibly owed her longevity to being employed on more minor routes than Liverpool to Douglas which was by now the province of fast, turbine steamers. She had been built of iron by the Barrow Shipbuilding Co. Ltd. Breakers were Smith and Houston at Port Glasgow, who paid £5,920 for her. Her First World War Service largely involved carrying troops mainly between Southampton and Le Havre. On one occasion in February 1917 the steel floats on one of her paddle wheels hit the conning tower of a German submarine which had tried to torpedo her, leading inevitably to a claim of sinking the U-boat.
[All: J. and M. Clarkson collection]

No article about paddlers in the north west would be complete without examples of the Manchester Ship Canal's fleet of paddle tugs, and first is *Rixton* (158/1905) (upper). With her sister *Eccles* (158/1905) she was built by J.T. Eltringham at South Shields. After fifty years' service her hull was still fit for use as a barge in Liverpool docks.

The Ship Canal operated the six paddle tugs which they had built alongside their screw tugs, with the paddlers invariably taking the stern line, as *Rixton* is doing here. The paddle tugs were designed so that their port and starboard paddles could operate independently, making them extremely manoeuvrable. Because of their shallow draft they were also able to work effectively close in to the Canal's bank. However, as bow tugs they were next to useless. Their broad beam made them heavy to handle and slow to respond to the movement of the tow.

Note the MSC railway running close alongside the Canal and an unusual telegraph pole in the background. *[World Ship Society Ltd.]*

In contrast with *Rixton*, *Barton* (186/1903) (lower) looked derelict when Manchester photographer Cliff Parsons came across her in October 1948, and she was officially withdrawn in 1949, the first of six paddle tugs to go. *Irlam* and *Barton* were the first pair of paddle tugs built for the Canal, by J.P. Rennoldson and Sons Ltd at South Shields. *[Cliff Parsons/World Ship Society Ltd.]*

CROSSED THE BAR
Obituaries of two Ships in Focus contributors

Murray Robinson

Only few people are bestowed the gift of twin talents being able to draw what they are writing about and to the highest standard. Murray Robinson of New Zealand greatly enjoyed having both. Growing up on the shores of Wellington Harbour his interest in shipping was more than just accepting it as part of the daily backdrop to life. His godfather, a rising star ship-master in the Union Steamship Company, enhanced his knowledge: Murray's degree in history achieved at Victoria University of Wellington ensured his quality of research reached a standard which he never allowed to be compromised. But for his eyesight he would have had a career that would have taken him to the highest in the Royal New Zealand Navy: his interest in defence matters enabled him to combine a career in the Army's reserve force for 24 years with that of the civil service. When career and family life allowed, Murray recorded the profiles of merchant ships that through the 20th century served New Zealand, Australia and beyond. His quest for accurate ships' plans drew our interests together and lead to two co-authored books. Murray's level of draughtmanship has produced a collection of drawn profiles that will be his monument. At the age of only 62 he died at the home that he, his wife Louise and two young daughters had created on the Tasman Sea coast north of Wellington. Murray joins the pantheon that records readably and visually the golden age of merchant shipping.

Andrew Bell

Murray and Andrew were joint authors of 'A Tasman Trio: Wanganella - Awatea – Monowai' and 'Shaw Savill's Magnificent Sisters'.

Peter Newall

Peter grew up in Cape Town where began his interest in ships, and particularly passenger liners, about which he became a recognised expert. Moving to the United Kingdom, he pursued a career in marketing and publicity with British Airways and its predecessor BOAC. On his retirement he adopted a second career as a maritime researcher and author, and also befriended many well-known figures in the field, including Ambrose Greenway to whom he was connected through his first marriage and Laurence Dunn, whose collection of photographic prints he bought on Laurence's death. In addition to a number of articles, Peter wrote and illustrated 'Cape Town Shipping' and 'Union Castle Line', and three books for Ships in Focus Publications: 'Mauretania: Triumph and Resurrection', 'Orient Line; a Fleet History' and 'Cunard Line: a Fleet History'. Peter very much knew his own mind when it came to writing, illustrating and designing books. Even if we sometimes disagreed over detail, the Ships in Focus team developed a great respect for Peter's work, and we believe his three histories and fleet lists may well represent the last word on the companies involved. Peter was also always very generous about us using his photographs.

In his last few years, cancer took a toll both of his health and output, but he completed for Seaforth Publishing a book which he was uniquely qualified to write and illustrate, 'Ocean liners: an Illustrated History', which he lived long enough to see published. We offer our condolences to Julie Newall.

FROM SAIL TO STEAM: THE BELFAST COAL TRADE

Ian Wilson

Unearthed in a box file recently, and far predating even the concept of electronic records, was research I began over 40 years ago: a study of the switch from sail to steam in the huge coal import trade to Belfast. I can see my plan was to extract the arrivals each January at three-yearly intervals from 1869, still the world of sail, until 1899, by which time even a quick glance at the arrivals showed almost 100% by steamers. The project involved copying out the reliable daily columns of the 'Belfast News Letter'. Unsurprisingly, I never finished it. I got as far as January 1884 when 89 of the 168 colliers were steamers, as opposed to only five of the 184 in January 1869: from less than 3% to over half in 15 years. Despite the incomplete nature of my work, clearly the crucial years of technological change were covered, and it is worth revisiting this short era to appreciate what elements were combining to precipitate such change in coastal shipping. I also listed all the loading ports – a huge number in Scotland, England and Wales, large and small – which gives added interest.

The Belfast coal trade

Belfast is the only industrial city in the British Isles without coal nearby. Although industries developed in other Irish cities, Belfast with its huge mills, factories, ropeworks and of course shipyards was in a different league. The population tripled between the 1820s and 1860s, partly owing to the massive influx caused by the Irish potato famine in the 1840s. Coal for industrial and domestic use was essential, and sea was the only route. In 1869, when our story begins, very little had changed in the coal trade in the previous century, despite steam passenger vessels becoming an everyday sight in the 1820s. A fleet of sailing coasters were engaged, mainly from Ayrshire and Cumberland. On New Year's Day 15 of the 28 came from Maryport alone. But owing to the prevailing westerly winds, the coal fleet could be bottled up. Days thus passed with no colliers. The 'Maryport Chronicle' of 16th February 1861 reported: 'The gale which commenced on Friday night has not been equalled for fury and intensity within the memory of the oldest seaman...the consequence was that the harbours of Maryport, Whitehaven and Workington were crowded with coal-laden vessels... when the wind was observed to change, an unusually large fleet put to sea, upwards of 80 from Maryport, and we are informed that 140 left Whitehaven...'

There was just one regular steam collier, appropriately called *Black Diamond* (259/1864). She is the only steamer I came across built of wood, at Troon in 1864. It was from there she traded, being owned by the Gauchalland Coal Company, who had pits at Galston near Kilmarnock, and transported their coal to Troon via what had been Scotland's pioneer railway. She is the single vessel which appears in each of the six Januarys surveyed, always loading at Troon.

So, it would seem, here was a situation ripe for the introduction of the evolving steam cargo vessel. But it was not as simple as I, for one, thought at the time I was compiling this. On the one hand, there were the technological advances that were bringing more economical use of space ratio between engines, bunkers and cargo hold, but on the other, profit could not be expected from the bigger investment in steam if discharge was to continue to be by the swarming gangs of manual coal 'whippers' who serviced the sailing ships with their smaller hatches, and could only be relied on for 80 tons or so per day. Harbour cranes are not a subject much covered, but the synergy between the arrival of Belfast's first steam cranes in the 1870s, the link of the coal quays to the Belfast and County Down Railway for onward transport and the increasingly attractive investment in steam colliers is a clear one. Still today, massive container ships cannot be built without massive cranes to handle their freight quickly. (I submit that the history of Victorian shipping has not taken enough account of firms, notably Rodman and Priestman, pioneers of efficient cranes. Priestman introduced the first grab cranes in 1875 though there is no evidence of them being present in Belfast in the period in question).

Steam ascendant

The numbers of sailing colliers with evocative names like *Cheshire Witch*, *Morning Light*, *Happy-go-Lucky* and *Red Rover* begin to diminish as the 1870s progress. This is the decade that sees coastal steamship builders begin to fit compound engines, more efficient than the early simple steam engines. By the close of the decade, broadly similar steam coasters on regular trades were becoming established. Previous steam collier arrivals at Belfast tended to be random, often relatively large tramps accepting a coastal cargo like the *Lindsay* (1,116/1866) on 21st January 1875.

A postcard of Queen's Bridge, Belfast with an assembly of sailing vessels beyond. *[Author's collection]*

This day saw the highest influx of colliers in my survey: 51, 49 of them sail – 19 from Troon alone. The other steamer was one of the earliest dedicated to the coal trade, the *Kirkless* (387/1865) of the Wigan Coal and Iron Company, like the *Black Diamond* part of an overall coal business rather than a coastal tramp as most of the later steamers were. She was named after the Kirkless mine at Aspull in Lancashire. The *Kirkless*, built of iron by the forgotten yard of Bowdler at Wallasey, loaded most regularly at Garston, but also came from Fleetwood, Silloth and Liverpool. The important Wigan Coal and Iron Company did a big trade to Belfast, continuing - always from Garston - with the *Balniel* of 1886, named after one of the titles of the Earl of Crawford, a founder of the company. Very long-lived, a tribute to the iron construction of McIlwaine and Lewis, Belfast, and the last link with these times, she braved a varied career to say the least until towed from Carrickfergus to Lancaster in 1974 for demolition (now of course 'recycling'!).

The earliest steamers in the trade included a third type, as well as colliery ships and random tramps. Occasionally seen were vessels normally on coastal liner routes with general cargo. Two of John Bacon's fleet arrived in January 1875 the *Plantagenet* (726/1869) twice, from Swansea and Briton Ferry, and the *Jane Bacon* (609/1865) from Briton Ferry. The *Italia* (410/1869) is another interesting example. The first cargo vessel owned by the Belfast Steamship Company, she was acquired in response to the undercutting of rates by non-members of the Irish and English Traffic Conference. When not carrying general cargo, she was employed in other coastal trades, as seems to have been the case with one of the rivals, *Torca* (344/1875), unusually a steamer built in Drogheda, by the Grendon foundry.

So from 7.7% steam in 1872, three years later 16.2% of the January 1875 total shipments arrived in steamers, then there is a jump in 1878 to 29 %. This January sees easily the biggest overall number – 272. The *Black Diamond* and

Balniel (460/1886), seen above at Preston in the spring of 1910 as *Londoner*, was built for Wigan Coal and Iron Co. Ltd. As a result of her use as a gun runner in 1914 when named *Clyde Valley* there was a move to preserve her in Northern Ireland after she was retired by Newfoundland owners in 1968, but this came to nothing. The sailing vessel in the background is the Liverpool built and owned *Dynomene* (1,949/1882) which was laid up at Preston for several months in 1910. Seen at Lancaster on 26th August 1974 (right), *Clyde Valley* was later scrapped there despite problems with pollution.
[J. and M. Clarkson]

Sunlight (388/1868) is not recorded as having traded with coal to Belfast in Ian's samples, but as a contemporary of *Plantagenet* and *Jane Bacon* in the Bacon fleet she was capable of doing so. Built and given her original, simple steam engine by Lawrence Hill and Co., Port Glasgow, she remained with Bacon, until 1913, having been given a compound engine in 1883. Sold to France as *Menhir*, she was wrecked on a voyage from Messina to Piraeus in January 1920. *[Roy Fenton collection]*

Kirkless soldier on, and notable among the steamers joining them now are those in the growing fleet of the Antrim Iron Ore Company. Founded in 1872 to extract ore from their mine at Parkmore on the Antrim plateau, it seems likely the company had significant shareholders in common with the Belfast Steamship Company. The names of their early acquisitions begin to appear in the coal fleet such as the *Ardclinis* (161/1870) and *Cargan* (168/1873). The latter was one of the growing number of steam coasters appearing from the Paisley yard of Fullerton, then establishing their role as coaster specialists. Two other regular steamers of this time, *Ardeer* (294/1871) and *Glengarnock* (205/1870), were Fullerton products. And, like the Antrim vessels, the names were associated with local industry, in their case Ayrshire ironworks. It was an age of expanding industry, with which shipping was intertwined.

Parkmore (261/1880) was the sixth ship built for or bought by the Antrim Iron Ore Company, whose coasters carried coal to Belfast in the late 1870s. *Parkmore* was built and engined in Belfast by McIlwaine and Lewis, and traded for the iron ore company until sunk in collision in Belfast Lough in January 1914. Raised and repaired, as *Cliffmore* she steamed on for other Belfast owners until a stranding in the Firth of Forth in May 1924 left her a constructive total loss, fit only for scrap. *Parkmore* was photographed, along with the Belfast-owned barque *Charger* (1,060/1856), in the 1875-built Hamilton Graving Dock alongside which was the enormous engine works of Harland and Wolff. *[Welch Collection, Ulster Museum]*

Casualties of the coal trade

The *Ardeer* made the last of many calls on 15th January 1884. Eleven days later, she sailed from Workington bound for Chatham but never arrived. She was posted missing. Losses among the collier fleet, sail and steam, did occur but relative to the huge number of ships at sea they were low. The overall number seems bad, but only out of context. This was the period of the introduction of the Plimsoll Line. Casualty returns to the Board of Trade were published from the early 1870s. So, the Victorians took shipping safety very seriously, as witnessed by the weighty proceedings of a number of select committees through the era. It is in fact surprising that more sailing ships were not lost in these winter months in the Irish Sea. Inevitably, some were. The Dutch-built schooner *Goldfinder* (77/1847) of Belfast went missing with her five crew having left Ayr with 152 tons. The inquiry heard that the weather was bad, she was overloaded and also had four or five tons of loose cargo on deck. The tiny lugger *Ellen* (25/1835) of Strangford foundered in the North Channel on passage from Ayr. 'This vessel was old and unseaworthy and sprang a leak, giving her crew barely time to escape'. The 52-year-old brig *Blair* (88/1819) foundered with all four crew off Islandmagee, County Antrim in February 1871, again coming from Ayr. But cases like this were increasingly rare – and it is worth noting the longevity of many of the sailing coasters. (The 100gt *Eliza*, a brig which brought two cargoes from Troon in January 1869, had been built in Whitehaven in 1792). The worst loss I have come across relating to a steamer was the missing *Bow Fell* (294/1882). Only completed at Port Glasgow on 24th October 1882, this iron vessel left Troon for Belfast on 3rd November and disappeared with a crew of twelve. She belonged to Hume, Smith and Company, Liverpool, whose *Rydal Fell* (601/1881) and *Wans Fell* (308/1882) often appear in the arrivals in these years. A few months before, the schooner *William Brocklebank* (131/1872) belonging to the well-known Postlethwaite family of Millom, also went missing 'supposed foundered during the heavy gale of 14 October' en route from Swansea.

The two oldest steamers which appear amongst the daily colliers date from 1857, the *Lizzie* (328/1857), built at Birkenhead and the *Robert Burns* (130/1857), a product of Seath's yard, Rutherglen. These were still the pioneering years for cargo steamers. In 1875, the *Lizzie* was another loss, though everyone got ashore safely when the wind changed as she lay in a dangerous anchorage, sheltering on passage with 340 tons from Swansea. She anchored under the lee of St John's Point, County Down, with the gale from the south east, but when it moved to the south west it was prudent to row to shore and sure enough the *Lizzie* dragged her anchor. The inquiry found that no blame should attach to the master, a Guernsey man with the resounding name of James Fixott Chevalier, 'who acted in concurrence with his officers'. This Manx steamer belonged to the Laxey Steamship Company, who may well have been associates of the Great Laxey Mine with its famous wheel, a tourist attraction to this day.

Steam dominant

The *Robert Burns* deserves a special mention, although she was a regular only in January 1878 when she brought four cargoes from Irvine. The enterprising merchant John Forsyth of Downpatrick owned her from 1866 until his death in 1883, and variously employed her in carrying cattle and general cargo to Workington with coal back, coal to Belfast and even on at least one celebratory occasion in July 1868 passengers on an excursion to Douglas! Before the complement joined at Quoile Quay near Downpatrick, then Killyleagh and Portaferry, Forsyth had conscientiously organised for all traces of coal and cattle to be cleaned away. (One wonders how many of the rules of the killjoys of the Maritime and Coastguard Agency this would break today?).

As the century progressed, steamers like the *Robert Burns*, just 120 gross tons and 106 feet in length, were inevitably superseded by larger and/or more efficient coastal colliers. One variety that was just too small to be economic on this trade was the 'puffer'. However, several interesting prototypes of the classic 66-foot vessel do appear, such as the *St. Rollox* (59/1866) which is recorded once, from Kirkintilloch on 24th January 1872. Kirkintilloch and the name Hay as builder and owner became synonymous with puffers, but the *St Rollox* pre-dates even them, arriving from the yard of Hill, Port Glasgow, in 1866. She must have been one of the first to have a loadline and other essentials to be allowed to trade outside Clyde limits. A small number of coal cargoes came by sail or steam from Kirkintilloch on the Forth and Clyde Canal, confined of course to vessels under 66 feet because of the locks, and a few also from the major canal harbour, Port Dundas, no doubt coal from the central Scottish fields brought via the linking Monkland Canal. There was a colliery at Kirkintilloch owned by the Gardner family and their steamer *Lizzie Gardner* (75/1873), one of Hay's first products, makes a single appearance in January 1881, from Glasgow.

It is worth noting here that the *Balniel* has a close challenger as the survey member with the greatest longevity, the *St Rollox*. The former recorded 88 years, the *St Rollox* 84, latterly around the port of Middlesbrough until 1950.

A coaster often quoted as a significant prototype is the *Agate* built by Seath in 1878 for William Robertson's Gem Line as their first genuine coaster after 'puffers' and the small *Amethyst* (113/1870). In the 21 years since building the *Robert Burns*, Seath much altered her three-mast design,

Unsurprisingly, photographs of ships from the 1850s are very scarce, and we are lucky to have this one of *Robert Burns*. She was registered at Newry between 1860 and 1870, and again between 1883 and her sale for breaking up in 1906. *[Author's collection]*.

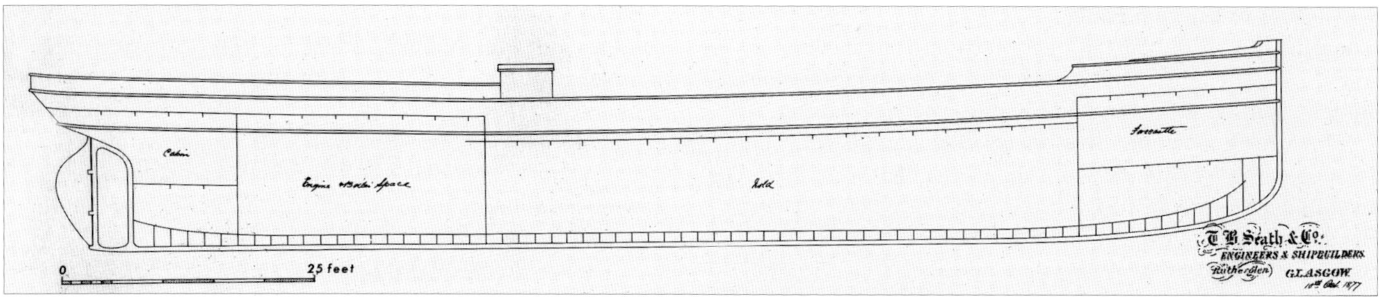

A drawing from Seath's yard of Robertson's *Agate* (184/1878). She would have looked much like *Olderfleet*, shown below. *Agate* was wrecked in the Kenmare River in February 1911. *[Courtesy Charles Waine]*

constructed her more heavily and installed a compound engine by King of Glasgow, rather than the simple engine by Inglis also of Glasgow. Sure enough, the *Agate* appears three times in January 1884, all from Glasgow.

By January 1884 then, the majority of arrivals are steamers, 53 %. Great change has taken place in 15 years. Appearing are many names of new coasters that go on to long careers: *Owain Tudur* (227/1882), *Olderfleet* (213/1880), *Sylfaen* (350/1883), *W.S. Caine* (155/1883). The variety of loading ports is not quite so wide as the smaller places are overtaken by progress, but still there are names forgotten as coal ports today: Neath, Porthcawl, Llanelly, Mostyn, Silloth, Girvan and Bowling.

Questions still arise though: how come certain sailing ship owners made the transition to steam and not others? What factors were involved? John Kelly, Belfast's most prominent collier owner, progressed out of sailing ships listed here like the *Agnes C. James* (214/1859) as did

Iron-hulled steam coasters trading with coal to Belfast in the 1880s are better represented in the photographic record, and three examples are shown.

Right: *Owain Tudur* was built and engined at Llanelly for Liverpool owners of Welsh extraction, and was photographed at Bristol between 1908 and 1916 whilst owned by Rix in Hull. Later renamed *Peggy Grieve*, she was broken up at Grays in Essex in 1929, her 47th year. *[Bristol Series/J. and M. Clarkson]*

Bottom: *Olderfleet* beached, just possibly at Rochester. A few feet longer than *Agate* also built by Seath's Rutherglen yard just two years previously, and also engined by William King of Glasgow, she is representative of the earliest design of single-hatch steam coasters with half-height forecastle, a single mast and no wheelhouse. Lengthening by a modest 10 feet in 1894 helped ensure her survival with various Clydeside owners until 1938. *[Roy Fenton collection]*

Sylfaen was built by Fullertons at Paisley for a single-ship company managed by quarry owners Kneeshaw, Lupton and Company, and brought coal across the Irish Sea whilst not in the stone carrying trade. She is seen, again at Bristol, as *Earlford* of Mann, Macneal of Glasgow, a name she carried from 1905 to 1915. Renamed *Jerseyman* by Cardiff owners, she was lost in the English Channel in February 1915, either mined or sunk by the submarine *UB 19*, depending on which source one believes. *[Bristol Series/J. and M. Clarkson]*

No account of the Belfast coal trade in steam days would be complete without mention of John Kelly, even though he did not join the ranks of steam coaster owners until 1890. Nevertheless, his *Cultra* (332/1884) - the oldest steamer to ever join his fleet - would have been seen in Belfast with coal in the 1880s as William Grainger's *Theme*, part of a fleet which delighted in short names beginning T, including *Tolka* (245/1867), *Topic* (248/1881) and *Thesis* (378/1887). Kelly bought her from Grainger in 1912 but sold her back in 1914 when Grainger reinstated the name *Theme.* A member of her crew in this short period remembered an aged, bowler-hatted Grainger coming down to the quay and poking at the ship with his stick. She was dreadfully slow, but was the pride and joy of her master, Captain Templeton. As shown, she was probably in original condition, with minimal bridge structure. Bought by the Antrim Iron Ore Company in 1915, as *Glenaan* she had her bridge raised, but offered no more protection to her crew (see page 1). Another great survivor, she was lost on a ballast voyage from Belfast to Glasgow in January 1932. *[Bristol Series/J. and M. Clarkson]*

William Grainger's first *Topic* (248/1881) was sold to Liverpool owners in 1888, but he almost immediately ordered a larger replacement from the same yard, that of McIlwaine and Lewis, Belfast who was Grainger's preferred builder. The second *Topic* (382/1889) lasted long enough to be photographed in Grainger's ownership when she visited Bristol. Grainger's casualty rate was quite high, five steamers lost out of 11 owned, and *Topic* (2) was to be numbered amongst them on 17th June 1913 when she struck Gipsy Rock, part of Tuskar Reef, and sank. She was on a voyage from Garston to Waterford with coal. *[Bristol Series/J. and M. Clarkson]*

William Barkley and Alexander King, both later absorbed by Kelly, and Hugh Craig, but the great majority never built or acquired a steamer. No doubt the capital cost was prohibitive, or of course the owner or majority shareholder in the 64 share system may have had no family successor.

One interesting figure whose life and business has been studied is William Hinde (1823–1890), a native of Maryport who married and settled in Carrickfergus, coming ashore from being a coasting skipper. His fleet grew from his first brig the *Thomas Connolly* (122/1837) until he became the agent for Lord Lonsdale's Cumberland collieries and by 1878 had added four more sailing vessels. Hinde went into steam with the *William Hinde* (264/1880) from McIlwaine and McColl of Belfast, soon adding the *Maria A. Hinde* (822/1883). Interestingly, a family historian suggests he was also a major shareholder in the Antrim Iron Ore Company. A detailed study of the rise of the maritime entrepreneurs in a port city would very likely uncover such correspondences. Having progressed even further to establish the Hinde Line for passengers and cargo to Whitehaven, he died in 1890, but son-in-law Lancelot Shaw who took over proved not to be such an astute businessman and with Hinde's sons having emigrated to Australia, the firm including its name was sold. The author can recall, from schoolboy walks round the docks in the 1960s, the faded Hinde sign on the shed which the Whitehaven steamers would have served.

So that was one of the last links with the Victorian coal trade. Now almost no-one knows where their coal comes from – mainly Russia I am told. The study I made does keep raising questions. How did the port deal with up to 50 colliers in a day? Did steamers have precedence? There can have been no compulsory pilotage, but a host of watermen or 'hobblers' were needed to get the sailing vessels to their berth. How were enough men hired to discharge, when one day no coal came, and other days a fleet arrived? How was the whole trade organised? It was probably the case that the skipper came ashore to submit his paperwork at the Custom House (still there today) and then at a coal exchange a coal factor arranged the sale of the cargo. Many days saw cargoes arriving from six or seven different ports. Presumably there was a constant stream of telegrams going backwards and forwards placing orders and confirming departures. (Perhaps the ubiquitous e-mail which business now uses is simply an update of the ubiquitous Victorian telegram – and the postal service was much better than today.)

It is not possible to know if the *Black Diamond*, launched by the Portland Shipbuilding Company of Troon on 19th October 1864, was the first steam collier to arrive in Belfast. However, she was certainly the first regular one. On 28th May 1892, inward in fog, she grounded at The Gobbins, Islandmagee, a rocky stretch of the coast she had passed a thousand times. She became a total loss. In her 28 years massive changes in the shipping scene had happened, as my project, dusty and incomplete as I found it, reveals.

William Hinde's second *Minnie Hinde* (409/1891) at Whitehaven about 1900. Built at Belfast by McIlwaine and Lewis for Hinde's daughter Maria Shaw, she was sold to owners in Lerwick as *Norseman* during 1904 as the Hinde fleet was run down. She was sold again just three years later, this time to the Bolivian Government. Although renamed *Explorador*, she never made it to Bolivia, as in March 1908 on her delivery voyage from London she was wrecked in Manaos harbour. *[Author's collection]*

MARGARONIS FAMILY SHIPOWNING

Malcolm Cranfield

The Margaronis family is one of the oldest Greek shipping families, originating in Vrontados on the island of Chios. The branch involved with shipping descended from Hadji Sideris Margaronis (1797-1866). His son, Pandelis Isidoros Margaronis (1841-1926), owned sailing ships and in 1900 purchased the family's first two steamers, *Despina* (1,223/1890) and *Iro* (ex-*Normanton*, 2,491/1899). These were followed in the early 1920s by *Aghios Marcos* (4,598/1910, built as *Hamm* for Deutsch-Australische D.G. of Hamburg) and *Andreas K.* (3,536/1903 built as *Sierra Morena* for Thompson, Anderson and Company, Liverpool). Around 1930 these were transferred to his four sons Anastasios (1864-1957), Isidoros, Georgios and Dimitris Margaronis, all of whom had served as masters on Pandelis' sailing ships.

Pandelis Margaronis also took a financial interest in two ships which Kulukundis bought in 1926, *Perseus* (4,688/1906 ex *Heliopolis*) and *William McAllum* (4,764/1906, ex *Salatis*), both of which were broken up in Italy in 1932 at the depth of the great depression

Dimitris Margaronis

In 1931 Dimitris Margaronis bought *Socrates* from Lamport and Holt, and renamed her *P. Margaronis*, placing her management with Michalos and Company in London. As mentioned in the caption, she was an early war loss. Post-war, Dimitris built up a large fleet of ships, many ex-British, listed below. His business was based in Athens with the Victoria Steam Ship Co. Ltd. acting as London agents. From about 1976, presumably on his death, the company name became John D. Margaronis and Sons. Post-war his funnel colours were blue with a black top and large red letter M.

Socrates (4,979/1913) (right) was built by Russell and Company, Port Glasgow for the Liverpool, Brazil and River Plate Steam Navigation Co. Ltd., better known as Lamport and Holt. When their entanglement in the Royal Mail Group debacle hit them badly, Lamport and Holt were forced to sell off ships, and Greek families such as Margaronis were willing buyers at bargain basement prices. *Socrates* became their *P. Margaronis*, as photographed arriving at Avonmouth (below).

By now in war colours, early in March 1940 *P. Margaronis* sailed from Antwerp for Boston, and was last heard of on the 8th. It was later discovered that she had been torpedoed south west of Land's End the next day by *U 28* with the loss of her entire crew. *[B. and A Feilden, Bristol Series, both J. and M. Clarkson]*

Fleet of Dimitris Margaronis post-war				
Name	**Former names**	**gt/ built**	**Bought**	**Disposal**
Despoina	*Rookley*	4,998/1940	1956	Sold 1966, b/u 1971
Polyxeni (1)	*Gaspesian Park*	7,159/ 1945	1954	Wrecked 1965
Efcharis (1)	*City of Portsmouth*	7,219/1943	1959	1971
Eftychia	*Riverton*	7,307/1943	1960	Sold 1965 b/u 1969
Efdemon	*Amsteldiep*	7,176/ 1943	1961	b/u 1968
Efdromos	*Maritsa, Lindekerk*	7,176/1943	1966	Wrecked 1970
Pantelis	*Temple Hall*	8,003/1954	1969	Sold 1977, wrecked 1981
Efcharis (2)	*Patagonia, Harpalyce*	10,296/1958	1972	Sold 1983, b/u 1983
Polyxeni (2)	*Fernmoor, Streambank*	6,326/1958	1973	Sold 1982 b/u 1983
(renamed *Banglar Polyxeni* from 1973 to 1977 on charter to Bangladesh)				
Demarg	*Bermeo*	9,107/1964	1975	r/n *Floriana* 1983, b/u 1984
Polyxeni (3)	*Al Farwaniah*	9,859/1972	1984	b/u 1994

A Doxford 'Economy' type motor ship, *Rookley* was built for Stephens, Sutton Ltd. of Newcastle in 1940. Dimitris Margaronis bought her jointly with A.A. Fardis in 1956, registering her in Greece as *Despoina*. After ten years she was sold to Italian owners who put her under the Panama flag as *Jumbo*. Renamed *Iris II* in 1970 she was broken up at Sveti Kajo, near Split in 1971. *[J. and M. Clarkson]*

Seen arriving at Durban, *Efcharis* (1) was launched by Bethlehem Fairfield at Baltimore as *Henry van Dyke*, but was completed for charter to the Ministry of War Transport as *Samhain*, managed by Ellerman and Bucknall. In 1947 her managers acquired her, and as *City of Portsmouth* she become one of eleven 'Liberties' scattered across the Ellerman group. She was bought by Dimitris Margaronis in 1959 to become his first *Efcharis*. Laid up in Piraeus in December 1970, she was broken up a few months later in Greece. *[Trevor Jones]*.

British owners were allowed to build for their own account during the Second World War provided they did so to a existing design. *Riverton* was a Burntisland steamer, built for a company managed by R. Chapman and Son of Newcastle. In 1960 Dimitris Margaronis bought her to become *Eftychia*, flagging her in Greece. Sold in 1965 she spent four years with Hong Kong owners under the Panama flag as *Boaz* before demolition at Kaohsiung. *[D.W. Harris/ Author's collection]*

Caledon Shipbuilding and Engineering Co. Ltd. were well known for building high class cargo liners for Alfred Holt, but they also turned out very workmanlike tramps, such as Lambert Brothers' *Temple Hall*. She was sold to Dimitris Margaronis in 1969 to become *Pantelis*, again flagged in Greece (above). Well maintained, she found another Greek owner in 1977 as *Telamon*, but on 31st October 1981 she sprang a leak off Lanzarotte and, although beached, was later declared a constructive total loss. Most of her wreck was still ashore at Arrecife in April 2018 (right). *[Malcolm Cranfield; Dirk Septer].*

Photographed at Durban, the second *Efcharis* (above) looked rather ungainly, due to a lengthening in 1967 whilst with her original owners, J. and C. Harrison Ltd. as *Harpalyce*. Dimitris Margaronis bought her in 1972, initially renaming her *Patagonia*, changing this to *Efcharis* in 1974. He sold her to Dubai-based Global Shipping (Private) Ltd. in 1982 to become *Intra Trophy*, as which she was broken up in India in 1983 following grounding damage. *[Author's collection]*

Polyxeni (2) (middle) had been owned by two well-established British owners, Bank Line, for whom she was built by Doxfords as *Streambank*, and Runciman, who ran her from 1971 to 1973 as *Fernmoor*. Dimitris Margaronis initially chartered her to Bangladesh as *Banglar Polyxeni* (photographed off Lagos in 1976, waiting to discharge her cargo of Spanish cement) removing the prefix in 1977 (bottom). Sale in February 1982 to Dubai-based principals saw registry change from Piraeus to Valletta before she ended up as *Intra Triumph* with a Gadani Beach ship breaker in April 1983. *[Middle: Author, bottom: Trevor Jones collection]*

The rather ugly name *Demarg* was an acronym for Dimitris Margaronis, whose first name was sometimes spelt Demetrios. The ship was a product of a Spanish shipbuilder, who had completed her to an interesting design as *Bermeo*. Margaronis bought and renamed her in 1975. Laid up in Amsterdam in June 1982, she emerged one year later under the Maltese flag as *Floriana* only to proceed early in 1984 to Gadani Beach. *[Chris Howell]*

The third *Polyxeni* was bought in 1984 from the Kuwait Shipping Company for whom she had been built in 1972 as *Al Farwaniah*. She was a product of Khersonskiy Sudostoitelny Zavod, Kherson at a time when the U.S.S.R. was marketing merchant ships of the 'Poltava' type to overseas buyers. Their main success was with the Kuwait company, who took 16. After ten years with Dimitris Margaronis and his successors, *Polyxeni* began to be demolished at Alang in May 1994. Her photograph was taken whilst berthing at T Jetty, Durban in December 1991. *[Trevor Jones].*

Three brothers

In the 1930s, Anastasios, Isidoros and Georgios Margaronis jointly acquired three ships, *Pandias*, *Nellie* and *Mount Rhodope*, all illustrated and described below. Management was placed with the London-based Rethymnis and Kulukundis and from 1937 the ships were registered under the Oceanos Maritime Steam Ship Company. In 1935, Isidoros Margaronis independently took a part interest in the Kulukundis-owned *Mount Parnassus* (3,654/1915). She was built at South Shields as *Headcliffe* for G.T. Readhead's Cliffe Steam Ship Co. Ltd. Sold to Latvia in 1936, as *Baltenland* she was sunk by a Russian submarine in 1941.

Angola (4,962/1912) was built for Maclay and Mcintyre of Glasgow, and is seen as *Baygola*, one of many ships bought during the First World War by the Bay Steamship Co. Ltd., a company owned by the French Government. Bought by the three Margaronis brothers in 1931 and renamed *Pandias* she was torpedoed by *U 107* on 13th June 1941 with the loss of 11 lives whilst on a voyage from Newport to Alexandria with coal and government stores. *[Roy Fenton collection]*

Photographed at Vancouver on 30th October 1936, *Nellie* (4,784/1913) was built as *Mottisfont* at Sunderland for Harris and Dixon Ltd, London (right). After being sold to Russia in 1915 and returning to British registry in 1918, in 1933 she was bought and renamed by Isidoros Margaronis, with his two brothers taking an interest in 1935. She was managed by Rethymnis and Kulukundis Ltd. in London. *Nellie* also became a war loss, torpedoed by *U 607* on 14th October 1942 with the loss of 32 lives while on voyage from Trois Rivières to the U.K. with a cargo of steel and timber. *[Walter E. Frost/City of Vancouver Archives]*

Mount Rhodope (5,182/1919) (below) was launched as *War Gull* for The Shipping Controller, but was delivered to Elder Dempster as *Boutry*. Purchased in 1934 when her owners were desperately selling off expensively-bought tonnage, she proved an excellent investment for the Margaronis brothers, surviving the Second World War and not sold until 1957 becoming *Captain Giorgis*. She was broken up three years later. *[Bristol Series/J. and M. Clarkson]*

Margaronis post-war

In 1952 the family's interests were divided, and a ship owned by Pandelis A. Margaronis (son of Anastasios), the Fort and Park type *Santa Calli*, was transferred to cousins Pandias, Sideris and Pandelis Georgios. Meanwhile, in 1954, they acquired from Cunard the Liberty *Vandalia* which became *Sideris*.

In 1957 Pandias joined with Pandelis Georgios to create the Margaronis Navigation Agency Ltd. in London to operate the *Sideris* and two newly-built sister ships, *Vrontados* and another *Calli*. Two smaller, older vessels given the names *Urania* (2,749/1929) and *Marinda* (2,734/1948) were acquired in 1964. Broken up in 1972 they were replaced by the *Ingramar* (5,078/1954), herself sold for further trading in 1976. A new *Sideris*, the former Blue Funnel bulk carrier *Antenor* (16,406/1972), was purchased in 1978 and sold in 1989. Another bulk carrier, given the name *Pandias* (21,426/1984), was the company's last vessel, operated between 1986 and 1999. A split of family interests in about 1977 saw Pandelis Georgios leave the company and Pandias being joined in its management by Dr. I. Margaronis. Funnel colours were grey with a black top and red letter M within a red circle.

In 1977 Pandelis Georgios created Malborough Shipping Co. Ltd. in London, taking over control of the *Vrontados* from his brother and then buying from P&O the *Strathtay* which was renamed *Zak*. Meanwhile his sons G.P. and J. Margaronis had joined the company. The 1974-built SD14 type ship *Belle Rose* was purchased in 1983 to trade as *Belle* until 1991 while between 1985 and 1988 another SD14, the *Nour*, was managed by Marlborough on behalf of Islamic Investment Shipping (One) S.A.

For just three years from 1988 two Spanish built general cargo ships, *Maestro* and *Vrontados* were operated by Malborough. This company's last ship, the SD14 type *Kos* (9,241/1972, built as *Cosmopolit*) was in the fleet from 1990 to 1992, in the first few months named *Agios Markos*. Funnel colours were grey with a black top and blue letter M within a blue circle.

The Vancouver-built *Fort Venango* was bought in 1949 to become *Santa Calli* (7,166/1943) for Pandelis A. Margaronis who registered her in Panama under the title Compania de Navegacion San George S.A. In 1952, on transfer to the brothers Pandias, Sideris and Pandelis G. Margaronis, her name was shortened to *Calli*, remaining flagged in Panama. Six years later she found a German buyer and traded as *August Thyssen* until broken up at Hamburg in 1962. *[Fotoflite incorporating Skyfotos, BW13781]*

Although launched in Los Angeles as *Granville Stuart*, this Liberty never carried the name in service, as on completion she was loaned to the United Kingdom as *Samaritan* (7,219/1943). From 1947 she ran for Cunard as *Vandalia* and in 1954 was bought by Pandias Margaronis who put her under the Liberian flag as *Sideris*, seen here arriving at Avonmouth in September 1970. She was delivered to breakers in Barcelona in May 1971. *[Author]*

Named after the town from which the family came, *Vrontados* (8,637/1956) was built in Osaka and although owned by different companies under the Liberian and Panama flags, remained with the Margaronis family until broken up in Taiwan in 1980. *Vrontados* is seen above arriving at Durban in February 1974 to load for Ellesmere Port. *[Trevor Jones]*

The second *Calli* (8,774/1957) was built in Osaka, a sister to *Vrontados* and her career was very similar, down to her also being broken up in 1980, in her case in India. *[Author]*

Bought and renamed in 1963, the motor ship *Urania* (2,749/1929) was surprisingly ancient. Rederi A/B Transatlantic, Gothenburg had her built by Eriksbergs M/V as *Hallaren*, and she worked for them for almost 30 years. In 1958 she could still find a Swedish buyer who renamed her *Annika*, although she was transferred to Panama registry in 1958. Pandias Margaronis continued with the Panama flag until *Urania* was broken up at Bruges in 1982, having been laid up at Zeebrugge for over a year. *[Author]*

Marinda (2,734/1948) had an unpromising start to life. Launched as a German-designed 'Hansa B' type standard ship by John Cockerill on 9th August 1944, she was scuttled at the Hoboken yard by retreating German forces on 4th September. She was refloated on 5th April 1945, repaired and completed as a motor ship by Antwerp Engineering Company as *Hainaut* for the Belgian Government, later being sold to her original managers, Armement Deppe S.A. Renamed *Birgitte Basse* on sale to Denmark in 1961, she was bought by Pandias Margaronis and renamed *Marinda* in 1963. She returned to Belgium in 1973 for demolition at Bruges. *[Author's collection]*

Pandias Margaronis' inspiration for bestowing the name *Ingramar* (5,078/1954) in 1973 probably came from her original name *Ingertre*, given by Jacob Kjøde A/S, Bergen, for whom she was built by A/S Fredriksstad M/V. A compound-engined steamer, she was in the fleet just three years before being sold to Nello Patella, Venice who put her under the Panama flag as *Ingrid 1* as depicted here. She was broken up in 1982 near Split by Brodospas. *[Author]*

The main claim to fame of *Sideris* (middle) was her being built in 1972 by Mitsui Engineering and Shipbuilding Co. Ltd. as *Antenor*, one of the 'Agamemnon' class bulk carriers for the Ocean Group. However, Blue Funnel Bulkships quite quickly realised their mistake in entering a market about which they knew little, and she was sold in 1978 to Margaronis as *Sideris*. Sold on to Norway in 1989 as *Solbulk* and subsequently returning to Greek ownership in 1996 as *Kyklades K*, she was broken up at Chittagong, Bangladesh in 2001. *[Fotoflite incorporating Skyfotos, 87689]*

Another product of Mitsui, this time from their Ichihara yard, was the bulk carrier *Pandias*, which was completed in 1984 as *Kepbay* and acquired a year later. Margaronis Navigation Agency held on to her until 1999, but she still had much life in her, and as first *Parnassos* and later *Santa Barbara*, she sailed on until an appointment with the breakers on Gadani Beach in November 2014. *[Fotoflite incorporating Skyfotos, 52910]*

One of the last British ships to join a Margaronis fleet was *Zak* (10,148/1962). She had been built as *Trebartha* for Hain Steamship Co., Ltd., London by Readheads at South Shields, a yard which had a remarkable relationship with the former Cornish company, who – prior to acquisition by P.&O. in 1917 – had never patronised another steam ship builder. In P.&O.'s search for corporate identity she had become *Strathtay* in 1975, but was sold in 1978 as *Zak* to the Marikog Shipping Co. S.A., Panama. The 'Mar' suffix was frequently used by the Margaronis family, and also featured in the title of their London-based company which managed *Zak*, the Malborough Shipping Co. Ltd.

Zak was laid up in the River Blackwater, Essex in June 1982, as seen in the top and middle photographs. The latter shows some much-needed repainting in progress, ultimately rather pointless as, emerging from lay-up in September 1984, she did not trade again but went to breakers in China where she was demolished during the next year. *[Dave Salisbury; Nigel Jones]*

Although Austin and Pickersgill tended to be resistant to amending their SD14 design, they sometimes found it expedient to bow to owner's wishes, as in the case of *Belle Rose* (8,327/1974) for the Mauritius Steam Navigation Co. Ltd., who specified a unique arrangement of masts and kingposts. The Margaronis brothers simply amended her name to *Belle* when buying her in 1983. The photograph shows her sailing from Liverpool on 21st April 1984. Following sale in 1991 she eventually found herself under North Korean ownership, and as *Jangdaesan* was wrecked off Karachi on 22nd July 1999. Although salvage was attempted it was quickly abandoned and she is reported to have sunk. *[Author]*

The SD14 *Nour* (9,214/1974) was managed by the Margaronis family's Marlborough Shipping Co. Ltd. from 1985 to 1988 (top). Her career was a complicated one, as she had been ordered by Hong Kong principals, but was completed as *Strathdare*, one of six SD14s for P&O. However, whilst on her maiden voyage she was sold to Ellerman Lines Ltd. and returned as *City of Exeter*. 1980 saw her move on to Greek ownership, as Lyras Brothers' *Phoevos*, going on to Pakistan ownership as *Safina-e-Barkat* in 1982. Margaronis management saw the name *Nour* painted up, but with new managers in 1988 this became *Zenith*. Her last name. *Nikolaos S*, was probably carried only for her final voyage to India for demolition which ended on 23rd December 1999. *Nour* was photographed approaching *Antofagasta*. *[Marc Piché collection]*

Maestro and *Vrontados* (9,660/1979) were sisters built by Astilleros Espanoles S.A. at Bilbao in 1979, each of which had carried three names prior to acquisition by Marlborough Shipping Co. Ltd. *Maestro* (middle) was bought in 1988 and *Vrontados* (bottom) in 1989, but in 1991 both were sold on, *Maestro* having her name pared down to *Estro*, although it was then briefly restored to *Maestro*. In both cases more names followed. Having become *Sunwind*, the former *Vrontados* went first, arriving at Gadani Beach in March 2004. The former *Maestro* lasted longer. Having become *Afamia*, her ninth name, dismantling beginning at Alang in October 2012. *[Both: Fotoflite incorporating Skyfotos, 82015, 96925]*

The third generation

Anastasios Margaronis had two sons, Christophoros (1905-73) and Pandelis A. Margaronis (1914-2000). The latter became a captain, serving on the family's ships during the Second World War. He then settled in New York and founded Poseidon Shipping, his brother Christophoros, a lawyer, overseeing the family's shipping interests and running the representative office in Piraeus. 1947 saw the acquisition of the Liberty type *A.J. Cassatt* (7,210/1944), renamed *Santa Ana*, nominally owned until 1965 by Compania de Navegacion San Martin S.A., soon followed by the Fort types *Santa Calli* (discussed above) and *Santa Despo*, both nominally owned by Compania de Navegacion San George S.A. Three more Liberty ships were acquired in the early 1950s, *Santa Venetia* (7,247/1944), *Santa Rosa* (7,176/1943) and *Santa Madre* (7,176/1944), the last-named replacing *Santa Despo* which was sold in 1955 for further trading.

In 1956 Pandelis A. Margaronis established the Liberian company Santa Maria Shipowning and Trading Company S.A. which had nominally owned his first newly-built ship, named *Santa Maria* (9,966/1956) and operated until 1974 under the title of A. Margaronis, Sons and Co. Ltd. Sister ship *Santa Despoina* (9,939/1957), sold in 1959, was placed in the ownership of Compania de Navigation San George S.A.

Two further new ships, *Captain Anastassis* and *Santa Constance*, were operated until 1976 and a larger ship, *Santa Alicia* (13,841/1964) until 1979. These ships were all Greek-flagged and nominally owned by Santa Cecilia Co. S.A. of Panama. Pandelis A.'s last ship, named *Santa Pola* (11,363/1968), purchased second hand in 1973 and nominally owned by Santa Madre Compania de Navegacion. S.A. of Panama, was sold for further trading in 1981. Funnel colours again featured a large red letter M.

During the 1950s several Greek ship owners felt it necessary to leave the United States and Pandelis A. Margaronis followed them in 1961, settling in Bermuda.

Christophoros Margaronis remained in Piraeus to pursue his maritime law practice and look after the family's business interests in Greece. His son, Anastasios C. Margaronis, briefly worked with his uncle Pandelis in Bermuda during the late 1970s. In 1980 Anastasios joined his cousin Simeon P. Palios, managing director of Diana Shipping Agencies S.A., a successful company based in Athens which Simeon had formed in 1972 and they managed a fleet of fifty large bulk carriers trading as Diana Shipping Inc. as well as Panamax and post-Panamax container ships under Diana Containerships Inc. Anastasios C. Margaronis acts as the president of both companies which are listed on the New York Stock Exchange and the NASDAQ, respectively.

Although their fleet was never particularly large, the Margaronis family are a fine example of a Greek shipping dynasty which survived the vicissitudes of the shipping industry by carefully operating relatively modest ships, not over-extending themselves, but gradually updating their fleet both in terms of age and ship type.

Santa Despo (7,189/1943) was photographed at Vancouver, where by coincidence she had been built by West Coast Shipbuilders Ltd. as *Fort Astoria* (top). Pandelis A. Margaronis owned her from 1948 to 1955, when she went to associates of Rethymnis and Kulukundis as *Mount Ithome*. She was broken up at Santander in 1967. *[City of Vancouver Archives]*

Seen in the Welland canal *Santa Maria* (9,966/1956) (bottom) was the first ship built for Pandelis A. Margaronis and was also special in being fitted with steam turbine machinery which gave her a speed of almost 16 knots. Builders were the Uraga Dock Co. Ltd. at Yokosuka. Perhaps her fuel-hungry machinery condemned her to a relatively short career, as after a respectable 18 years with the Margaronis family's Liberian ship owning company Santa Maria Shipowning and Trading Company S.A., she was towed from Kuwait to Karachi in August 1974 and sold to Gulf Shipping Lines Ltd. who renamed her *Jayem* but sent her direct to breakers at Gadani Beach. *[Fred Miller II]*

Seen in New Zealand waters (top), *Captain Anastassis* (8,717/1960) was delivered in 1960 by the Uraga Dock Co. Ltd., by when Pandelis Margaronis was using the Chios-based Santa Cecilia Co. S.A. to register his ships under the Greek flag. As the careers of the ships described here suggest, the Margaronis fleet seemed to be well enough run to have avoided many peacetime casualties, although this was not the case once their ships were sold. *Captain Anastassis* went to other Greek owners in 1976 as *Evangelia*, and on 2nd December 1979 was damaged by fire south of Crete whilst on a voyage from Trieste to Basrah with flour and timber. Towed to Piraeus, she was declared a constructive total loss and in October 1980 broken up at Cartagena. *[J. and M. Clarkson]*

Another product of Uraga Dock, *Santa Constance* (8,772/1960) (middle) went to another Greek owner in 1975 as *Golden Seagull*, but on 16th April 1978 she stranded and caught fire 55 miles north of the port of Assab in Eritrea whilst on a voyage from Constantza to Haiphong with a cargo of urea. Once the fire had burned out she was refloated on 29th April, but was subsequently declared a constructive total loss and broken up at Kaohsiung where she arrived under tow on 9th March 1979. *[David Pemberton/Author's collection]*

Bought and renamed in 1973, *Santa Pola* (11,363/1968) (bottom) had been built for Olav Ringdal, Oslo by Bremer Vulkan at Vegesack as *Ringvard*. As the last ship owned by Pandelis Margaronis, in 1980 she moved without change of name and registered ownership to the management by Diana Shipping Agencies which Anastasios C. Margaronis had recently joined. Sold in 1981 to become *Telfair Trader*, she was broken up at Gadani Beach in 1985. *[George Wilson]*

REMEMBERING *KHALIJ CRYSTAL*

Tony Breach

I had a little chuckle when reading the caption to the photo of *Khalij Crystal* ('Record' 63, page 186) describing her to be 'in superb condition'; she is a ship that I knew quite well and the history of her latter days is interesting.

During her last years with the Shaw, Savill and Albion Co. Ltd. as *Zealandic*, she was time chartered to the Uiterwyk Corporation of Tampa, a company with whom I was master from 1976 until their financial collapse in 1982. While in that service she was employed carrying meat and offal from Great Lakes ports to Northern Europe. The management were not at all happy with the ship and her condition was rapidly deteriorating as virtually no maintenance was done. A photograph shows corrosion of the hull above the water line. Following the end of the charter period in 1980 she was sold to Greek owners who renamed her *Port Launay* and I understand that they soon discovered her problems and quickly put her up for sale.

In 1981 she was sold to Cobalt Shipping Inc. of the Gulfeast group who renamed her *Khalij Crystal* with Liberian registry. I have no idea of how she traded during her first three years with Gulfeast but I later found out that eventually charterers could not be found due to her appalling condition. This was bad news as Gulfeast's Monaco-based reefer company, UniMarine, had recently expanded with time charters of several new, Japanese-owned ships and was doing quite well in the market. UniMarine, whose president, Bo Rammer, was formerly a senior manager of Salen Reefer Services, demanded that the ship be upgraded or sold resulting in the ship getting a coat of white paint in 1983. In March of 1984 I was offered the position as master and was given a photograph which looked quite nice and I accepted the offer. This photograph appears to have been taken at the same time and possibly from the same platform as yours at Cape Town. The ship had lost a cargo of apples and eggs from France to Red Sea and Persian Gulf ports and the Asian master, mate, chief engineer and reefer engineer were fired and replaced by British officers who joined the ship at Durban during a bunker call en-route to the Falkland Islands.

The photograph opposite indicates pretty much how the ship looked on our joining. During our first day on board the ship had an oil spill which was fortunately contained on deck although this caused other problems as the main deck was wood sheathed. We were somewhat dismayed but these things happen and we were determined to do our best. The Mate came to me and reported that there were rats in the storerooms and I called the agents to have the local exterminator's service. We also found out from the junior officers that the two cranes could be luffed for access to the hatches but could not be used for lifting cargo and that the Stülcken derrick was very dangerous. I also wrote a report to the ship managers in Hong Kong describing the condition of the ship and requiring her to be repaired and upgraded. My own opinion was that, due to the awful appearance of the ship, the local authorities should have made an inspection of the ship and dealt with the housekeeping problems a least. We did our best with what we had.

We sailed to the Falklands and went on-hire to our Polish squid fishing charterers at the extremely low rate for March of US 27 cents per cubic foot per month. They only had sufficient product to fill the lower holds and tried to fix a cargo of citrus to Europe from Uruguay. In conjunction with UniMarine I advised against it as the ship's cargo circulating cold air fans were of insufficient power to handle citrus fruits. During unberthing we were struck by a Polish mother ship causing the loss of the port lifeboat and damage to a Samson post and some bulwarks. I was able to persuade the Poles to supply four inflatable life rafts and have three masters to issue a

Zealandic was launched on 4th November 1964 by Alexander Stephen and Sons Ltd., Glasgow and delivered to Shaw, Savill and Albion Co. Ltd. in March 1965. She was photographed arriving at Hobart, Tasmania. *[David E. Kirby/Russell Priest collection]*

certificate of seaworthiness (which was later accepted at the Panama Canal, Poland, Rotterdam and Le Havre with a second-hand boat supplied at Brest). We sailed from the Islands through the Magellan Strait and the Chilean Archipelago and loaded horse mackerel from another Polish factory ship under way 200 miles of the coast of Chile; an interesting operation. Then to Europe via the Panama Canal. In Poland the charterers met with me and offered $100,000 to the owners as payment for the damage if they then scrapped the ship; a good deal I thought but the owners disagreed. We discharged and sailed for Rotterdam.

The photograph of the *Khalij Crystal* in 'Record' 63 was taken, I think, whilst arriving at Rotterdam where she was dry-docked for survey and repairs. To cut a long story short, the contact damage was repaired but the ship had some very old and corroded bottom damage for which the owner's superintendent requested I write in the logbook that we had grounded in the Falklands. I informed him that would be totally stupid as the damage was so old and in any case I would not risk my ticket for that. The Lloyd's Register surveyor also knew of unrepaired collision damage to the hull topsides which had occurred when she was in the Great Lakes in her Uiterwyk days. There was a condition of class for this but there was no copy in the ship's file; now that was interesting - when and where did it go missing? The mind boggles.

We loaded meat and dairy products at French ports for Alexandria where I left the ship to take care of the discharge of two further vessels for UniMarine and returned to their office as Port Captain. The Mate became Master and took the ship to Pakistan for scrapping and the company lost the $100,000 they could have had. Nobody had been paid for months and I was personally owed just over $10,000 as was the Chief Engineer. Unimarine gave me some money as well as free accommodation in Monaco and I could contact the Chief Engineer by radio and his wife by telephone. Prior to leaving the ship I had discussed this with the Chief and he would not allow the engine to be started in order to beach the ship until I could confirm that his and my money was in our respective banks. Each workday I would call my bank in the UK to see if the money had arrived and the Chief's wife to see if his had as well. If not I would call Hong Kong who for about two weeks assured me daily that 'It has been paid today'. What I did not know was that the Mate who was a Pakistani who had relieved the British Mate at Rotterdam and was now the Master had not been paid from his previous ship, and was keeping her offshore in international waters and working closely with the Chief to ensure that everyone was paid. Eventually we all got our money as far as I know and the ship was beached. I continued with UniMarine as Port Captain in the office and abroad as necessary until the company folded in 1975.

In retrospect I think the paintwork of *Khalij Crystal* might have been in superb condition but it certainly covered up a disastrous mess. One other thing: the funnel was constructed of aluminium and its connection to the steel had corroded and when the ship was rolling heavily it moved a little and groaned a lot. My cabin was situated abaft the wheelhouse right underneath and it was quite noisy at times.

Her last years as *Zealandic* saw her, along with her Vickers-built sister *Laurentic* (7,964/1964), chartered to Uiterwyk Lines. In this photograph, taken on the New Waterway on 28th June 1979, she looks in better condition than the author remembers her. *[George Garwood/World Ship Society Ltd.]*

Two photographs of *Khalij Crystal* in the New Waterway in June 1984. Note that her port lifeboat is missing, destroyed in a collision with a Polish mother ship whilst loading squid in the South Atlantic. *[Tony Stacey/World Ship Society Ltd.]*

PUTTING THE RECORD STRAIGHT

We welcome letters, additions, amendments and photographs relating to features in *any* issues of 'Record': this year's column has letters referring to issues in 2016, which were overlooked in last year's issue, and several even older references. They are presented in roughly chronological order of the issues to which they refer. Senders of e-mails are asked to provide their postal address. Letters may be lightly edited.

Empire Bittern (8,546/1902) a US Coast Guard photograph dated 23rd October 1943, before her somewhat ignominious end on the beach at Arromanches. *[Roy Fenton collection],*

What finally happened to *Empire Bittern*?

Recently a friend lent me a holiday snapshot looking out over the sea wall at Arromanches at the remains of Mulberry B. The time can be assumed to be summer in either 1946 or 1947. On the horizon at centre left, gleaming ghostly white, there is a large, single-funnelled ship. Examination under a magnifying glass reveals that she has five masts (three before the funnel and two abaft it). As has already been established ('Record' 47, page 191, where there is a similar photograph), *Empire Bittern* was the only five-master present at D-Day (or anywhere else for that matter), so this can only be that ship. Another telling point is that in both images it can be seen that she has broken in two between the third mast and funnel.

I've tried might and main to find out what eventually happened to the hulk, but to no avail. Were the two halves patched, raised and towed away to the scrapyard, or was she dismantled in situ? Would any of your contacts know the answer?

The erstwhile *Iowa* and her history have always been a favourite shipping topic of mine. She had such a wonderfully varied career, and carried at different times livestock, emigrants, troops, cotton and other important cargoes in peacetime and during both world wars. Yet she was hardly altered throughout. Truly a tribute to her builders, Harland and Wolff, Belfast. Why no sisters? Her original owners, White Diamond Steamship Co. Ltd. of Liverpool (Warren Line) were a relatively small concern, and possibly could not afford to build a consort for such a large vessel. I have never come across a photograph of the ship in her early guises as *Iowa* and *Bohemia*, only drawings.

ROBERT LANGLOIS, Feu Follet, Maisons au Compte, Vale, Guernsey, GY3 5HF

NDL ships in 'Record'

I can confirm that Tore Nilsen's comment (page 127 in 'Record' 58) on the photograph on page 10 of issue 57 is indeed 'a very near miss'. The photograph is of the *Targis* (5,952/1915), which features on page 39 of Arnold Kludas' book on Norddeutscher Lloyd (NDL). As related in Duncan Haws' book on Henderson and Bibby and the Dutch book on Vereenigde Nederlandsche, the *Targis* was already prone to fire. According to the Dutch book when on fire in November 1923 as *Rijperkerk* she had to be deliberately sunk by a French monitor at Bastia. The wreck was later sold by the underwriters to the Roland Line of the NDL group, which was somehow near at hand, as she was built for the Hamburg-Bremer Afrika-Linien (HBAL), another part of the NDL group. Duncan Haws is wrong in suggesting she was never delivered, as she was completed in January 1917, but was subsequently laid up. The kingposts on the forecastle were probably added during the repairs before she returned to service in 1925.

In 'Record' 58, page 79 there are two photographs of another NDL ship: *Dundalk Bay* ex *Nürnberg*. In 1948-9 she repatriated Shanghai's German community. I got this information about 20 years ago from a late former colleague of mine. He remembered that the voyage back to Europe was prolonged by countless engine troubles.

When looking at the photographs on page 79 it is hard to believe that for a while 1,024 passengers (in stark contrast to the original 28 first class passengers) would be carried, because in these images of 1954 there are only a few differences from her pre-war appearance: two large lifeboats added at bridge deck level, radar and a lengthened funnel. The row of portholes beneath the superstructure is shorter than one may expect of a migrant ship. As can be seen on the enclosed copy of her wartime photo as *MRS 12* (mothership for minesweeping launches) at that time there were portholes at numbers 2 and 3 holds, probably for the additional crews for the launches.

The *Phoenix* in 'Record' 60, page 255, is the German vessel (999/1913) built for the Argo Line, Bremen (again closely connected with NDL) for their British service. So she was already a regular caller at Hull before the First World War. Surviving the conflict she resumed her owner's British service in 1920. In 1922-3 the Argo Line and its services and ships were taken over by the Roland Line, another company in the NDL group. In 1926 the Roland Line was totally taken over by the NDL group, but retained their funnel colours (buff with a black top, like the *Targis*). I have enclosed two photos showing *Phoenix* leaving Hamburg in the late 1930s in the colours of the reformed Argo Reederei to which she was transferred in 1933. The only difference, except for the funnel colours, is that the first lifeboat (at least on the starboard side) is gone. Becoming a Sperrbrecher (mine destructor vessel) with the Kriegsmarine she was scuttled in August 1944 when the retreating German troops blocked the French Atlantic ports.

ECKHARD MUND, Agathenstrasse1, 20357 Hamburg, Germany

Nürnberg as the minesweeper mother ship *MRS 12. [Eckhard Mund collection]*

Photographed leaving Hamburg in the 1930s, the *Phoenix* of Argo Line is positively identified as the *Phoenix* on page 255 of 'Record' 60. *[Eckhard Mund collection]*

Eckhard kindly provided extensive documentation about the Targis, *and the editors can only apologise to him for failing to include his information earlier. She was built by J. Frerichs & Co., Einswarden as* Wolfram *for the Hamburg-Bremer Afrika Linie of Bremen, but was claimed by Great Britain in 1919. In 1921 she became the* Netley Abbey *of the little known David Steamship Co. Ltd. (D.G. Pinkney and Company, managers), London. In 1921 they sold her to Vereenigde Nederlandsche Stoomboot Maatschappij, The Hague, Netherlands who renamed her* Rijperkerk. *The first fire referred to occurred on 17th November 1923 at Bastia during a voyage from Natal and Mombasa to Marseille and London with a cargo of bark, maize, coconut oil and ivory. The next day she was scuttled by gunfire to extinguish the fire. Refloated on 3rd March 1924, she was declared a constructive total loss, but was sold to Roland Linie A.G., Bremen and re-built as* Targis. *The photograph in 'Record' 57 shows* Targis *after she caught fire on 17th July 1930 in the South Atlantic and shortly before she foundered two days later. She was on a voyage from Valparaiso to Antwerp and Hamburg with general cargo including nitrate and copper. Ed.*

Swords or crosses?

At the time of writing the article on Gulf Shipping the funnel markings of *Fexl Glory* were a mystery ('Record'62, page 91). It has now been suggested that the markings are in fact crossed swords, not crossed letters X. The Saudi coat of arms has a pair of crossed swords beneath a script that proclaims God as Allah and Muhammad as the Prophet, so if I am correct, these markings may indicate a further Saudi connection in the beneficial ownership of some of the Gulf operated ships

MALCOLM CRANFIELD, 8 Foxcover Road, Heswall, Wirral L60 1YB

Of identity and anchors.

You write these articles - you're bound to get feedback!

Re the *Skerryvore/Coath*, 'Record' 63, page 165. I can't explain the fidded masts. Apart from that she seems to be the same ship as *Coath* in 'Record' 10 page 122. Note that both have Admiralty pattern anchors, i.e. in keeping with the 1882 model. In both photos the ships have the shortened funnel. But, the *Coath* in 'Record' 11 page 150 has modern, stockless anchors and seems more likely to be the 1898 model; she still has the tall funnel and appears to lack the prominent deckhouse aft. The *Exe* in 'Record' 63, page 169 is also radical, not only in hull design, but in possessing stockless anchors if the original fitting from 1887; *Princess Irene* and *Princess Sophia,* 'Record' 63, page 166, both of 1891, having the older type.

JOHN ANDERSON, 523 Louise Road, Ladysmith, British Columbia V9G 1W7, Canada

Salvesen 1: whaling at Olnafirth

On page 232 of 'Record 64' there is a fascinating little article about the Salvesen hulk *Black Boy* at Olnafirth in the Shetlands.

There are two published accounts of Salvesen and its ships. The first was *Salvesen of Leith* by Wray Vamplew, published by Scottish Academic Press in 1975. Although Graeme Somner had given Dr. Vamplew some assistance in matters relating to ships owned by the company, the book was really an economic history of the company in which individual ships featured only from time to time and there was no intention to cover the fleet as a whole. Graeme and I thought it was a pity that no fleet list existed, particularly as Graeme's research for the book had effectively given him access to nearly all that he needed. I was then working for Salvesen and persuaded the Salvesen board to underwrite the publication of a detailed fleet list entitled 'From 70 North to 70 South', published by Salvesen in 1984. Graeme supplied all the details of the ships and sourced many of the photographs; I wrote the text and sourced some additional photographs from the company's archives. For both of us, it was a labour of love.

We did not cover hulks so the *Black Boy* and a couple of others did not feature in our book. On the other hand, Dr. Vamplew has some interesting background on the *Black Boy* and the Olna whaling project. It includes an undated photograph (plate 48, opposite page 85) of the whaling station with the *Black Boy* alongside the pier (by then more substantial than shown on page 232 of Charles Simpson's article), taken after the hulk's prominent funnel had been repainted in Salvesen colours - and the latter includes the pre-1915 black top. As an aside, I wonder whether the hulk had retained her boiler (but not her propulsion machinery) so that she had steam-raising capability for operating winches and the like, which would have necessitated the retention of the funnel.

Salvesen is perhaps best-remembered by many for its involvement in Antarctic whaling but that was not the start of its whaling ventures. The company had been Scottish agents for Norwegian producers of whale oil from the early 1880s but in the very late 1890s it took its first small-scale steps into whaling in Norway and Iceland. It ordered its first whale-catcher, from a Norwegian yard, in 1903. Those early ventures were not particularly successful but Christian Salvesen's son Theodore was convinced of the longer-term potential for whaling. A Norwegian whaling company had established a small whaling station on the Shetlands in 1903 and Theodore persuaded his partners to invest in a new whaling station at Olnafirth. Although Christian was by now in his late-seventies, he was still very much the firm's driving force and he backed Theodore's judgment against the other sons who had different ideas about new capital investments. As an aside, it was Christian, a few years later and by then in his eighties, who supported Theodore's plan to start whaling in the Antarctic.

Theodore identified the site in Olnafirth (sheltered but close to the open sea) which he reckoned was ideal but there was substantial local opposition. He won the day because of the firm's policy of totally reducing the whales rather than discarding the carcasses after extracting only the blubber. Behind the scenes he had already placed the orders for the factory buildings and their equipment and Dr. Vamplew suspects he had already purchased the *Black Boy* before the end of 1903 (that would tie in with the closure of the ship's registry taking place in December 1903). A considerable embarrassment to Theodore came in a classic instance of the left hand and the right not being in synch: having told the Marine Superintendant's Department to proceed with all speed with the hulking of the *Black Boy* on Tyneside in preparation for her being towed to the Shetlands, he forgot to put a halt to the plans. In the midst of the most delicate negotiations with the County Council, during which he had assured them that the company's plans would not be started until permission had been given, the tug arrived at Olnafirth with the *Black Boy* in tow. Permission was not granted until a Government enquiry had reported, which was fortunately in Salvesen's favour. Another bone of contention was that the whale catchers at Olna all flew the Danish flag: the Danish authorities in Iceland had insisted that all whalers operating there must be registered in Denmark so Salvesen kept the Danish flag so that it could switch vessels at will between Iceland and the Shetlands. The Shetland licence was delivered in May 1904; the whaling station opened on 1st June; the first shipment of oil was taken away on 15th June.

The Olnafirth station continued in relatively profitable circumstances until the development of Scapa Flow as a major naval base and the outbreak of the First World War. The Admiralty was worried about the constant movement of small vessels to and from the whaling station and was also concerned that, in poor visibility, its own guns might mistakenly shoot at a Salvesen vessel. It closed down the whaling operations in 1915 and requisitioned the buildings which were used for naval purposes for the duration of the war. With typical bloody-mindedness, the Admiralty did not de-requisition the station until too late for anything to be done for the 1919 season so work did not start again until 1920. Having had several seasons of inactivity, the local opposition to whaling operations started again with a vengeance and the objectors managed to force an official enquiry by the Fishery Board for Scotland. It reported that no further whaling should be permitted once the current concessions expired in 1923 but the Government failed to introduce the necessary legislation. The station at Olnafirth remained reasonably profitable for a few more seasons but it closed permanently in 1929 largely because cheaper and more plentiful whale products were coming from the Antarctic. There is no record of what happened to the *Black Boy:* as she was a floating asset, she was probably towed away for scrapping rather than incurring the further wrath of the Shetlanders by being left as a derelict item at Olnafirth.

This involves no original research: it is all culled from various chapters of Vamplew's book.

COLIN MENZIES, 17 Bickenhall Mansions, London W1U 6BP

Salvesen 2: joint ventures with Harrisons (Clyde) Ltd.

You will recall that I worked for Christian Salvesen for fourteen years in the 1970s and early 1980s. The lower two pictures on page 226 of 'Record' 64 struck an immediate bell with me: one of them was owned by Voreda Steamship Company while the other was named *Virgilia*. Both were part of the Gow, Harrison group of companies about which you give a brief background in the captions.

When I joined Salvesen, the chairman was Sir Max Harper Gow (Max is the common Scottish shortening of the name Maxwell when it is used as a Christian name). His mother had been a grand daughter of Christian Salvesen; his father had been a member of the Glasgow ship owning Gow family. Max was an enormously likeable and successful man with a great sense of humour and virtually unerring business sense: the approachable exterior could often mask his keen sense of business drive. Salvesen had recently taken on the management of the two coasters *Virgilia* (1,437/1970) and *Voreda* (1,437/1971) which had just been built in the Netherlands for Harrisons (Clyde) Ltd., the re-incarnation of the former Gow, Harrison partnership. At the same time, Salvesen had commissioned a new bulk-carrier from a Japanese shipyard; she was given the traditional Gow, Harrison name of *Verdala* (14,771/1968) and placed under the management of Harrisons (Clyde).

I once asked Max (who was aware of my interest in shipping) about this slightly odd cross-fertilisation between the two companies. He began to explain confidently but it tailed off into several loose ends from which I concluded that he had slightly forgotten the ins and outs of the original arguments. I think it boiled down to this. Harrisons (Clyde) had become largely involved in deep-sea bulk-carriers and wanted to diversify: they had decided to look at coasters but felt they had no management expertise in running such tonnage so they had contracted Salvesen (who ran a fleet of then-modern coasters on the UK-Norway line together with the coastal tramps of A.F. Henry and MacGregor) to run the Harrison investment in coasters. Similarly Salvesen, although already owning one deep-sea bulk carrier (but she was on a long-term time charter), wanted to dip its toe

Virgilia in Salvesen colours, approaching Eastham. With her sister *Voreda* she was built to a standard Dutch design by N.V. Scheepwerven Gebr. Van Diepen at Waterhuizen. *[J. and M. Clarkson]*

further into the waters of deep-sea ship owning and therefore put Harrisons as managers of the new ship, as it was felt they had the relevant experience and expertise. Underneath it all there was some kind of arrangement to pool the management costs of the three ships.

Whatever the reason (and if Max had got himself slightly confused over the details, I have anyway forgotten the finer points), the arrangements did not last for long. The new *Voreda* was sold by Harrisons to Dutch coaster owners after only four years. Similarly the new *Virgilia* was sold by Harrisons after five years to other British owners, although Salvesen continued as the managers (under an entirely separate arrangement) on behalf of the new owners for a further eight years. Also after five years, the *Verdala* was brought under Salvesen's own management but she was sold 18 months later to Bibby Line as *Shropshire* and had no further Salvesen connection. In other words the three ships arrived in this odd management pool at much the same time and the arrangements were all ended five years later: I have a recollection that the two owning companies had agreed to give the new arrangements five years to see if they were worthwhile and concluded that they were not.

COLIN MENZIES, 17 Bickenhall Mansions, London W1U 6BP

Putting 'Record' 64 straight

Bartrams did not manufacture main engines, so it is incorrect to attribute them as suppliers of the machinery of *Flimston* of Evan Thomas Radcliffe ('Record' 64, page 224). Blairs of Stockton-on-Tees did that, as they did for a lot of the vessels Bartrams built at the time (certainly for this owner).

JOHN LINGWOOD, 53 Rothbury Road, Newton Hall, Durham DH1 5PF

Geest ships from Greenock

The following Geest ships featured in 'Record' 64 were built at the Cartsdyke Yard at Greenock (formerly Greenock Dockyard) which was taken over by Scotts in 1965. But as Scotts merged with Lithgows in 1969 they were actually built by Scott Lithgow Ltd.: *Geest-tide* of 1971, *Geestcrest* and *Geestland* of 1972 and *Geest Star* of 1973.

However, *Geestcape* and *Geesthaven* were built by Greenock Dockyard at Cartsdyke prior to it being merged with Scotts. The latter operated the Cartsburn Yard at Greenock.

JIM POTTINGER, 1 Jesmond Cirle, Bridge of Don, Aberdeen AB22 8WX

Muskoka* and *Implacable

It might be the result of a typo, but the building year you give for the *Muskoka* (1911) is out by exactly 20 years ('Record' 2017, page 122). She was launched by Richardson, Duck on 5th October 1891, two months after a sister (*Oweenee*) for the same owner. The same builder launched two slightly smaller barques for Liverpool owners in 1892, and there was a positive surge in sailing ship construction on the Clyde, particularly in the Russell and Company yards at Port Glasgow and Greenock in the early 1890s. As an upshot, it might be better to describe *Muskoka* as one of the last generation of large commercial sailing ships, rather than as a 'latecomer'.

The other point relates to the caption of the photograph of HMS *Implacable*. As *Duguay-Trouin*, she was one of four French ships of the line which escaped to sea after the battle, but (after some losses and recaptures caused by the storm which followed the battle) another five ships of the line escaped back to Cadiz and were still there in 1808, when the Spanish seized them after they declared war on France. (A number of smaller craft - five frigates and two brigs - also escaped back to Cadiz). I doubt that 'Record' is the place for a diversion into Napoleonic War naval history, but for the sake of completeness, the fates of the 18 French ships of the line were as follows:

Lost in the battle or the following storm (9): *Bucentaure*, *Redoubtable*, *Indomptable*, *Fougueux*, *Intrepide*, *Aigle*, *Swiftsure*, *Achille*, *Berwick*.

Escaped into the Atlantic but then captured off Cape Ortegal on 4th November 1805 (4): *Formidable*, *Scipion*, *Duguay-Trouin*, *Mont Blanc*.

Escaped back to Cadiz and captured there by the Spanish in 1808 (5):
Neptune, *Heros*, *Pluton*, *Algeciras*, *Argonaute*.

The stern gallery of HMS *Implacable* is preserved and displayed at the National Maritime Museum.

MALCOLM COOPER, 12 Harvest Lane, Thames Ditton, Surrey KT7 0NG

Glen Rosa*, not *Cambria

I can, indeed, as you suggested, identify the un-named paddle steamer in the photograph on page 233 of 'Record' 64. She is P. and A. Campbell's *Glen Rosa*, built in 1877 for services to Arran on the Clyde, as her name suggests. She was sold in 1881 to London owners, changed hands in London several times before being sold for service on the Sussex coast in 1893. Captain Alex. Campbell, one of the two brothers who founded P. and A. Campbell (which became a limited company in 1893), purchased her on his own account in 1897 but sold her on to the company in 1898, in whose service she remained until called up for war service in 1917. After the war she was found not worth reconditioning and was scrapped in 1920.

During her whole career she, perhaps surprisingly, retained her original name: appropriately for the Campbell brothers whose origins were on the Clyde, and who named three of their later, purpose-built ships with the *Glen* prefix. *Glen Rosa* operated for the While Funnel Fleet, at different times, on the Bristol Channel, Southampton and the Sussex coast. She

Left: *Glen Rosa* of 1877, photographed whilst operating on the South Coast. The photograph is attributed to E.A. Schwerdtfeger & Co., London, but the card was printed at their Berlin works.

Right: *Cambria* of 1895 was, as Reverend Bird points out, a very different vessel from *Glen Rosa*. *[Both photographs: World Ship Society Print Colection]*

retained her appearance as shown in your photograph until Easter 1911. In May of that year she was built up aft with a full-width saloon on the main deck and a promenade deck atop the saloon, much improving her accommodation. The photograph was therefore taken some time between 1897 and Easter 1911, but I cannot be more specific than that.

I am indebted for most of this information to Chris Collard's series of books on P. and A. Campbell's White Funnel Fleet and to Frank Burtt's 'Steamers of the Thames and Medway'.

The guess that the photograph might be that of the *Cambria* was rather wide of the mark. *Cambria* was a very different ship: purpose-built for Campbells in 1895, she was larger and more heavily-built than *Glen Rosa*, with a continuous promenade deck from stem to stern and a fully enclosed main deck. She was scrapped in 1946 after Admiralty service in the Second World War. I can distinctly remember sailing on her, at the age of seven, in 1939, from Cardiff to Ilfracombe with my grandfather.

REVEREND NORMAN BIRD, 35 Woodcock Court, 258-266 Woodcock Hill, Harrow HA3 0PN

Loss of the *Diamant*

Diamant ('Record' 2017, page 67 to 82) had been seized by the advancing German forces in the inner dock at St Malo on 21st June 1940 and, after repairs to damage done when she was abandoned by her Belgian crew, she entered service carrying supplies and equipment to the German troops who occupied Jersey and Guernsey.

Her end came on the 20th September 1942 while bound from Granville to St Peter Port, Guernsey. With the weather worsening on reaching Corbiere Point on Jersey's south west coast she was unable to make headway with both wind and tide against her. Her master decided to go about and seek shelter in St. Helier Harbour. On making her approach she turned to port rather late and was blown on to the Dogs Nest Reef on the eastern side of the fairway leading to the port. She was carrying a full cargo of stores and equipment for the occupying forces plus a number of troops returning to duty after shore leave.

The German Harbour Captain (Kapitan Hartmann) ordered the St Helier Lifeboat *Howard D* to be launched and to proceed to the scene, but by the time she arrived off the Dogs Nest *Diamant* was almost completely submerged with most of those on board having already been rescued by patrol boats of the Harbour Protection Flotilla. On cruising around the lifeboat discovered three men on a low head of rock but were unable to reach them. *Howard D* then returned to harbour and towed out a small rowing boat which, manned by two lifeboat men, rescued the three men. In the meantime a further seven were discovered actually sitting on the Dogs Nest beacon but the lifeboat was unable to reach them, due to the darkness and the heavy swell. However, she stood by until daylight and rescued five men, the other two having been washed away during the night. It is known that 22 men were lost, but it is believed there were as many as 500 on board that night.

Diamant soon started to break up. Her cargo included eggs, fruit and vegetables plus large quantities of prepared timber including doors, window frames, roof trusses which were parts of the numerous large huts that were being built on the islands. I remember my father bringing home a complete window frame which had come from the wreck: this was later incorporated into our garden shed.

DAVE HOCQUARD, Les Cotils des Pelles, Petit Port, St. Brelade, Jersey

Petrolea identified

John Pryce has identified the tanker illustrated on page 126 of 'Record' 2017 as the Russian-flagged steamer *Petrolea*, completed in 1888 by the Motala Company of Gothenburg for Ludvig Nobel of St. Petersburg. In 1890 the Nobel organisation renamed her *Ludwig Nobel*, and in 1891 sold her to Johan Bryde, Sandefjord, Norway who renamed her *Drageren*. Bryde was in the whaling business, and used her to carry whale oil. On such a voyage from Inhambane, Mozambique to Rotterdam she was wrecked on Fungo Rock, 45 miles south of Delgado, on 18th November 1912.

Michael notes that she brought the first cargo of oil in bulk to the Thames about 1890, discharged at Atlantic Wharf at Bow after pipelines had been laid beneath the streets. The cargo of one thousand tons came from Libau, Russia (where *Petrolea* was registered) and was handled by Lane and Macandrew of London.

Putting Black Ships straight

I found a small mistake in the history of the *Bratton Castle*: as *Mount Taurus* ('Record' 2017, page 37). She also sailed under Greek flag after 1935/36 (she was chartered by the Swiss Government from 11.10.1939 till 10.01.1941 and then she sailed under Greek flag). See Lloyd's Register and http://www.test.swiss-ships.ch/reeder/reederlist-ch-foreign-flag/kta-ausland-charter-liste.html https://uboat.net/allies/merchants/ship/2438.html

MARKUS BERGER by e-mail

In common with most compound words, the normal German practice for naval (and indeed all other) ranks was to run the words together into one - thus the rank of most of the U-boat commanders mentioned in the article was spelled Käpitanleutnant. However, note that Oberleutnant zur See is correct, but the first name of the gentleman of that rank mentioned at the top of page 32 was Johannes - he was an ace who sank just over 150,000 tons of Allied shipping and had a Second World War U-boat flotilla named after him.

The author of 'Union-Castle's Black Ships, 'Record' 2017 pages 25 to 54) seems to have a bit of a negative opinion on First World War standard ships. In one sense, at least, they were better than he suggests they were - he gives their speed as 9.5 knots, but their registers consistently give a figure of 11.5 knots, which would seem better to match their engine specifications.

There might be a very good reason why there are no photos of *Rosyth Castle* (page 35) - the vessel's closed register in BT 110 and London customs house register entry in CUST 130 are unanimous in giving dates between the sequential renamings to *Rosyth Castle* and then to *Umlazi* which are less than a month apart - which would have given very little chance to photograph her in the former guise. I believe the confusion arises because the dates given in 'Record' more closely approximate to the date of the Board of Trade sanction for the name change, than the date of the change itself. Strangely, most of the dates given in the vessel entry in 'Record' are out of line with those in BT 110/CUST 130, so for the sake of completeness, I have reproduced the official ones below:

28.11.1918: Registered at London (427/1918) as WAR EARL.
3.11.1919: Sold to Union Castle.
17.2.1920: BoT sanction name change to ROSYTH CASTLE.
22.3.1921: Transferred to Bullard King.
8.8.1921: Name changed to ROSYTH CASTLE in register.
25.8.1921: BoT sanction for name change to UMLAZI.
30.8.1921: Name changed to UMLAZI in register.
3.6.1936: Sold to the Tramp Shipping Development Co. Ltd.
26.6.1936: Transferred to the Campden Hill Steamship Co. Ltd.
29.9.1936: Renamed CAMPDEN HILL.
3.11.1937: Register closed on sale to Japan.

MALCOLM COOPER, 12 Harvest Lane, Thames Ditton, Surrey KT7 0NG

Putting 'Record' 2017 straight (1)

Page 41 *Boskoop* 21.6.1960. Avila is south of San Francisco in California. This should be Aviles, near Gijon in Spain.

Page 42 *Jean L.D.* The name on the ship is *Jean L-D* (*yes, but 'Lloyd's Register' renders it* Jean L.D. *Ed*). It is stated she is in neutrality markings in 1941. She was at Cape Town (Table Bay) from 23rd January to 23rd April 1941 and again from 16th June to 6th July 1941 but she is showing no signs of any wartime armament or life saving gear. The only time she was a neutral ship was when she was in Vichy service between late June 1940 and her capture and at that time she was named *Betelgeuse*. Is it possible these markings are for the Spanish Civil War 1937-1939 and the date is wrong? *(very possible. Ed)*

Page 49. The top photograph is of the *Tantallon Castle*, not the *Tintagel Castle*.

Page 125. To say *Torrid* was placed in Reserve in February 1919 and sold in 1937 gives the wrong impression. She was in Devonport Reserve 1919-1926. Commissioned for service in the first anti-submarine flotilla based on Portland 1st February 1927. Forward gun removed in 1927 and carried an experimental bomb thrower in number 1 gun position

The photograph of *Bratton Castle* of 1920 on page 37 of 'Record' 2017 showed her as completed with a particularly short funnel. This photograph, believed to be taken at Durban, shows her with a much taller funnel. The condition of the plates alongside her bunker hatch suggests she has been patched up after some calamity. *[Ships in Focus]*

1930-1933. Commissioned into the 19th Destroyer Flotilla, Mediterranean Fleet on 14th October 1935 and forward gun reinstated. Commissioned into reserve at the Nore 11th June 1936. Paid off into dockyard control 23rd October 1936. Handed over to T.W. Ward 27th January 1937 together with 21 other destroyers in exchange for the passenger liner *Majestic* (56,599/1921) which had been sold to Ward for demolition but which the Admiralty wanted to acquire to convert to a training ship for boys. The Admiralty was not permitted to buy the *Majestic* and so they had to exchange an equivalent tonnage of old warships to effect the acquisition. The *Torrid* was wrecked while under tow to Ward's Hayle yard for breaking. The *Majestic*, renamed *Caledonia*, was converted at Southampton and towed to Rosyth, arriving 23rd April 1937. On 29th September 1939 she caught fire, was completely burnt out and sank alongside her berth in shallow water. She was scrapped down to the waterline *in situ* and in July 1943 the remainder of the hull was refloated and towed to Inverkeithing for final demolition.
BOB TODD by e-mail,

Putting 'Record' 2017 straight (2)
The photo of *Drover* on page 64 was taken in Liverpool's Trafalgar Branch Dock (now sadly infilled to make way for the B&I car ferry terminal). In the background of the shot you can see the CEGB Clarence Dock Power Station (extreme left), the Liverpool Overhead Railway elevated structure (to the left of the bow) and Tate and Lyle's sugar refinery in Love Lane (right of shot) - closed in 1980. Sadly all of those three features have been totally wiped out.

The reference to the acquisition of vessels from the fleet of Burton's Barges of Liverpool on page 104 is indeed intriguing. Page 34 of the January 1960 edition of 'Sea Breezes' contained an account of the liquidation sale of this barge fleet. From this, I can only speculate that the two motor barges acquired by Milford Haven Marine Services were the steel *Ellesborough* of 1921 (a former steamer converted to diesel in 1937 by her builders W.J. Yarwood and Sons Ltd. of Northwich) - which 'Sea Breezes' records as being sold for £475 at auction to Marine Reclamation of Connah's Quay (possibly being resold rather than being broken up) and the wooden motor barge *W.L. Burton* built by Burtons at their own yard at Bromborough Pool in 1940 - which 'Sea Breezes' records as being sold for £1,775 to a T.M. Morgan of Cardiff (the highest price paid for any of the craft on offer at the auction) and again possibly sold on, being a speculative purchase.

The only 1933-built barge I can find in Burton's ownership was the wooden *Ada Burton* (2) (again built at their own yard at Bromborough Pool) and according to the 'Sea Breezes' article no bids were forthcoming for the 12 wooden barges offered for sale at the auction. So - if indeed this is the craft that became *Pembroke Mallard* - it must have been obtained at a bargain price - as a remnant post auction!

It would therefore be most interesting to learn if the author of the article on R.S. Hayes of Pembroke Dock can shed any further light on the earlier history/confirmed original identity of *Pembroke Mallard*, *Pembroke Cormorant* and *Pembroke Pelican*.

Page 126. *Newlands* was the vessel that delivered the death blow to the River Mersey's Egremont Ferry service to Liverpool. On the night of May12th/13th 1941 *Newlands* is reported to have drifted into the pier connecting the floating stage to the shore - and demolished it for the second time in its history. The ferry service had actually been suspended as a wartime economy measure before the collision, but it was never restored post war and the entire structure was subsequently demolished as a result.
NIGEL BOWKER, 9 Poulton Green Close, Spital, Wirral, Merseyside CH63 9FS.

Majestic at Southampton, 27th February 1936. For another three weeks until *Queen Mary* (80,773/1936) entered service on 21st March, she was to remain the largest ship in Cunard's fleet. *[R.A. Snook/F.W. Hawks]*

A splendid view of *Majestic* taken in 1934 by the renowned photographer Kirk of Cowes. What became of his negatives no one knows but in the 1990s some at least were in a collection in the south of England. *[J. and M. Clarkson collection]*

EUXINE SHIPPING CO. LTD.

Ken Garrett

Euxine Shipping Co. Ltd. was incorporated in London in 1932 although the major shareholders, the Dutchmen W.F. van der Zee and W.F.H. van der Zee, both had addresses in Paris, one of them later moving to Switzerland. This is perhaps not surprising given the earlier international nature of the business. Quite when this Dutch family set up their business in the Levant remains a mystery and there are stories but little fact. One of these stories links them with river steamers on the Nile but no real evidence of this seems to exist. If something came to light, it would, of course give rise to the next inevitable question.

Operations in Smyrna

The first mention of the Dutch van der Zee family that I have found shows William Frederick Henry van der Zee as the manager of the Turkish-registered steamer *Rhodes* in 1911. Although the port of Adalia, now Antalya, is mentioned, later operations seem to have been located at Smyrna. This was a flourishing, cosmopolitan port city and trading centre within the Ottoman Empire. Most of the rich merchants were Greek, French, British or other christian Europeans, many of whose families had been in the area for several generations. There was also an American presence and they, amongst other things, ran a hospital. The town itself was opulent with restaurants, hotels, clubs, schools, hospitals and even an opera house. Most of the foreign merchants lived in large houses outside the town and commuted to their offices on their own railway. The city was apparently a remarkably tolerant place with Greeks and Turks living and working amicably side by side.

Amongst other things, these émigré families were involved in finance, commerce, mining, manufacturing and the preparation and export of dried fruit, the Van der Zee family were involved in their shipping activities but also had coal mining interests at Zonguldak on the Turkish Black Sea coast. This must have been good business because practically everything from coal and grain to manufactured goods were imported by sea and the dried fruit and other locally manufactured goods were exported by sea. These Levantine merchants were a rather patrician bunch and made sure that their workforce was well treated. This probably set the locals on a higher prosperity level than most in the region. It is interesting to note that old alliances die hard and after the Second World War, in 1945 the van der Zees were joined on the board of Euxine by Edward Halley Whittall, a member of another former and very senior Smyrna merchant family. The writer was at a navigation college in 1950 with Edgar Giraud, a member of another of these families.

Almost inevitably this seemingly idyllic situation in Smyrna could not last and began to deteriorate with the breaking up of the Ottoman Empire after the First World War. The local Turkish governor was remarkably tolerant and obviously realised the value to Turkey of a prosperous Smyrna but unfortunately politics intervened. The leaders of the victorious British, French and US powers discussed the situation in the Levant and Middle East, but in the end only vacillated. A Greek attempt to conquer the country ended in disaster for the Greeks and a confidence in their new national identity for the Turks. In September 1922 the Turkish army laid waste to the port and although many citizens were evacuated there was a very high death toll. This really was the end of the matter and the port was soon renamed Izmir.

In the years before 1922 the registration of the ships had a bi-national character. Some were registered in Smyrna but flew the Dutch flag; other Smyrna-registered ships flew the Greek flag. The situation immediately after 1922 becomes even more confusing and for a while the van der Zee business and the ship registration seems to have been located in Alexandria, Egypt. Later there appears to have been a very limited return to Smyrna although this could have been due to inaccurate or unreliable contemporary recording in a confused political situation. Later still, and here the facts are not in dispute, the company moved to Rotterdam.

Euxine in London

Unlike the land-based merchants of Smyrna, van der Zee had an advantage and with the exception of any coal mines he might have owned was easily able to move his assets to safer areas and engage in trade elsewhere. The business moved, first to Rotterdam and then, apparently following a disagreement with the Dutch tax authorities, to London, where the Euxine Shipping Co. Ltd. was incorporated on 26th February 1932. The funnel mark and house flag clearly show the Dutch provenance as can be seen from the illustration (see endpapers). Although Euxine Sea is the ancient name for the Black Sea this seems to have been of less importance for the company's operations than the Mediterranean although van der Zee is known to have retained an interest in the coal trade from Zongulduk in northern Turkey but whether as a shipper, agent, mine owner or perhaps all three is less certain. Most of the company's trade seems to have involved voyages from the UK or near continent to the Mediterranean. A ships' agent with the van der Zee name was still active in Izmir well into the 1980s, at least indicating that some connection might have been retained.

From the very early days there was contact between the company and Lambert Brothers in London. Two ships were purchased from the London company in 1913 and the very short period of ownership by Lambert seems to indicate that they were acting more in the role of sale and purchase brokers or agents than ship owners. This contact was maintained in one form or another throughout the life of the company.

When the company moved to London the four vessels of the contemporary fleet, namely the dry cargo steamers *Christine* and *Carol*, and the steam tankers *Helka (3)* and *Myriel*, were all transferred to the London register. Four more ships were purchased before the start of the Second World War, the *Hendrik*, *Helena Margareta* (2), *W. Hendrik* and *Christine Marie*, all continuing the style of using family names or their diminutives initiated with the *Helena Margareta* in 1913. Of these eight ships, one was sold and one, the *Hendrik* was stranded on the Spanish coast before the outbreak of war leaving a fleet of six when hostilities commenced in 1939.

Second World War losses

These Euxine ships could be described as handy-sized and were pretty much in the front line from the start with the *W. Hendrik* the first of the company's war losses on a voyage from Halifax to Newcastle when sunk by enemy aircraft in late 1940. She was followed in 1941 by the *Helena Margareta* (2) sunk by torpedo from the German submarine *U 107* while on a voyage in the other direction from the Tyne to Takoradi. Both the tankers were requisitioned as water tankers and the *Helka* was bombed and sunk by enemy aircraft off Sollum on passage from Alexandria to Tobruk presumably loaded with fresh water for the troops there. Her sister *Myriel* was damaged by a torpedo from the submarine *U 431* but managed to get to Alexandria where she was used as a fresh water ship until sold after the war. The loss of these ships was made up in terms of tonnage by the management of three ships for the Ministry of War Transport. But the tragic loss of 34 men could not be made up.

It is interesting to note that in addition to the war losses the company was particularly affected by the loss of the *Hendrik* which stranded, as mentioned before, on the Spanish coast just west of Gibraltar in April 1935. It was still being felt 12 years later when, as recalled by the Fourth Engineer on the first voyage of the new *Hendrik* in 1947, he was ordered to stop the engine during the forenoon watch while a wreath was thrown overboard to the west of Gibraltar. The occasion does not tally with any of the war loss dates or other events giving considerable credence to his recollection that it was the new ship saluting her older, unfortunate namesake.

Of great concern to the van der Zee family was the loss at sea of the young H. Henry William van der Zee in December 1941. Twenty three years of age, he was the son of Willem Hendrik and Christine Marie van der Zee. By this time it would seem that the family, or at least the younger generation, had become anglicised. He was a Temporary Sub Lieutenant, RNVR and was on passage from Tobruk to Alexandria to join HMS *Nile*, the naval shore establishment and headquarters there. He was on board the British steamer *Shuntien* (3,059/1934) in Convoy TA 5/M when she was torpedoed by the German submarine *U 559* and sank on passage from Tobruk to Alexandria. Also on board were between 800 and 1,100 prisoners of war (reports, official and unofficial vary) and 40 of their military guards, mainly from the Durham Light Infantry together with some sick and wounded soldiers from their own battalion. Many of the survivors, including Henry van der Zee, were picked up by the British corvette HMS *Salvia* (K.97), one of the convoy escorts. Tragedy struck again and the *Salvia* was torpedoed by *U 568* the next day with heavy loss of life including Henry van der Zee. His name is commemorated on the Naval War Memorial at Chatham.

The basic balance sheet shows that the Euxine fleet at the outbreak of war stood at six vessels. During the war three were lost by enemy action but three vessels were managed on behalf of the Ministry of War Transport. Two of these were returned to their pre-war owners shortly after the end of hostilities and one was retained leaving the fleet at four vessels. The three managed ships were the Norwegian *Cetus*, the former Finnish *Modesta*, and the former Spanish *Empire Tees*. This last ship had had an exciting if chequered life under several flags until captured by the British in 1943 as will be described in her fleet list entry.

The Mediterranean trade

Shortly after the war, a new company, Mediterranean Coasters Ltd., was incorporated with more or less the same directors and bareboat chartered the *Empire Pattern*. The ship was managed by the parent Euxine Shipping. She was a Type B steam coaster destined for service in the Far East and originally managed by the Singapore Straits Steamship Co. Ltd. It seems that on her outward passage she did not get past the Mediterranean before the war ended and was taken over in Alexandria in July 1946. Originally the ship was bareboat chartered for three years but was in fact purchased after two years and promptly sold to Elder Dempster Lines Ltd. of Liverpool in 1948.

Post-war, the average deep-sea officer formed the impression of smart and well found ships on regular short voyages and naturally the company was on the list of

The Euxine-managed *Empire Tees* not only survived the war but found a British owner, Shamrock Shipping, willing to trade her as *Clonlee*, seen here. *[Fotoflite incorporating Skyfotos/Roy Fenton collection]*

potential employers for officers having become disenchanted with very long periods on articles. Sometimes these could extend to two years in duration. But the conditions of service on many short sea and Mediterranean cargo liners, including some of the Euxine fleet, were a drawback to many, particularly younger officers. These Section B contractual conditions were by no means harsh but lacked many of the advantages of the Section A Agreements. The most important of these were; generally higher wages and seniority increments, continuous employment, paid study leave, extra leave, sick pay and a number of other minor but important benefits. One of the drawbacks concerned the taking of leave. In Section A with the benefit of continuous employment it was normal procedure for an officer to be reappointed at the end of his leave but in Section B this was not necessarily the case. It generally depended on the supply of officers. In times of shortage, a company would try to coax a return to work as soon as possible but in times of plenty it could end up with a return to the 'Pool', or a company rota system because an appointment would not be made until a serving officer decided to take some leave and thus create a vacancy.

In the immediate post-war years there were many foreign officers and ratings mainly from the Baltic republics and Poland who had managed to remain west of the Iron Curtain and having sailed on the side of the Allies were allowed to continue. Naturally it was not wise for them to sail to any ports in the communist bloc, nor for that matter to the USA while Senator McCarthy was conducting his purges. Euxine employed a number of Latvian seafarers and because of all the political problems they tended to remain on board and unlike their British counterparts were not particularly concerned with leave.

Even within such a modest fleet the crews varied from the good to the not-so-good. Some, particularly the masters, were exemplary characters while others apparently had a weakness for the bottle. One of the better ones was Captain Owen T. Jones whose name pops up frequently and is always referred to in the most complimentary terms. He was in command of the *Helena Margareta* when she was torpedoed and sunk by the German submarine *U 107* in April 1941. Twenty seven of the crew were lost but he managed to take to a boat with eight other survivors and was eventually rescued a week later and taken to Gibraltar. For his seamanship, good management and bravery in a difficult situation he was awarded the Lloyd's War Medal. After the war, in command of the *Hendrik* on her maiden voyage it was he who saluted the earlier ship of that name off Gibraltar. Later he was in command of the *Henzee* from new until, against his better judgement, instead of retiring he took her on a delivery voyage to Hong Kong where he died of a heart attack on arrival.

Outward bound the ships carried general cargo to eastern Mediterranean ports and military stores for the British forces along the Suez Canal and also for the Arab Legion in Aqaba. Even in the early 1950s it was as well not to mix trading with Arab and Israeli ports and this political factor became ever more serious, making trade, even with neutral flag ships, an economic nonsense. This was exacerbated when a black list was maintained in Damascus of ships that had visited Israeli ports. A listed ship would not be allowed entry to an Arab port but more seriously would not be allowed to transit the Suez Canal. Owners sometimes made surreptitious name changes in attempts to outwit the office in Damascus with varying degrees of success.

Homeward bound, iron and other ores, various minerals, marble in both slab and chip form were carried. None of the ships were reefers but those with mechanical ventilation would carry fruit. A regular cargo from the Mediterranean to the UK was esparto grass in bales. The freight rate for this was on the low side indicating that the company was relying on the outward freight to cover the costs of the round voyage. To maximize the homeward earnings, if stability criteria permitted, it was often also carried on deck. It was generally loaded in places like Sfax, Sousse or Nemours in North Africa and it would be discharged at Granton or other east coast Scottish ports, Sunderland, with smaller amounts being taken to ports in the Thames and Medway, Bristol Channel, Mersey and Glasgow. It was generally used in the manufacture of quality art paper and paper for glossy magazines.

Generations of deck officers came to know about it through standard questions in their examinations where, given the hold capacities and stowage factors of esparto grass and something much heavier; marble chips or iron ore for example, they were required to work out the quantity of each in each hold to completely fill the ship down to her marks.

Esparto grass apparently grows like a weed and apart from its use in papermaking is used in a number of artisanal products, for example sandals and straw bags. However, for carriage at sea it does have its fair share of problems. Firstly and probably the least important is that it can harbour various creatures, some harmful, others harmless; snakes, spiders, tortoises and so on. Secondly it is liable to spontaneous combustion and a deck cargo, even if covered by tarpaulins, would also be particularly susceptible to sparks from a steamer's funnel. Wisps of smoke coming from the cargo was not an uncommon sight. Thirdly, a deck cargo was capable of absorbing a considerable amount of water, certainly at least a third of its own weight. This added weight above the centre of gravity would reduce the ship's margin of stability already made worse by the consumption of bunkers from low down. Eventually the ship would list until she reached her angle of loll when due to the increase in waterplane area she would regain some positive stability. At one time it was not uncommon to see a ship listed to an almost impossible angle with wisps of smoke coming from the deck cargo plodding up the English Channel or North Sea. Attempts at firefighting with water had to be carefully considered lest it should adversely affect the already marginal stability. At worst of course the fire would cause the ship to be abandoned or capsize and sink. An example of this in April 1963 was the elderly steamer *Aghios Georgios II* (1,653/1916) which had a list and her deck cargo of the grass, loaded at Kenitra in Morocco, was well on fire. Her distress calls were picked up by the Everard vessel *Accruity* (465/1935) whose watchkeepers could actually see the casualty. Most of the crew were taken off by the ship's jolly boat and later transferred to the Eastbourne lifeboat. The ship itself drifted ashore in Pevensey Bay becoming a total loss and was later scrapped in Bruges.

Amongst seafarers, the given word was that esparto grass was used in making paper for banknotes but a little research has shown that this is most unlikely due to the nature of the fibres. But it was such a widely held belief that something must have suggested it. Could it perhaps have been the seafarers way of pointing the finger at unscrupulous ship owners who fixed the cargo in the certain knowledge of

A listing *Helka* (4) demonstrates one of the hazards of carrying esparto grass. *[Author's collection]*

what could happen, the banknote part of the yarn referring to the insurance payout if things really went wrong?

During the war the contact between Euxine and Lamberts became closer, probably due to the lack of senior British managers and directors. After the war, technical staff from Lamberts were involved in the specification and building of four new ships for the company. In fact these were the first and last ships ever built for Euxine. Almost certainly, the shipyards would have been responsible for the actual design that would follow the owner's specification in terms of dimensions, tonnage, accommodation and engine. For some reason Lamberts opted for oil-fired boilers and anachronistic triple-expansion steam machinery. Yet the hull and accommodation design certainly made one think that they were more economic and stylish motor ships. They were good looking ships but engine rooms and accommodation were noted for being uncomfortably hot, particularly in the summer.

Two shipbuilders were involved in building the post war ships; Burntisland Shipbuilding Co. Ltd. and William Pickersgill and Sons Ltd. The machinery was made by the North East Marine Engineering Co Ltd., whose engines were notably reliable, particularly if operated by experienced engineers. Although their numbers were reducing there were still sufficient men with steam 'up and down' experience around that the company would not have had a recruitment problem. Indeed, this might have been part of the reasoning behind the choice of such outdated and inefficient machinery. Two of the new ships were registered in Alexandria under the Egyptian flag. Both were fully managed by Euxine in a move to curry a little favour in the region. The arrangement did not last very long and both ships were sold to a Swedish owner in 1950. Later, in 1954, one ship reverted to the British flag and Euxine ownership. The other went further east and was purchased by an Indian company.

The company had sold all its ships and apparently ceased trading by 1967. However, by 1968 the name must have been acquired by Lambert Brothers who used it to register a couple of large ships. Although really not much to do with the original Euxine company they have been included in the fleet list for completeness. This arrangement seems to have run its course by 1975 and the company was dissolved shortly afterwards.

One of the last ships built for management by Euxine was *Terica*, seen here at Malta after sale to Yugoslavia as *Titov Veles*. *[World Ship Society Ltd.]*

Fleet list

1. **RHODES** 1911-1912
O.N. 79141 507.49g 313.22n.
173.8 x 24.6 x 13.2 feet (registered dimensions).
C. 2-cyl. steam engine made by the shipbuilder.
12.4.1878: Completed by R. Steele and Company, Greenock (Yard No. 105) for James Currie and Alexander Blackwood, Leith as ULVA.
Registered 8/1878 in Leith.
11.1883: Owners became James Currie, Donald Currie and Thomas Cockerton, London.
13.11.1894: Net tonnage became 291.76.
17.3.1899: Sold to the Leith, Hull and Hamburg Steam Packet Co. Ltd (J. Currie and Co., manager), Leith.
23.2.1907: Sold to O. Loulou, Adalia, Turkey.
1911: Sold to Hari Omer Lutfi Ferahli ve Ortaklari (W.F. Henry van der Zee, manager) Adalia, Turkey and renamed RHODES.
*1911:*Sold to Lulu Faragliari and Company, same manager, Adalia, Turkey.
1912: Sold to the Archipelago American Steamship Company (G. Farkovh, manager), Smyrna. Registered in Smyrna and renamed NEVADA, under the US flag.
24.5.1913: While leaving Smyrna, bound for Adalia, the ship left the channel to avoid collision with a Russian steamer and entered a minefield. Her bow struck a mine, a minute later another and yet another within a couple of minutes and she sank immediately. She had a crew of 40 and was carrying 200 passengers. Only 80 persons were saved.

2. **HELENA MARGARETA (1)/ELENA MARGARITA** 1913-1918
O.N. 120840 2,537.53g 1,556.25n.
300.0 x 40.2 x 19.4 feet (registered dimensions).
T. 3-cyl. steam engine made by the shipbuilder.
2.1890: Completed by Palmers' Shipbuilding and Iron Co. Ltd., Newcastle-upon-Tyne (Yard No. 635) for E.D. Vlassopulo, Ithaca, Greece as AMALIA VLASSOPULO.
1894: Sold to Foscolo, Mango and Company, Constantinople, Turkey and renamed GEORGIOS P. BOUBOULIS. Registered in Piraeus, Greece.
28.3.1905: Sold to Joseph Hoult, Liverpool and renamed BENAN. Registered 22/1905 in Liverpool.
22.2.1907: Sold to The Steam Transport Co. Ltd. (Joseph Hoult, manager), Liverpool.
16.4.1913: Sold to Lambert Brothers Ltd., London.
19.5.1913: Acquired by W.F. Henry van der Zee, Smyrna, Turkey and renamed HELENA MARGARETA. Registered in Smyrna. Dutch flag.
1914: Owner became Henry van der Zee, Smyrna, Turkey and renamed ELENA MARGARITA. Registered in Smyrna, Greek flag.
1918: Sold to A. Capparis and G. Gregos, Piraeus, Greece.
1919: Sold to the Oriental Shipping Co. Ltd. (A.A. Capparis, manager), Piraeus.
1924: Sold to P.G. Callimanopulos, Piraeus, Greece and renamed GRIGORIOS C.
1934: Broken up in Turkey.

3. **HELKA (1)/ELKA** 1913-1918
O.N. 82669 2,128.28g 1,346.94n.
281.2 x 38.0 x 23.8 feet (registered dimensions).
C. 2-cyl. steam engine made by Blair and Company, Stockton-on-Tees.
8.7.1881: Completed by T. Turnbull and Son, Whitby (Yard No. 71) for G. Pyman and others, Whitby as FLORENCE.
Registered 4/1881 in Whitby.
14.9.1881: Register transferred to London, 123/1881.
18.4.1894: Re-engined with a T. 3-cyl. steam engine made by Thomas Richardson and Sons, West Hartlepool.
22.8.1898: Owner became London and Northern Steamship Co. Ltd. (Pyman Brothers Ltd., manager), London.
3.5.1912: Sold to Lambert Brothers Ltd., London.
11.10.1913: Acquired by W.F. Henry van der Zee, Smyrna, Turkey and renamed HELKA. Registered in Smyrna. Dutch flag.
1915: Renamed ELKA. Registered in Smyrna, Greek flag.
1918: Sold to J. Charapoulos, Piraeus, Greece.
19.4.1918: Torpedoed and sunk by German submarine U 34 in the Mediterranean Sea 20 miles off Adra. She was on a voyage from Marseilles to Dakar.

4. **WILLEM FREDERIK** 1913-1915
O.N. 87256 1,225.01g 755.45n.
248.2 x 33.2 x 17.3 feet (registered dimensions).
C. 2-cyl. steam engine made by the shipbuilder.
10.8.1883: Completed by R. Steele and Company, Greenock (Yard No. 128) for James Currie, Edinburgh, Thomas Cockerton and Donald Currie, London as TORTONA.
Registered 21/1883 in Leith.
17.3.1899: Sold to the Leith, Hull and Hamburg Steam Packet Co. Ltd. (J. Currie and Co., manager), Leith.
25.6.1908: Sold to G. Papadakis, Syra, Greece and renamed AGHIOS SPYRIDON.
1913: Acquired by W.F. Henry van der Zee, Smyrna, Turkey. Renamed WILLEM FREDERIK. Registered in Smyrna. Dutch flag.
1915: Sold to L. Albino, Genoa, Italy and renamed VINCI.
1920: Sold to Luigi Schiaffino fu A., Camogli, Italy.
1924: Sold to Greek owners and renamed AGIOS SPYRIDON.
1924: Broken up.

5. **HELKA** (2) 1923-1924
O.N. 142360 1,221.60g 735.77n 1,692d.
230.0 x 33.0 x 17.6 feet (registered dimensions).
T. 3-cyl. steam engine made by Maatschappij Fyenoord, Rotterdam, Netherlands.
4.1903: Completed by N.V. Werf voorheen Rijkee and Co., Rotterdam (Yard No. 108) for N.V. Hollandsche Stoomboot Maatschappij, Amsterdam, Netherlands as SCHELDESTROOM. Registered in Amsterdam.
30.3.1918: Taken over by the Shipping Controller, London (William Brown, Atkinson and Co. Ltd., Hull, manager). Registered 105/1918 in London.
16.4.1919: Reverted to original Dutch owner and registry.
1923: Acquired by W.H. van der Zee, Smyrna, Turkey and renamed HELKA. Registered in Smyrna.
1924: Sold to Administration de Navigation à Vapeur Turque, Constantinople, Turkey. Renamed ZONGOULDAK. Tonnages became1,222g, 736n. Registered in Constantinople.
1928: Name amended to ZONGULDAK. Registered in Istanbul.
1930: Owner restyled Turkiye Seyrisefain Idaresi, Istanbul, Turkey.
1934: Sold to Denizyollari Idaresi, Istanbul.
1935: Sold to Kirzade Mustafa ve Huseyinmunir (Kirzade Sevkiye, manager), Istanbul.
1938: Sold to Turk Silepcilik Sirketi, Istanbul. Registered in Istanbul.

Helka (2) as the Dutch *Scheldestroom. [www.marhisdata.nl]*

1939: Sold to Komur Kolektif Sirketi ve Ahmet Hamdi, Istanbul.
1942: Sold to Ahmet Kalaycioglu ve Ortaklari, Istanbul. Registered in Istanbul.
1944: Sold to Yusuf ve Seyfi Kolektif Sirketi, Istanbul.
1948: Sold to Ahmet and Yusuf Kalaycioglu Arisan, Istanbul. Registered in Istanbul.
1952: Owner became Ahmet and Yusuf Kalaysioglu, Istanbul.
7.3.1954: Sank after a collision in fog with the Turkish steamer YOLAC (3,489/1922) in the Black Sea four miles off Kefken in position 41.19 north, 30.23 east while on a ballast passage from Istanbul to Zonguldak.

6. **HELENA** 1923-1933
O.N. 124333 1,301.44g 782.92n 1,880d.
234.7 x 34.5 x 15.1 feet (registered dimensions).
T. 3-cyl. steam engine made by Richardsons, Westgarth and Co. Ltd., Sunderland.
24.4.1907: Completed by Blyth Shipbuilding Co. Ltd., Blyth (Yard No. 135) for Furness, Withy and Co. Ltd., West Hartlepool as LUDWORTH. Registered 12/1907 in West Hartlepool.
27.2.1923: Acquired by W.H. van der Zee, Alexandria, Egypt. Renamed HELENA. Later registered in Smyrna, Turkey. Dutch flag.
1933: Sold to Zisan Hanum, Madam Kir Zade Mustafa and others (Kir Zade Sevki ve Ssi, manager), Istanbul, Turkey and renamed ATILLA.
1936: Sold to Haci Selimzade Hamdi ve Serikleri, Istanbul.
1953: Sold to Mehmet Kazanci ve Serikleri, Istanbul.
1957: Sold to Ahmet ve Mehmet Kosar Kollektif Sirketi, Istanbul and renamed KOSAR.
1968: Broken up.

7. **CHRISTINE/CHRISTINE MARIE (**1) 1923-1936
O.N. 145720 1,882.98g 1,173.45n.
279.3 x 40.1 x 18.3 feet (registered dimensions).
T. 3-cyl. steam engine made by Richardsons, Westgarth and Co. Ltd., Sunderland.
1910: Launched by Irvine's Shipbuilding and Drydock Co. Ltd., West Hartlepool (Yard No. 490) for G.V. Turnbull and Company, Leith as LAMORNA.
1910: Sold and completed for Scheepvaart Maatschappij 'Gylsen' (J. D'Haene and Co., manager), Antwerp, Belgium as GRAANHANDEL.
1912: Manager became Mercantile and Shipping Co. Ltd., Antwerp, Belgium.
1916: Sold to Lloyd Royal Belge S.A., Antwerp and renamed COLOMBIER.
19.12.1922: Sold to Abbey Line Ltd. (F. Jones and Co., manager), Cardiff and renamed TINTERN ABBEY. Registered 36/1922 in Cardiff.
5.2.1923: Sold to Lambert Brothers Ltd., London.
12.3.1923: Acquired by W.H. van der Zee, Alexandria, Egypt and renamed CHRISTINE. Later registered in Smyrna, Turkey. Dutch flag.
18.5.1934: Acquired by Euxine Shipping Co. Ltd., London and renamed CHRISTINE MARIE. Registered 55/1934 in London.
28.5.1936: Sold to Lovisa Angfartygs A/B (A/B Nordstrom and Co. O/Y., manager), Lovisa, Finland and renamed INGA.
17.12.1940: Sank in the Kiel Canal after a collision with the Danish steamer SILKEBORG (1,806/1915). The wreck was removed on 28.12.1940.

8. **HENDI** (1) 1927-1931
O.N. 102746 2,445.17g 1,545.79n.
290.0 x 43.0 x 16.5 feet (registered dimensions).
T. 3-cyl. steam engine made by Thomas Richardson and Sons Ltd., West Hartlepool.
11.4.1896: Completed by R. Ropner and Son, Stockton-on-Tees (Yard No. 319) for J.S. Allinson and others, West Hartlepool as DOROTHY. Registered 9/1896 in West Hartlepool.
2.1.1906: Sold to the Seaton Shipping Co. Ltd., West Hartlepool.
5.5.1906: Sold to Mawson Shipping Co. Ltd. (A. Mawson and Co., manager), Cardiff. Renamed MILLWALL. Registered 13/1906 in Cardiff.
12.7.1913: Sold to Dorothy Shipping Co. Ltd. (Moller and Company, manager), London.
5.11.1915: Renamed SAGITTARIUS.
18.11.1915: Owners renamed Sagittarius Shipping Co. Ltd., London.
20.3.1917: Sold to the London and China Steamship Co. Ltd., Shanghai, China.
15.8.1919: Sold to N.G. Livanos, Chios, Greece. Renamed ARCHANGELOS.
1924: Sold to G. Ktistakis, Chios.
1927: Acquired by W.F. Henry van der Zee, Smyrna, Turkey and renamed HENDI. Registered in Smyrna, Dutch flag.
19.1.1931: Beached following a collision at Zonguldak, Turkey whilst carrying coal. Declared a compromised total loss.
21.4.1931: Refloated and taken to Istanbul for demolition.

9. **HELKA** (3) 1930-1941 Trunk deck tanker.
O.N. 162725 3,471.17g 2,457.19n 4,600d.
325.9 x 47.2 x 22.6 feet (registered dimensions).
T. 3-cyl. steam engine made by the shipbuilder.
12.1912: Completed by Rotterdamsche

Upper: *Christine. [Jochen Krusmann]*
Lower: *Hendi* (1) as *Millwall. [Bristol Series]*

Top: The tanker *Helka* (3). *[www.marhisdata.nl]*
Middle: *Myriel* as *Wieldrecht*. *[www.marhisdata.nl]*
Bottom: *Carol Dorian* under her first name, *Helmsdale*. *[Bristol Series/J. and M. Clarkson]*

Droogdok Maatschappij N.V., Rotterdam, Netherlands (Yard No. 33) for N.V. Maatschappij Stoomschip 'Mijdrecht' (N.V. Phs. Van Ommerens Scheepvaart Bedrijf, manager), Rotterdam, Netherlands as MIJDRECHT. (Classed for carrying petroleum in bulk).
3.1918: Requisitioned by the United States Government and operated under the U.S. flag by the U.S. Shipping Board.
4.1919: Returned to owner.
1930: Acquired by N.V. Rederij W. Hendrik van der Zee, Rotterdam, Netherlands and renamed HELKA.
21.6.1932: Owner became the Euxine Shipping Co. Ltd., London. Registered 69/1932 in London.
11.11.1940: Requisitioned by the Ministry of War Transport, London for military service as a water tanker.
25.5.1941: Sunk by enemy aircraft near Sollum on passage Alexandria to Tobruk.

10. **MYRIEL** 1930-1946 Trunk deck tanker
O.N. 163302 3,560.45g 2,112.99n 5,100d.
331.7 x 47.3 x 22.6 feet (registered dimensions).
T. 3-cyl. steam engine made by the shipbuilder.
11.1913: Completed by Rotterdamsche Droogdok Maatschappij N.V., Rotterdam, Netherlands (Yard No.38) for N.V. Maatschappij Stoomschip 'Wieldrecht' (N.V. Phs. Van Ommerens Scheepvaart Bedrijf, manager), Rotterdam, Netherlands as WIELDRECHT. (Classed for carrying petroleum in bulk).
3.1918: Requisitioned by the United States Government and operated under the U.S. flag by the U.S. Shipping Board.
6.1918: Transferred to the U.S. Navy and renamed NOTS (# 2519).
4.1919: Returned to the owner.
1930: Acquired by N.V. Rederij W. Hendrik van der Zee, Rotterdam, Netherlands and renamed MYRIEL.
7.11.1932: Owner became the Euxine Shipping Co. Ltd., London. Registered 138/1932 in London.
3.9.1940-16.1.1946: Requisitioned by the Ministry of War Transport, London for military service as a water tanker.
14.5.1946: Register closed. Vessel considered a constructive total loss.
1947: Sold to 'Citmar', Compagnia Italiana Trasporti Marittimi, Genoa, Italy, repaired and renamed MIRIELLA.
1955: Broken up by Cantieri Navali del Golfo, La Spezia, Italy after being laid up since the previous year.

11. **CAROL DORIAN** 1931-1938
O.N. 123188 3,164.58g 2,026.97n 5,600d.
330.5 x 49.0 x 14.4 feet (registered).
T. 3-cyl. steam engine made by the shipbuilder.
28.9.1907: Completed by A. Rodger and Co. Ltd., Port Glasgow (Yard No. 403) for Strath Shipping Co. Ltd. (Downing and Sutherland Ltd., manager), Cardiff as HELMSDALE. Registered 22/1907 in Cardiff.
18.3.1931: Acquired by W.H. van der Zee, Alexandria, Egypt and renamed CAROL.
17.10.1932: Acquired by the Euxine Shipping Co. Ltd., London and renamed CAROL DORIAN. Registered 129/1932 in London.
25.8.1938: Sold to C. Strubin and Co. Ltd., London and later renamed LAKE HALLWIL.
6.2.1939: Sold to A. Inkapool, E. Jakobsen and others, Tallinn, Estonia.
20.1.1941: Requisitioned by the Ministry of Shipping, London (Harper, Mathew and Co. Ltd., Cardiff, manager). Registered 12/1941 in London.
1941: Reportedly renamed SIGNE but this is doubtful.
7.1.1942: Renamed INGMAN.
11.1943: Manager became China Trading Co. Ltd., London.
12.4.1944: Manager became Christian Salvesen Ltd., Leith.
9.6.1944: Scuttled as a blockship off Normandy to form part of Gooseberry No.3 Harbour.
21.8.1944: Register closed.
12.8.1945: Raised and towed to Newport for demolition by John Cashmore Ltd.

12. **HENDRIK** (1) 1934-1935
O.N. 128484 3,928.09g 2,529.70n 6,500d.
340.6 x 50.5 x 24.7 feet (registered dimensions).
T. 3-cyl. steam engine made by Richardsons, Westgarth and Co. Ltd., Hartlepool.
15.9.1908: Completed by R. Stephenson and Co. Ltd., Hebburn-on-Tyne (Yard No. 116) for the Gwladys Steamship Co. Ltd. (Percival Samuel and W.T. Symonds, manager), Cardiff as GWLADYS. Registered 13/1908 in Cardiff.
6.1.1914: Sold to Universal Steam Navigation Co. Ltd. (Percival Samuel and W.T. Symonds, manager), Cardiff.
1917: Owner and manager relocated to London. Registered 17/1917 in London.
29.12.1923: Sold to Regier Shipping Co. Ltd., London.
14.10.1924: Renamed CROMERTON.
16.12.1925: Sold to Anglo Commercial Shipping Co. Ltd., Newcastle-upon-Tyne (Regier Shipping Co. Ltd., London, manager).
9.6.1927: Sold to T.E. Evans and Co. Ltd., London.
13.10.1927: Renamed PURLEY DOWNS.
15.10.1934: Acquired by Euxine Shipping Co. Ltd., London.
15.11.1934: Renamed HENDRIK.
15.4.1935: Ran aground on the Spanish coast just west of Gibraltar in position 35.57 north, 05.29 west while on passage from Antwerp to Alexandria with a general cargo.

13. **HELENA MARGARETA** (2) 1935-1941
O.N. 164556 3,316.48g 2,062.88n 5,400d.
326.6 x 48.2 x 22.9 feet (registered dimensions).
T. 3-cyl. steam engine made by George T Grey, South Shields.
3.1915: Completed by A.Vuijk and Zonen, Capelle, Netherlands (Yard No. 432) for Stoomvaart Maatschappij 'Hillegersberg' (Vinke and Co. manager), Amsterdam, Netherlands as LARENBERG.
3.1918: Requisitioned by the United States Government and operated under the U.S. flag by the U.S. Shipping Board.
4.1919: Returned to the owner.
2.12.1935: Acquired by the Euxine Shipping Co. Ltd., London and renamed HELENA MARGARETA. Registered 182/1935 in London.
28.1.1940-8.4.1941: Requisitioned by the Ministry of War Transport, London for commercial service.
8.4.1941: Sunk by the German submarine U 107 in position 33.00 north, 23.52 west while on ballast passage from the Tyne to Takoradi.

14. **W. HENDRIK** 1937-1941
O.N. 139235 4,360.16g 2,710.66n 6,900d.
360.5 x 52.2 x 27.6 feet (registered dimensions).
T. 3-cyl. steam engine made by Richardson Westgarth and Co. Ltd., Middlesbrough.
9.3.1925: Completed by Furness Shipbuilding Co. Ltd., Haverton Hill-on-Tees (Yard No. 78) for the North of England Steamship Co. Ltd., West Hartlepool as TYNE BRIDGE. Registered 3/1925 in West Hartlepool.
6.3.1934: Sold to New Era Steamship Co. Ltd., Cardiff.

Upper: *Gwladys* in Manchester: the ship that eventually became *Hendrik* (1) photographed during the First World War. *[C. Downs/Roy Fenton collection]*
Lower: *Helena Margareta* (2). *[World Ship Society Ltd.]*

Christine Marie (2) as Houston's *Hesperia*. *[B. and A. Feilden/J. and M. Clarkson]*

19.9.1934: Renamed MARY WALTON. Registered 7/1934 in Newcastle.
22.2.1937: Acquired by the Euxine Shipping Co. Ltd., London and renamed W. HENDRIK.
17.3.1940-3.12.1940: Requisitioned by the Ministry of War Transport, London for commercial service.
3.12.1940: Sunk by German aircraft in position 56.26 north, 12.20 west while on voyage from Halifax to Newcastle with timber and steel.

15. **CHRISTINE MARIE** (2) 1938-1947
O.N. 144661 3,895.01g 2,379.58n 7,047d.
384.5 x 52.0 x 22.5 feet (registered dimensions).
T. 3-cyl. steam engine made by the shipbuilder.
1919: Completed by Flensburger Schiffsbau Gesellschaft, Flensburg, Germany (Yard No. 351) for 'war reparations' as PATRIA.
21.7.1920: Owner became the Ministry of Transport (Royal Mail Shipping Co. Ltd., manager), London. Registered 404/1920 in London.
22.2.1921: Sold to the British and South American Steam Navigation Co. Ltd., Liverpool. Registered 79/1921 in Liverpool.
3.5.1921: Renamed HESPERIA. Registered 289/1921 in London.
9.2.1938: Acquired by the Euxine Shipping Co. Ltd., London.
24.3.1938: Renamed CHRISTINE MARIE.
17.4.1940-22.3.1946: Requisitioned by the Ministry of War Transport, London for commercial, liner, coasting and short sea tramp services.
25.3.1947: Sold to Cargueros Panamenos

S.A., Panama (Lambert Brothers Ltd., London, managers) and renamed COSTA RICA. Registered in Panama.
1947: Sold to A/B Ledsund, Mariehamn, Sweden and renamed LEDSUND.
21.11.1959: Arrived at Hong Kong for demolition by Omega Shipping Co.

16. **CETUS** 1940-1945
O.N. 142866 2,693.37g 1,361.68n.
313.9 x 44.2 x 17.9 feet (registered dimensions).
T. 3-cyl. steam engine made by J.G. Kincaid and Co. Ltd., Greenock.
19.4.1920: Completed by Murdoch and Murray Ltd., Port Glasgow (Yard No. 269) for Pelton Steamship Co. Ltd., Newcastle-upon-Tyne as MOTO. Registered 12/1920 in Newcastle.
1.12.1936: Sold to A/S Dampskibsselsk 'Neptun' (Hendrik Ostervold, manager), Bergen, Norway and renamed CETUS.
28.6.1940-1.10.1945: Requisitioned by the Ministry of War Transport, London for commercial, liner, coasting and short sea tramp services (Euxine Shipping Co. Ltd., London, manager).
1953: Sold to D/S Nautic (Aage Vollmond, manager) Copenhagen, Denmark and renamed LISE.
1956: Sold to Ertel Bieber and Co. G.m.b.H., Hamburg, West Germany and renamed J.C. ERTEL. Tonnages became 2,803g 1,587n.
1958: Re-engined with a 7-cyl. 4SA oil engine made by Maschinenbau Augsberg-Nürnburg A.G., Augsburg, West Gemany (M.A.N.).
1959: Lengthened to 347.3 feet. Tonnages became 3,223g, 1,781n, 5,157d.
1966: Sold to Deutsch Nordisch Schiffahrtgesellschaft (H.F. Cordes and Co., manager) Hamburg, West Germany and renamed GYDA.
1969: Sold to H.F. Cordes and Co., Hamburg and renamed GYDA C.
1972: Sold to Gyda C Shipping Co. Ltd., Famagusta, Cyprus.
1976: Sold to S. Kasmas and Brothers Co. Ltd., Piraeus, Greece and renamed GYDA.
1978: Sold to Romano Pagwan and Filli, Trieste, Italy for use as a storage hulk.
1979: Sold to Sidemar S.p.A., Trieste, Italy and arrived at Trieste for demolition on 28.2.1979.

17. **MODESTA** 1941-1942
O.N. 139187 3,831.91g 2,299.44n 6,300d.
346.5 x 50.8 x 23.55 feet (registered dimensions).
T. 3-cyl. steam engine made by the North Eastern Marine Engineering Co. Ltd., Sunderland.
8.1.1917: Completed by Joseph Priestman and Co. Ltd., Sunderland (Yard No. 258) for The Gulf Line Ltd., London as MODESTA. Registered 6/1917 in London.
23.6.1920: Sold to A/S Iverans Rederi (Iver An Christiansen, manager) Christiania, Norway.
16.6.1926: Sold to Leeston Shipping Co. Ltd., Cardiff. Registered 96/1926 in London. Tonnages became 3,848.57g, 2,408.55n.

Built as the British collier *Moto*, the name *Cetus* had been bestowed by Norwegian owners in 1936. She is seen on the Thames (top) and post-war in the English Channel (upper middle). We then see her after considerable rebuilding and conversion to a motor ship as the German *J.C. Ertel* (lower middle) and finally (bottom) as *Gyda C* on 26th March 1975 under the Cyprus flag. *[Top; World Ship Society Ltd., upper middle and bottom; J. and M. Clarkson, lower middle; Roy Fenton collection]*

30.9.1933: Sold to J.W. Paulin, Wiborg, Finland.
22.10.1941: Acquired by the Ministry of War Transport (Euxine Shipping Co. Ltd., manager), London. Registered 35/1941 in Glasgow. Tonnages 3,848.54g, 2,402.44n.
29.9.1941-25.4.1942: Requisitioned by the Ministry of War Transport, London for commercial service.
25.4.1942: Sunk by enemy submarine in position 33.40 north, 63.10 west whilst on a voyage from Trinidad and St. Thomas to New York with bauxite.

18. **SEBASTIAN/EMPIRE TEES** 1944-1950
O.N. 143504 3,023.76g 1,835.67n 5,256d.
331.3 x 46.8 x 23.9 feet (registered dimensions).
T. 3-cyl. steam engine made by the North Eastern Marine Engineering Co. Ltd., Sunderland.
15.3.1920: Completed by J. Blumer and Co. Ltd., Sunderland (Yard No. 253) for the Claymore Shipping Co. Ltd., Cardiff as DAYBEAM. Registered 14/1920 Cardiff.
13.2.1929: Sold to F. Sainz e Inchaustegui, Bilbao, Spain and renamed SEBASTIAN.
1933: Sold to Marques del Real Socorro, Bilbao and renamed AZTECA.
1936: Reported requisitioned by the Basque separatist administration and renamed ITXAS-ALDE. Also reported to have been registered in Mexico and renamed AZTECA for a period.
27.7.1937: Captured by the Spanish nationalist cruiser ALMIRANTE CERVERA in the Bay of Biscay. Returned to her former owners and renamed SEBASTIAN.
1941: Sold to Compania Comercial Maritima de Transportes S.A., Madrid, Spain.
31.10.1943: Seized by the destroyer H.M.S. TYNEDALE (L96) seven miles off Tortosa Lighthouse while on passage from Valencia to Sete with a cargo of iron ore. Taken in prize to Gibraltar under the provisions of the 'Trading with the Enemy Act'.
7.4.1944: Taken over by the Ministry of War Transport (Euxine Shipping Co. Ltd., manager), London. Registered 11/1944 in Gibraltar.
24.8.1944: Registered 278/1944 in London and renamed EMPIRE TEES. Tonnages became 3,100.82g, 1,819.23n.
11.9.1946: Owner became the Ministry of Transport (Euxine Shipping Co. Ltd., manager), London.
20.1.1950: Sold to Compania Maritimos Tees, Panama and renamed TEES.
19.1.1952: Sold to Shamrock Shipping Ltd., Larne and renamed CLONLEE. Registered 3/1952 in Belfast. Tonnages became 3,099.62g, 1,816.46n.
21.10.1954: Sold to Muzaffer Taviloglu, Yacub Uzener and Muhittin Topcuoglu, Istanbul, Turkey and renamed SELAMET. Registered in Istanbul.
4.4.1968: Arrived at Istanbul for demolition by Bozmacilaz Tic ve San Ltd. at Haskoy where work commenced on 26.4.1968.

19. **EMPIRE PATTERN** 1946-1948
O.N. 169148 973.79g 370.67n 1,175d.
214.8 x 36.7 x 11.6 feet (registered dimensions).
T. 3-cyl. steam engine made by the shipbuilder.
4.7.1945: Completed by Smiths Dock Co. Ltd., Middlesbrough (Yard No. 1153) for the Ministry of War Transport, London (Singapore Straits Steamship Co. Ltd., Taunton, manager) as EMPIRE PATTERN. Registered 1/1945 in Middlesbrough.
27.7.1945-12.10.1945: Requisitioned for service in the Liner Division.
13.10.1945-16.6.1946: Requisitioned for service as a Cased Petrol Ship.
17.6.1946-31.7.1946: Requisitioned for service in the Liner Division.
31.7.1946: Bareboat chartered to Mediterranean Coasters Ltd. (Euxine Shipping Co. Ltd., manager), London for three years.
12.8.1946: Owner became the Ministry of Transport (Euxine Shipping Co. Ltd., manager), London.
31.10.1948: Acquired by Mediterranean Coasters Ltd., London. (11.00).
31.10.1948: Acquired by Euxine Shipping Co. Ltd., London. (15.00).
2.12.1948: Sold to Elder Dempster Lines Ltd., Liverpool.
9.2.1949: Renamed FORCADOS.
11.9.1962: Sold to S. Leriotis and I.D. Anghelatos, Piraeus, Greece and renamed BARBALIS.
1966: Sold to G. Tzortzis and C. Sykias, Piraeus, Greece and renamed AGIA VARVARA.
8.12.1966: Sank in heavy weather off Cyprus whilst on a voyage from Ashdod and became a total loss.

20. **HENDRIK** (2) 1946-1962
O.N. 180978 2,269.56g 1,127.62n 3,840d.
330.3 (l.o.a) x 45.2 x 19.4 feet.
T. 3-cyl. steam engine made by the North Eastern Marine Engineering Co (1938) Ltd., Sunderland.
11.10.1946: Completed by William Pickersgill and Sons Ltd., Sunderland (Yard

Upper: The Euxine-managed *Empire Tees* is seen in the Surrey Commercial Docks in 1955 late in her very long career as the Turkish *Selamet*. *[Roy Fenton collection]*
Lower: *Empire Pattern* was sold to Elder Dempster in 1948 for service in West Africa as *Forcados*. *[Ships in Focus]*

No. 303) for the Euxine Shipping Co. Ltd., London as HENDRIK. Registered 367/1946 in London.
2.11.1962: Sold to Marservicio Compania Naviera, Panama and renamed MARLINDO.
1966: Sold to Marcrecida Compania Naviera S.A., Piraeus, Greece and renamed NAFTILOS.
1970: Sold to Naviera Amazonica Peruana S.A., Lima, Peru and renamed YACU MAMA. Registered in Iquitos.
19.6.1974: Went aground in the River Amazon off Ilha Jupatituba during a voyage from Callao to Iquitos and later broke up.

21. **MEMNON/HENDI** (2) 1947-1950 and 1954-1962.
O.N. 186090 2,022.98g 1,072.06n 3,700d.
323.5 (l.o.a) x 44.5 x 19.8 feet.
T. 3-cyl. steam engine made by Hall, Russell and Co. Ltd., Aberdeen.
2.1947: Completed by the Burntisland Shipbuilding Co. Ltd., Burntisland (Yard No. 318) for the Egyptian Shipping Co. S.A.E., Cairo, Egypt (Euxine Shipping Co. Ltd., London, manager) as MEMNON.
1950: Sold to Rederi A/S Transatlantic (Per Carlsson, manager), Gothenburg, Sweden and renamed BOREN.
23.6.1954: Acquired by the Euxine Shipping Co. Ltd., London and renamed HENDI. Registered 135/1954 in London.
12.7.1962: Sold to Maritime Enterprise Co., Panama and renamed ERIKA.
1964: Sold to S. Baxivanis, Piraeus, Greece and renamed STEFANOS M.
1969: Sold to Velba Maritime Corporation S.A., Piraeus, Greece and renamed VELBA.
1971: Sold to Velan Shipping Co. Ltd., Famagusta, Cyprus.
3.8.1973: Went aground when entering Alexandria. Reported to have been renamed DIRFUS and sailed on 26.1.1974 for demolition at Piraeus, Greece.

Hendrik (2), Euxine's first post-war delivery (above) and as the Greek-owned *Marlindo* (below). *[Roy Fenton collection; Author's collection]*

The Euxine-managed *Memnon* at Butler's Wharf in the Pool of London on 11th July 1949. *[G.A. Osbon/World Ship Society Ltd.]*

Left: *Memnon* after transfer to Euxine ownership as *Hendi* (2). *[Ships in Focus]*

Middle: *Helka* (4) on the Thames, 2nd May 1953. *[Len Sawyer]*

Bottom: The Egyptian-flag *Nefertiti. [Roy Fenton collection]*

22. **HELKA** (4) 1947-1967
O.N. 181813 2,111.17g 1,106.59n 3,640d.
323.5 (l.o.a) x 44.4 x 19.8 feet.
T. 3-cyl. steam engine made by Hall, Russell and Co. Ltd., Aberdeen.
24.12.1947: Completed by the Burntisland Shipbuilding Co. Ltd., Burntisland (Yard No. 322) for the Euxine Shipping Co. Ltd., London as HELKA. Registered 464/1947 in London.
18.7.1963: Register transferred to Hong Kong.
1967: Sold to Sparko Shipping Co. S.A., Piraeus, Greece and renamed ANNA MARIA.
1.1973: Sold to shipbreakers at Piraeus after being laid up in the port since 18.7.1971.

23. **NEFERTITI** 1948-1950
O.N. 196661 2,276g 1,121n. 3840d.
330.3 (l.o.a) x 45.1 x 19.4 feet.
T. 3-cyl. steam engine made by the North Eastern Marine Engineering Co (1938) Ltd., Sunderland.
5.1948: Completed by William Pickersgill and Sons Ltd., Sunderland (Yard No. 309) for the Egyptian Shipping Co. S.A.E., Cairo, Egypt (Euxine Shipping Co. Ltd., London, manager) as NEFERTITI.
1950: Sold to Rederi A/B Transatlantic (Per Carlsson, manager), Gothenburg, Sweden and renamed ROXEN.
1954: Sold to Bharat Line Ltd., Bombay, India and renamed BHARATKESARI.
1967: Sold to Bukhsagar Shipping Pvt. Ltd., Bombay, India and renamed BANDE NAWAZ.
1975: Sold to Hind Shipping Agencies Ltd., Bombay and renamed VAISHNAVI.
15.6.1977: Went aground off Dwarka Lighthouse in position 22.17 north, 68.56 east during a voyage from Hoddeidah to Sikka and was abandoned as a total loss. Sold to G.G. Shipbreakers, Bombay for demolition.

Henzee of 1948 with a full deck cargo of army trucks (above), and a rare view of her on the Manchester Ship Canal (right). *Henzee* as the Greek-flagged *Olga* discharging in Surrey Commerical Docks on 20th September 1965 (below). *[Fotoflite incorporating Skyfotos; K. Cunnington; J. and M. Clarkson]*

The Spanish-built *Terica* (above) had a short career with Euxine, but spent 14 years with Atlantska Plovidba of Dubrovnik as *Titov Veles* (right). A regular visitor to British ports, she was photographed at Eastham on 31st May 1979. *[J. and M. Clarkson, L. Schofield/World Ship Society Ltd.]*

24. **HENZEE** 1948-1964
O.N. 182000 2,371.79g 1,183.58n 3,760d.
330.3 (l.o.a) x 45.2 x 19.4 feet.
T. 3-cyl. steam engine made by the North Eastern Marine Engineering Co (1938) Ltd., Sunderland.
14.8.1948: Completed by William Pickersgill and Sons Ltd., Sunderland (Yard No 310) for the Euxine Shipping Co. Ltd., London as HENZEE. Registered 275/1948 in London.
1.11.1963: Register transferred to Hong Kong.
1964: Sold to Olga Shipping Co. S.A., Piraeus, Greece and renamed OLGA.
1969: Sold to Nestor Compania Naviera S.A., Piraeus, Greece and renamed NESTOR.
1977: Sold to Tzonis Ltd., Elefsis, Greece who commenced demolition on 20.7.1977.

25. **TERICA** 1962-1967
O.N. 302871 1,597.61g 647.88n 2,460d.
85.45 x 13.14 x 5.25 metres (draft 6.02 metres in closed shelter deck mode).
2,414.94g 1,220.49n 3,078d.
6-cyl. 2SA Gotaverken-type oil engine made by Empresa Nacional 'Elcano' Valencia, Spain.
8.2.1962: Completed by Empresa Nacional 'Elcano', Seville, Spain (Yard No. 76) for the United Levant Line Ltd. (Euxine Shipping Co. Ltd., manager), London as TERICA. Registered 28/1962 in London.
6.1.1967: Sold to Atlantska Plovidba, Dubrovnik, Yugoslavia and renamed TITOV VELES.
1981: Sold to Pisco Shipping Co. Ltd., Gibraltar. Renamed HAIDER A and registered in Gibraltar. O.N. 385118. Tonnages became 1,472g, 651n/2,324g, 1,236n, 3,078d.
8.1983: Broken up by Van Heyghen Freres S.A., Ghent, Belgium.

26. **DUNSTER** 1968-1969
O.N. 186140 7,847.57g 4,376.07n 10,351d.
138.64 x 17.73 x 8.29 metres.
4-cyl 2SA Doxford oil engine made by David Rowan and Co. Ltd., Glasgow.
15.10.1954: Completed by Lithgows Ltd., Port Glasgow (Yard No. 1084) for the Temple Steam Ship Co. Ltd. (Lambert Brothers Ltd., manager) London as TEMPLE LANE. Registered 210/1954 in London.
31.7.1968: Sold to Euxine Shipping Co. Ltd. (Lambert Brothers Ltd., manager), London. Tonnages (CSG/OSG) now 7,700.72g, 4,191.84n/5,294.72g, 2,650.74n.
1.8.1968: Registered 26/1968 in Hong Kong.
21.7.1969: Registered 322/1969 in London and renamed DUNSTER.
8.8.1969: Sold to Leopard Shipping Co (1969) Ltd., Gibraltar and renamed DEUTERORNIS.
16.10.1969: Register transferred to Gibraltar.
1971: Sold to Felicity Shipping Co. S.A., Piraeus, Greece and renamed HUMANITY.
1973: Sold to Fidelity Maritime Co. Ltd. (Tremco Maritime and Trading Co. Ltd., manager), Piraeus, registered in Famagusta, Cyprus and renamed LAURICE FIDELITY.
1975: Sold to East Aegean Navigation S.A., Piraeus, Greece. Registered in Panama and renamed AEGEAN NAVIGATOR.

Lambert's *Temple Lane*, seen at Cape Town, was transferred to nominal ownership by Euxine Shipping Co. Ltd. in 1968 and subsequently renamed *Dunster* for a matter of weeks. *[Ships in Focus]*

1977: Sold to Northwave Navigation S.A., Piraeus, Greece and renamed NORTH WAVE.
11.4.1978: Laid up in Alexandria.
21.4.1981: Taking in water and beached.
1985: Condemned and presumed broken up locally.

27. **TEMPLE ARCH** 1969-1978
O.N. 338023 13,543.39g 7,990.77n 22,658d.
160.86 x 22.92 x 9.77 metres.
Two 9-cyl. 2SA oil engines made by English Electric Diesels Ltd., Ruston Engine Division, Lincoln.
4.11.1969: Completed by A/S Horten Verft, Horten, Norway (Yard No. 166) for Euxine Shipping Co. Ltd. (Lambert Brothers Ltd.), London (Scottish Ship Management Ltd., Glasgow, manager) as TEMPLE ARCH. Registered 488/1969 in London.
12.1973: Re-engined with two 8-cyl. 4SA oil engines made by Stork-Werkspoor Diesel N.V., Amsterdam.
1975: Manager became Whitco Marine Services Ltd., London.
5.12.1978: Sold to Jacamar Shipping Co. Ltd., Limassol, Cyprus and renamed SOLITAIRE.
1978: Sold to Leila Maritime Co. Ltd., Naples, Italy. Registered in Limassol, Cyprus and renamed LEILA. O.N. 381029.
1979: Owner relocated to Lisbon, Portugal.
1982: Manager became Socomar S.r.l., Naples, Italy.
1983: Manager became Mediterranean Shipping Co. S.A., Geneva, Switzerland.
1986: Sold to Cia. Naviera Francesca S.A., Panama.
1988: Sold to Silver Dolphin S.A., Panama. Registered in Panama and renamed GHADEER.
1990: Manager became Petra Navigation and International Trading Co. Ltd. (Tourist International Investments Co. Ltd), Amman, Jordan.
1993: Sold to Royal Kris Maritime S.A., Singapore. Registered in Panama and renamed ROYAL KRIS.
6.8.1994: Sailed from Inchon, South Korea bound for China to be broken up.

Temple Arch approaching the Tasman Bridge, Hobart, Tasmania bound for Risdon to discharge phosphate. *[Kingsley Barr/Russell Priest]*

Top: The 'old' RMS *St Helena*, formerly the Canadian *Northland Prince* (3,150/1963), served St Helena from 1977 to 1990. Thereafter she was briefly renamed *St Helena Island*, becoming *Avalon* later in 1990, *Indoceanique* in 1993 before being broken up at Alang in 1996. *[Ian Shiffman]*

Middle: *Centaur* (7,070/1964) served the island whilst *St Helena* (1) was requisitioned during the Falklands conflict. *[Ian Shiffman]*

Bottom: Still in excellent external condition, *Centaur* leaves Cape Town for the last time, bound for Singapore. Her funnel colours have been painted out. As the Chinese *Hai Da* she was broken up in China sometime earlier this century. *[Ian Shiffman]*

A NEW SHIP FOR ST HELENA

Andrew Bell

Curnow Shipping always knew that the original *St Helena*, built in Vancouver in 1963 with a gross tonnage of 3,150 tons, was too small to serve St. Helena and Ascension Island with terminal ports at either end of a 6,000 mile route between Avonmouth and Cape Town. The vital requirement after the abdication of Union-Castle Line in October 1977 was to get a replacement ship into service as quickly as possible: this was achieved within ten months. During the charter of the 'old' RMS *St Helena* to the Ministry of Defence for the period of the Falklands war and after (May 1982 to September 1983) there was once again an urgent need for a replacement ship to be St Helena's link to the world. My previous employers (1957-1974) Ocean Transport and Trading had just retired their 1964-built, 7,070 gross tons *Centaur* from the trade for which she had been specially built, Western Australia to Singapore and Malaysia. Curnow Shipping arranged a time charter as soon as she came out of Blue Funnel's SEA service with Curnow providing the hotel service crew. The charter ran from September 1982 to December 1983 and gave St. Helena a taste of what a bigger ship could provide. Unabashed, Curnow Shipping fuelled this desire on St. Helena and also explained how it could be done - whilst keeping the British Government's Overseas Development Agency in the picture. In 1986 Governor Dick Baker initiated the process that led to the new RMS. This became public knowledge when, one Sunday morning, he made a phone call to me. This was confirmed in a telex received on the Monday morning. This succinct document - thereafter always referred to with us at Curnow Shipping as 'The Purple Telex' - set the parameters for a ship to be newly built and Curnow Shipping's role in it: this was something that was to later settle many an argument. The new ship was to be provided by the British Government as aid to St. Helena with a 20-year net subsidy. There was to be no capital repayment: this was a very generous package. Curnow Shipping was to continue to be involved for three years after delivery, having worked up the new ship once in service. Tactically this sustained Curnow Shipping's increasingly important plan to create a cadre of local Saints' to man their own St. Helena ship at all levels.

Consultations

Through competitive tendering, Three Quays Marine Services - at that time a subsidiary of P&O - was chosen to design and superintend the building of the new ship. Curnow Shipping had previously used another firm of naval architects, Burness Corlett of Basingstoke, who were quite sure that the contract was theirs and in the bag but I had warned them not to be too greedy. And they were. During the summer of 1986 Three Quays rapidly got to work. The Overseas Development Agency backed Curnow Shipping's idea that two successive consultative sessions should be held on board the 'old' RMS when the ship was at Avonmouth. These took place on Saturdays and there was an open invitation to anyone involved in the St. Helena service. Everyone from crew members to port agents, from cargo shippers to travel agents, through to the St. Helena Government's London Representative, and even insurance underwriters and HM Customs came along. And they were not just lured by the alcohol-free lunch. The sea staff were particularly expansive and contributed much data, and many ideas. Ideas came from not just the 'old' RMS and experience gained from the *Centaur* but particularly valuable were those from Union-Castle's ships, for at that time Curnow Shipping had been greatly helped by some of that line's former staff who were now employed by us. Many will remember those star pursers Colin Deller, Jeannie Rollins and Geoff Shallcross, and the invaluable services of Dusty Miller in training catering crew members to the highest standards.

Ten weeks later, the meeting was repeated, this time the centre piece was Three Quays presenting their interpretation of what the outline design could be with as many as possible of 'The Good Ideas' that the naval architects could include. There was plenty of debate but the result was a surprising degree of overall agreement. This enabled Three Quays to very quickly complete the definitive design with the approval of both the Department of Transport and Lloyd's Register of Shipping. It was Curnow Shipping's stance that once this was done there were to be no amendments to the design. There were several made during the building of the ship but these were initiated by a very special person of whom mention is made later on in this story.

Design principles

The primary principles for the design of the new ship were based on two thirds of St Helena's and Ascension's imports coming from the United Kingdom and one third from South Africa and, of course, also the need for a widely-priced range of passenger accommodation in one class only, thus sharing all the public facilities. So the ship had to be able to carry 25,000 tons of cargo a year and an annual total of around 2,500 passengers.

A seaworthy hull had to be able to tackle the infamous Cape rollers in the South Atlantic and the winter storms in the North Atlantic while maintaining a service speed of 14 knots. This was to be done with twin diesel engines driving twin propellers. The accommodation had to be completely air conditioned with none of the processed air being recirculated, as this reduced the spread of germs that might affect public health on St. Helena where resistance is low. All the inter-island passengers were to be berthed in cabins which were specified to be better than British Rail's first class sleepers. It was insisted that there should be the capacity to generate as much fresh water as the ship would reasonably need; much experience of this type of plant had been gained in the 'old' RMS which had the necessary equipment fitted when she had been mother-ship for two minesweepers in the Falklands. Another lesson from this period was the importance of having the latest satellite communications system. Retractable fin-like stabilizers had been well proven so they too were specified. Right from the start the cargo spaces were designed to be capable of stowing containers. Special features were to include a sheltered space where animals could be carried. Two reliable cranes had to be sited to handle all the cargo carried and to be capable of being linked together to handle heavy lifts. Originally there was a set of derricks just in case the cranes broke down: as these never had to be used some brave executive, sometime after 2001, had them removed.

Suggestions made at the Avonmouth meetings included having the dining saloon, the main galley and the store rooms all on the same deck with stores loaded through their own hatchway. The main lounge was able to seat all the passengers at one time. Adjacent to the swimming pool there needed to be the sun lounge with a bar served by a full-scale pantry with a lift to supply it from the main galley and stores. Something really new at that time was a cabin with facilities for two disabled passengers. A dedicated children's room had stowage for toys and games. There had to be a shop with its own storage area. It would have been good to have a hairdresser but experience operating the *Centaur* proved that this could not, even for 188 passengers, cover its own costs. There were a whole host of details that went into the design such as the engineers' office on the boat deck having direct access to the engine room. There was to be one bathroom for the public use of elderly passengers. The radio room opened on to the navigating bridge. The officers' lounge had to be capable of hosting private parties. My particular contribution was that passenger baggage would be loaded into the accommodation through a platform in the stores hatch, a feature copied from the same feature on New Zealand Shipping's passenger liners. I also proposed that, adjacent to the two cabins for four cadets, there was a four-berth cabin with its own toilet and shower which was intended to take Prince Andrew School's senior students on trips to Ascension Island and Cape Town. The idea never caught on but the cabin was useful for berthing supernumeraries. These included junior officers from the Royal Navy who needed deep-sea time, and whose presence as part of the ship's company added much to the enjoyment of those onboard. It was no coincidence that these three cabins adjoined the area in which the senior officers were accommodated.

Arguments lost by Curnow Shipping during the design stage included the choice of whose main engines were installed. We wanted them built by F. Allen but the Overseas Development Agency had experience of Mirrlees machinery for aid-packaged power stations. The hull was designed so that the cargo area could be lengthened, but although this was agreed it was never implemented probably because of extra cost. There was a long-running disagreement between Curnow Shipping and Solomons – the shipping agency owned by the St. Helena Government – over the proportion of single berth cabins to the rest: the compromise was right down the middle of the numbers each party wanted.

Placing the building contract

The specification for the ship was widely circulated by Three Quays, but there was little interest from shipbuilders to produce such a one off. The UK yards who tendered were Brooke Marine at Lowestoft, Govan Shipbuilders on the Clyde and Hall Russell at Aberdeen. Govan were the favourites at £26,000,000 and who were building the *Norsea*, a 31,000 gross ton roll-on roll-off passenger ferry for P&O's North Sea Ferries. There was doubt about Brooke Marine who had never built anything larger than the *Bolton Abbey* (2,740/1958) 30 years previously. Hall Russell at £19m were widely considered as far too low: the price was seen as politically motivated. However the Treasury ruled for Hall Russell and let it be known 'If you don't place the order at Aberdeen, you won't get the money'.

There now comes into a leading role in the story Clive Warren, a man of great spirit and resolve who at the time was the Overseas Development Agency's head of section for the British Overseas Territories in the South Atlantic. Sensing that the Scottish Office was behind the choice of Hall Russell he wrung a quid pro quo out of them - all legally signed and binding - that if there was a cost over-run the Scottish Office would meet it; he was well advised by the Crown Agents who were the funding conduit to Hall Russell. Clive Warren had a dedication to St Helena and its people that can best be described as driving, purposeful and all done with a sharp good humour.

The contract was signed in London in December 1987 but as early as February 1988 it was sensed that Hall Russell were in trouble. However, with the new ship the only one on their order book, materials including steel and components were pouring into the yard which lay almost in the centre of the Granite City. The keel was laid by Mrs Gay Denbow (the St. Helena Government's Representative in London) in June 1988: it was in fact a large piece of the midships fuel tanks forward of the engine room and was placed on the keel blocks on one of which Gay had placed a St. Helena crown coin - it was vaporised when 5,000 tonnes of steel slid over it at the time of the launch.

The worst happened: in early November 1988 Hall Russell was placed in receivership by their bank. Taking the lead from Clive Warren in all but name, Three Quays were left managing the yard and building the ship which the Overseas Development Agency were definite about continuing. The possibility was considered of abandoning the order and breaking the ship up on the stocks, but she was around 20% complete. Clive Warren with the Crown Agents worked on the receivers to fund the work force and keep the construction going. A key event was the delivery to the yard of the two huge main engines, swathed in PVC: this was a visible act of confidence. Only six weeks after the bank had acted on 23rd December the Overseas Development Agency invited bids for the yard. Working over the Christmas and New Year holidays on a watch-on-stop-on basis, Clive Warren with his man at the Crown Agents and guided by Three Quays chose the A&P Group (at that time owned by Peter de Savary) and a new contract was negotiated to finish the ship, all done with not a day's work lost in the building of what was becoming the 'new' RMS.

From the earliest days Curnow Shipping had an engineer and a deck officer present in the yard at Aberdeen. Once a month members of the Curnow Shipping's management met at Aberdeen in what some people called contemptuously 'The Curtains Committee'. Ron Baxter and his wife Pat produced the master plan for all the interior decor based on a great deal of experience. A true Ulsterman, Ron had started his career in the yard of Harland and Wolff, Belfast in 1943 and by 1955 was the manager charged with building Union-Castle's *Pendennis Castle*. He so impressed the ship's owners that they offered him a career on the technical staff of British and Commonwealth Shipping, parent company of Union-Castle and Clan Line. Retiring early, Ron set up his own company and I had first been impressed with his company's work that had produced the muted interior splendour of Trinity House's flagship *Patricia* of 1982 which acted as deputy Royal Yacht at times. An example of Ron's worldly wiseness was that he advised us to order not less than 20% overrun of all the major items of soft furnishing materials so that well into the ship's lifetime we had the match of just what was being replaced: some of the public room carpeting being especially woven for the new ship. The intensity of the detail put in by the company's staff was considerable. Bob Wilson, the senior of our two radio officers, was given charge of just what was required and went in the radio room, which resulted in what I would claim to have been the most effective and habitable one afloat. Many of the paintings in the ship were reproductions from Trevor Hearle's private collection which featured St Helena: he was very generous in allowing access to what we thought we wanted. It was only after we had assembled the paintings to be reproduced and framed by a modest copy and printing works in Bridgenorth that we found out that the same company also worked for the Royal Collection at Windsor Castle.

Clive Warren had a lot of satisfaction in being involved in the building of the ship for which he was responsible and which he had actually saved. This meant him often attending the monthly progress meeting. On one of these we toured the ship as she was fitting out. We were in what was becoming economy-grade cabins on C deck, and he asked why was there no natural light? The answer came: 'there are no portholes.' 'Can they be fitted to the outboard ship's side cabins?' 'Yes. Let's have portholes where possible.' Three Quays were very keen to show a number of features they had designed into the *Norsea* so off to Hull we went to where the ship was turning around from having come in from Rotterdam. Looking aft from the bridge on a cold, bright morning after it had rained revealed that the bare steel deck stretching aft had contracted in the cold and looked like a rutted country lane. 'Is that what a steel deck can look like? We cannot have that around the swimming pool area. What is the alternative?' Came the chorus 'timber' and that is why the RMS might be the last merchant ship built in a British yard that had a teak deck laid. And it seems to have worn well.

The launch took place on a windy Tuesday 31st October 1989. The ship was to have been named by the Duchess of York but, with her father dying on his ranch in Argentina, she was substituted by Prince Andrew who flew himself from his Royal Navy ship, then on the west coast of Scotland, to Aberdeen. The Saint community came from far and wide to see their ship slide out of the vast building shed into the Dee and nudged to the nearby fitting out berth. There was also the Governor Robert Stimson: we never knew why Peter de Savary was absent. Curnow Shipping had little to do with organising the ceremony - unlike that when Princess Margaret named the old RMS at Southampton in September 1978. All we did was charter the British Midland aircraft that carried the London guests to the occasion and which nearly did not make it for Dyce Airport was affected that morning by wind shear!

Eleven months late and £13m over the originally contracted price, the ship was delivered on 30th October 1990, signed for by Rodney Young (at that time the ship's second officer and most senior Saint onboard and in Curnow Shipping's employment). This was after three weeks of satisfactory trials. It is said that no ship is ever finished in the builder's yard which was why the last details were completed by A & P Falmouth where RMS *St Helena* embarked 135 passengers invited for the overnight trip to Cardiff. It was a rough passage but it showed that the hull shape was sea kindly: the stabilizers worked and reduced the rolling. Three Quays' design also reduced vibration almost to nil. The new and old *St. Helenas* were berthed stern-to-stern at Cardiff so that some fittings and furnishing as well as ships' staff could be transferred: it was the only time they ever met. And when she sailed on 14th November 1990, the new RMS *St Helena's* career began.

St Helena fitting out at Aberdeen. *[James A. Pottinger]*

St Helena on trials with all tanks full. The deadweight cargo of 2,000 tonnes was seldom reached during the ship's commercial life. *[Author's collection]*

Above: *St Helena* at Cape Town on 21st November 1992. Designed to serve St. Helena from both the UK and South Africa, the ship built up a remunerative business by offering spare passenger berths between the terminal ports, giving St. Helena a modest number of tourists. *[Ian Shiffman]*

Below: *St Helena* at Cape Town on 7th December 2015. Later in the ship's career the St. Helena government required her to be based in Cape Town where all cargo from the UK was expensively transhipped. Using a long-haul ship on short-haul voyages increased the frequency of calls but drove the net subsidy required up from £1 million a year to over £4,000,000. *[Ian Shiffman]*

Above: *St Helena* preparing to sail from Cape Town on her last voyage to St Helena, with pipers on the quay (left) and just after casting off (right). Clearly shown in both photographs is the gym built at the base of the funnel on part of the little-used sports deck. *[Ian Shiffman]*

Below: *St Helena* sailing from Cape Town on 29th April 2018 as *MNG Tahiti* to begin a new career as the base ship for supplying parties of armed mercenaries to merchant ships proceeding through areas with a threat of piracy. The art collection as well as the Falkland's battle honours from the 'old RMS' had been landed at St. Helena. *[Ian Shiffman]*

STEEL SAILERS TO STEAM COASTERS: THE SHIPS OF WILLIAMSONS OF WORKINGTON

Roy Fenton

If a prerequisite for a successful iron shipbuilder was to have its raw materials close to hand, Williamsons of Harrington and later Workington were well qualified. What is now Cumbria had some of the United Kingdom's richest seams of iron ore, and a large iron and steel industry to turn the ore into plates and sections. There was also coal available from local collieries to power the machinery that was essential once building in iron began. Like many other builders, Williamsons prospered in the 19th century, but found the 20th too much of a challenge, and staggered on into the 1930s only by building largely for their own account. Nevertheless, Williamsons were responsible for some of the finest, large iron and steel sailing vessels built, exploiting a niche in the market which saw a temporary renaissance of sail. When this market inevitably declined, Williamsons partially re-invented themselves as a constructor of steam coasters. But their history was marked by periods when, to keep their yard working, the family had to fund the ships themselves. Although they built up and traded a small fleet of steam coasters, ultimately this was not a successful business model. This article reviews the history of this significant, if rather neglected, shipbuilder. The large sailing ships and the steam coasters built are listed, and fully detailed are those which were part of Williamsons' own fleet, latterly trading as the Northwest Shipping Co. Ltd.

Wood to iron

The business was founded by Whitehaven-born Richard Williamson (1800-1859) and also involved his younger brothers John and Hugh. The first vessel, the 60-ton wooden schooner *Union*, was completed at Harrington in 1839. Twelve of the first 17 hulls completed at Harrington were either for Richard or other members of the Williamson family, including his youngest brother William. On Richard's retirement in the 1850s, his son Thomas Williamson (1830-1909) took over and is first listed as an ship owner on completion of the yard's wooden barque *Lanercost* (358/1865). Now living at Harrington, Thomas had two sons, Richard W. (1855-1939) and Robert Hardy Williamson (1857-1938).

Richard served an engineering apprenticeship with Fletcher, Jennings and Company in Whitehaven, and after a few years at sea became manager of the Harrington yard in 1876, becoming chief partner in the company in just four years. In what was to be a remarkably long career, he not only ran the yard but was also a significant figure in the Institution of Mechanical Engineers, serving on its Council from 1917 to 1930.

In the 19th century, Williamsons gained something of a reputation for innovation, and in the 1860s they built wooden hulls under the cover of two large, open-sided sheds. This lost fewer days through bad weather, and may have meant that Lloyd's Register gave them a higher classification. The move to building in iron was undoubtedly made during Richard's management, and first saw the *Ann Gambles*, yard number 30, launched for Workington owners on 29th July 1862. Wooden and some composite hulls continued to be built until 1868, after which all construction at Harrington was in iron. Building in this material needed skills and equipment significantly different from those which sufficed for wooden hulls, and by no means all yards made the transition. But the advantages of iron were undeniable. Wood came in lengths limited by the size of the trees from which it was cut, and fastening these pieces end to end presented weaknesses. The realistic maximum size for a wooden ships was probably that represented by the 720 gross tons of *Yaratilda*, Williamson's yard number 21, built for the China trade in 1857. In contrast, iron plates and sections could be fastened by riveting, and as long as this was done well there was essentially no limit to how large iron hulls could get. Builders and owners of steam ships were amongst the first to exploit this advantage and as steam engines became more efficient and less coal-hungry, iron steamers began to offer serious competition to wooden sailing vessels. But owners and builders such as Williamson realised that the much larger sailing ships which iron construction made possible could compete with steam, especially on long-distance trades with relatively low-value bulk cargoes such as coal, ore, grain and fertilisers. Hence the 1870s saw something of a renaissance in construction of full-rigged ships and three- and four-masted barques of growing size. The accompanying table lists all iron and steel sailing ships over 200 feet built by Williamsons, and shows that even during the last years at Harrington the Williamsons were offering iron hulls to a

The sheds at the Harrington yard which allowed hulls to be built under cover. The hull on the right is reportedly *Parthia*, (yard number 60) which would date the photograph to just before her launch on 2nd June 1874. *[Cumbria Archive Services YDX69/7/41]*

standard size, particularly notable being a sequence of nine, from *Airey Force* (58), built to around 216 feet.

However, there are signs that in the late 1870s the Harrington yard was proving too small to build the largest iron hulls being demanded, with a 216-foot hull being the largest of which this yard was capable of comfortably producing. That the last of these, *Bellaport* (70) and *Oakhurst* (71), were built for Thomas Williamson suggests that outside orders for ships of this size were drying up, and it was therefore decided to move the yard to a new and larger site at Workington. The last vessel built at Harrington was Williamson's first steamer, the paddle tug *Florence* launched on 31st October 1879 for use at Maryport. The move inevitably caused a hiatus in construction, with the first hull from Workington, the iron ship *Grassendale*, not being launched until 19th January 1882. She was yard number 74: the sequence of the Harrington yard numbers being maintained at Workington. At 266 feet *Grassendale* was larger than anything built at Harrington, and was followed by an almost unbroken series of 12 ships built to this size. *Grassendale* was ordered by a new customer, R.W. Leyland and Company of Liverpool, whose large fleet of sailing ships was detailed in 'Record' 3, 4 and 5. Another Leyland order, again to the same size, *Garston* (78) of 1883 was the first hull in which both iron and steel were used, the first ship wholly built of steel was to be Williamson's own *Silvercrag* (89) of 1888. However, several of the steam coasters which the yard was now building, such as *Scale Force* (77) and *Black Rock* (96), reverted to a mixture of iron and steel, probably at the insistence of their rather conservative owners, the Kennaugh brothers and Alfred Rowland. In 1889, hull size was ratcheted up again with *Andelana* (92), which was followed by another 12 four-masted barques of between 304 and 308 feet, a sequence broken only by *Carmanian* (107), the last sailing ship built at the yard which had a 260-foot hull. Nothing anywhere near as large was to be built subsequently.

The steel four-masted barque *Pendragon Castle* (yard number 94) completed in 1891 for James Chambers and Co. Ltd. of Liverpool. She was sold to Hamburg owners in 1899 as *Lisbeth.* Laid up at Iquique in 1914, in 1921 she was allocated as reparations to France who almost immediately sold her back to Germany. Seen docking at Birkenhead and still as *Lisbeth*, she was broken up at Port Glasgow in 1927. *[B. and A. Feilden/J. and M. Clarkson]*

The steam coaster *Point Lynas* (yard number 166) ready for launching in September 1900. On completion in October she was registered as *Planudes* for owners in Middlesbrough. She went missing on a voyage from the Tyne to Trouville in January 1917, and is presumed to have been mined off Whitby on the 19th or 20th January. *[Cumbria Archive Services YDX69/7/39]*

Large iron and steel sailing ships built by Williamsons The somewhat arbitrary criteria for inclusion is length over 200 feet. Yard numbers from 74 onward were built at Workington.					
No	Name	Launch	Gross	Length	Built for
57	Ada Iredale	21.6.1872	1,032	243	P. Iredale and Co, Liverpool
58	Airey Force	15.3.1873	1,065	216	Sprott and Co., Liverpool
59	John Gambles	1.1.1874	1,066	216	J. Gambles and Co., Workington
60	Parthia	2.6.1874	1,063	215	W. Nicol and Co., Liverpool
61	Lupata	18.2.1875	1,069	215	Clark and Co., London
62	Inglewood	20.7.1875	1,077	215	J. Sprott, Workington
64	Geltwood	11.1.1876	1,091	216	J. Sprott, Workington
65	Aethelstan	28.4.1876	814	210	White, Foreman and Co., Liverpool
66	Aethelberht	19.8.1876	810	202	White, Foreman and Co., Liverpool
67	Crosfield	28.2.1877	811	199	Johnson, Sproule and Co., Liverpool
68	Mallsgate	26.5.1877	1,073	215	Fisher and Sprott, Workington
69	George Bewley	20.12.1877	1,071	207	J. Bewley and Co., Liverpool
70	Bellaport	1.7.1878	1,065	216	Thomas Williamson, Workington
71	Oakhurst	21.1.1879	1,068	216	Thomas Williamson, Workington
72	Oweenee	18.8.1879	1,145	227	B. McCorkell, Londonderry
74	Grassendale (1)	19.1.1882	1,842	266	R.W. Leyland and Co., Liverpool
75	Aigburth	5.8.1882	1,838	267	R.W. Leyland and Co., Liverpool
76	Crown of England	9.2.1883	1,839	267	Robertson, Cruikshanks, Liverpool
78	Garston	17.9.1883	1,852	267	R.W. Leyland and Co., Liverpool
79	Cumberland	27.3.1884	1,849	267	Thomas Williamson, Workington
81	Grassendale (2)	14.5.1885	1860	267	R.W. Leyland and Co., Liverpool
82	Lowther Castle	22.1.1886	1,868	262	Chambers
83	Lancaster Castle	18.10.1884	2,155	279	Chambers
85	Greystoke Castle	2.7.1886	1,878	262	Chambers
86	Silverdale	10.3.1887	1,920	264	R. Williamson and Son, Workington
87	Boadicea	17.10.1887	1,938	264	Brown, Jenkinson and Co., London
89	Silvercrag	29.3.1888	1,939	264	R. Williamson and Son, Workington
90	Aldebaran	8.9.1888	1,943	264	Boyes & Ruyter, Bremen
91	Wray Castle	19.2.1889	1,891	264	Chambers
92	Andelana	18.10.1889	2,512	304	E.F. & W. Roberts, Liverpool
93	Friars Crag	5.3.1890	2,512	304	Fisher and Sprott
94	Pendragon Castle	12.1.1891	2,510	304	Chambers
95	Vortigern	23.7.1891	2,529	306	Brown, Jenkinson, London
97	Caradoc	28.5.1892	2,531	306	Brown, Jenkinson, London
98	Conishead	6.10.1892	2,526	306	Bourke and Huntrods, Workington
100	Centesima	11.9.1893	2,949	308	R. Williamson and Son, Workington
101	Iranian	11.3.1895	2,958	308	R. Williamson and Son, Workington
107	Carmanian	19.4.1897	1,867	260	R. Williamson and Son, Workington

The second *Grassendale* (yard number 81) was built in 1885 for the important fleet of sailing ships owned by R.W. Leyland and Company, which were named after suburbs of Liverpool. She was sold to Finnish owners in 1900 and renamed *Imperator Alexander II* (Finland was still part of the Russian empire). Sold to Swedish owners and renamed *Ernst* in 1919. She was last seen heading east from Skagen on 24th April 1920 whilst on a voyage from Santos to Aarhus with a cargo of oil cake. She is believed to have hit a mine in the Herta Flak minefield, where her wreck was later located in position 57.45.5 north, 11.05 east. *[National Maritime Museum P294]*

Top: *Cumberland* (yard number 79) was built in 1884 for Thomas Williamson. He sold her to British owners in 1900, and as the Italian *Mater Misericordiae* she was dismantled in Italy during 1924. *[State Library of Victoria H99 220/410]*

Middle: *Silverdale* (86): see page 132. *[State Library of Victoria H99 220/528]*

Bottom left: *Wray Castle* (91) built for James Chambers and Company. As the Canadian-owned *Garthwray* she was wrecked outside Talca, Chile on 23rd April 1924. *[State Library of Victoria H99 220/993]*

Believed to be the *John Gambles*, yard number 59, launched at Harrington on the first day of 1874. *[Cumbria Archive Services YDX69/7/44]*

Steam coasters built by Williamsons					
No.	Launch name	Launched	GT	Feet	Initial owner
77	Scale Force	21.7.1883	229	130	W. Kennaugh Co., Whitehaven
80	Derwent	17.12.1883	267	111	J. Cassons, Whitehaven
84	Holme Force	22.6.1887	266	144	R. Williamson, Cockermouth and W. Kennaugh, Whitehaven
88	Stanley Force (1)	1.1.1890	373	152	W. Kennaugh, Whitehaven
96	Black Rock	17.9.1891	362	152	Alfred Rowland, Liverpool
99	Bell Rock	6.2.1893	368	153	Alfred Rowland, Liverpool
102	Queen's Channel	8.2.1894	370	153	John Edwards, Liverpool
110	Holmecrag	25.6.1895	390	153	R. Williamson and Son, Workington
111	Lodes	10.1.1898	396	154	Casebourne, Fowler, Middlesbrough
117	Brest Rock	22.10.1896	533	168	Alfred Rowland, Liverpool
118	Luddick	17.10.1898	530	168	Aberdeen, Newcastle and Hull Steam Co. Ltd.
130	Braeside	4.1.1900	261	129	Thomas Pinkney, Sunderland
139	Eden	4.12.1896	281	131	Carr and Co. Ltd., Carlisle
140	Nith	11.11.1897	279	131	Carr and Co. Ltd., Carlisle
144	Foy	23.6.1902	354	136	Toyne, Carter, Fowey
152	Volscian	20.7.1898	616	178	Rogers and Bright, Liverpool
154	Rock Channel	14.12.1898	431	154	John Edwards, Liverpool
155	Formby	29.5.1899	431	154	John Edwards, Liverpool
156	Fred	28.2.1899	312	141	T.G. Best, Liverpool
162	Gipsy	7.9.1899	634	183	Waterford Steamship Co., Waterford
165	Hamm	13.9.1900	633	183	D.P.H. Fuhrmann, Hamburg
166	Point Lynas	18.8.1900	542	166	G.V. Fowler, Middlesbrough
168	Cape York	10.1.1902	530	165	Dawson Brothers, Glasgow
169	Horn	22.4.1901	627	184	D.P.H. Fuhrmann, Hamburg
181	Seagull	18.11.1902	658	183	Shoreham Shipping Co., Shoreham
183	Slateford	9.10.1903	355	183	Mann, Macneal, Glasgow
184	Queenie	9.3.1905	352	136	A.H. Keep, London
185	Shad Thames	22.9.1902	549	165	M.A. Ray, London
186	Stock Force	2.5.1905	538	165	W. Kennaugh, Whitehaven
187	Pylades	11.8.1903	681	183	R. Williamson and Son, Workington
188	Voreda (1)	9.5.1906	509	183	R. Williamson and Son, Workington
190	Guanche	8.1.1904	257	121	Elders and Fyffes,
191	Calatum	24.9.1908	270	121	R. Williamson and Son, Workington
192	Stainburn	10.12.1903	405	142	Murphy and Sandwith, Workington
193	Galava	20.9.1906	400	142	R. Williamson and Son, Workington
194	Mary Emily	16.8.1904	350	136	Betson, Dublin
200	Colwith Force	21.6.1906	550	165	W. Kennaugh, Whitehaven
201	Voreda (2)	23.9.1907	559	165	R. Williamson and Son, Workington
206	Volpone	27.2.1907	531	165	Rogers and Bright, Liverpool
207	Volhynia	4.2.1908	531	175	Rogers and Bright, Liverpool
208	Ravonia (1)	4.2.1908	703	183	R. Williamson and Son, Workington
209	Petriana	22.2.1909	707	183	R. Williamson and Son, Workington
210	Skelwith Force	12.8.1908	562	165	W. Kennaugh, Whitehaven
211	Calcaria	20.9.1910	406	165	R. Williamson and Son, Workington
212	Glanoventa	13.1.1910	406	142	R. Williamson and Son, Workington
213	Wythburn	25.9.1911	420	142	Murphy and Sandwith, Workington
214	Aysgarth Force	18.4.1912	582	165	W. Kennaugh, Whitehaven
215	Volturnus	27.11.1912	615	175	Rogers and Bright, Liverpool
216	Ingstad	27.7.1910	773	183	Grifstad & Herlofson, Arendal
217	Deventia	20.5.1913	800	186	R. Williamson and Son, Workington
218	McElwain	8.1.1912	811	186	R.H. Ballantyne, Glasgow
219	Boro	17.6.1912	814	186	A/S Sorlandet, Arendal
220	Arleia	18.1.1915	795	186	R. Williamson and Son, Workington
221	Freshet	31.5.1915	794	186	E.H. Sollas, London
222	Stepney	18.7.1916	808	186	Commercial Gas Co., London
223	Volana	1610.1913	616	175	Rgrs and Bright, Liverpool
224	Galacum	14.9.1915	585	166	R. Williamson and Son, Workington
226	Cliburn	4.4.1916	440	166	Murphy & Sandwith, Workington
227	Lynburn	10.5.1917	587	150	Murphy & Sandwith, Workington
228	Stanley Force (2)	6.1.1920	586	166	W. Kennaugh, Liverpool
229	Dynamo	8.3.1920	809	186	Ellerman's Wilson Line, Hull
237	Ardshean	14.9.1920	804	187	Adam Brothers, Aberdeen
238	Levenwood	7.11.1923	803	187	Constantine, Middlesbrough
239	Ravonia (2)	26.1.1925	870	187	R. Williamson and Son, Workington
240	Homewood	20.10.1926	881	193	Constantine, Middlesbrough
241	Corinia	30.8.1928	870	188	R. Williamson and Son, Workington
242	Silvonia	12.2.1930	1,131	211	R. Williamson and Son, Workington
243	Sodality	2.4.1938	829	188	F.T. Everard and Sons Ltd., Greenhithe
	Sodality - after launching she was taken to Goole and completed as a motor vessel				

Sail to steam

Inevitably, the renaissance in sailing ship building was short-lived, as further improvements in the efficiency of steam ships threatened to drive sail from even the longest routes. Although big ships and barques remained just about viable for many years, owners could foresee their demise and the orders they gave to shipyards like Williamsons dried up in the early 1890s. The last from Workington was the *Carmanian* for the builders' own account launched as yard number 107 in 1897. Although steam coaster building at Workington had begun with the iron-hulled *Scale Force* for Kennaughs in 1883, it was yet to provide the work needed to keep the yard employed, and from 1893 a large number of barges and lighters mostly under one hundred tons, plus occasional non-cargo-carrying craft such as dredgers and hoppers were turned out, including a few with steam engines. From 1898, however, steam coasters became the yard's staple output, although lighters still figured amongst the list of yard numbers. Local owners, such as Kennaughs, Murphy and Sandwith, and Carrs of Carlisle accounted for some orders, but coastal ship owning in the region was declining, as centres such as Liverpool, London and Glasgow grew in importance. The later completions saw an increase in size, culminating in the 211-foot *Silvonia*, and these were particularly suited to the buoyant east coast coal trade, particularly out of Goole, and several gravitated there.

Unlike many other yards, Williamson's was not immediately turned over to naval construction in the First World War, and it continued to build coasters, although there is little sign of output being geared up to meet the growing demand for tonnage as war losses mounted. Eventually the Admiralty noticed the yard, and a number of 'Strath' class trawler hulls were ordered, six being completed, two of which were sold to commercial owners before completion. But the war indirectly led to the Williamson's demise as shipbuilders. Business was buoyant enough at the end of the war, with the *Stanley Force* (2), *Dynamo* and *Ardshean* delivered at top-of-the market prices during 1920. But with demand for steam coasters largely satisfied, and the onset of a severe depression in freight rates, there were but two further orders, both from Middlesbrough for the large coasters *Levenwood* and *Homewood*.

Presumably out of concern for the future, R. Williamson and Son Ltd. was incorporated as a limited liability company in 1923. Four ships were started for the builder's own account, of which they completed just three, one of these *Corinia*, seeing the launching ways collapse as she was launched on 30th August 1928. Thus the years 1921, 1922, 1924, 1927 and 1929 did not see a single launch at Workington.

Once *Silvonia* had been completed in July 1930, work was largely suspended on yard number 244, with the yard formally closing in 1932. The very last ship was left on the stocks until launched in April 1938, once trees and undergrowth had been cleared from the ways. She was then taken to Goole for installation of an oil engine, becoming Everard's *Sodality*, and the only motor ship ever built in Cumberland.

As with the iron and steel sailing ships, an attempt was made by Williamsons to offer steam coaster hulls in a number of standard lengths. This was not as successful, as many coaster owners had rigid size limits set by ports to which they habitually traded, including Dublin and Newry where the upper limit was about 145 feet (Williamson built 10 just inside this figure). However, from the accompanying table a pattern begins to emerge. A total of eight ships were sold with a length of 152 to 153 feet. Fourteen were built to the larger size of 165 to 168 feet, but the most popular range was 183 to 186 feet – relatively large for British coasters – which accounted for 20 completions. The outliers were two ships of 121 feet and one of 211 feet. The former include an oddity, the *Guanche* (190) built for Elders and Fyffes, and the latter the *Silvonia* (232), last completion for Williamson and clearly intended for the East Coast coal trade.

Left: *Derwent* was the second steam coaster built by Williamsons (yard number 80) . Note the particularly tall masts, a feature of Workington-built coasters for some years. She has the conventional raised quarter deck layout, but high bulwarks tend to mask this. Built for a locally-owned single ship company, she had a variety of managers before sale to Liverpool. In 1913 she was sold foreign, and survived under successive Danish, Norwegian and Belgian ownership until lost in collision off Flamborough Head on 15th February 1941 as *Marguerite*. *[Author's collection]*

Bottom left: Kennaugh's *Holme Force* (yard number 84) was sold in 1906 to Preston Corporation who used her to tranship cargo from ships anchored in Bog Hole off Southport and which were too deep-draughted to enter Preston Dock, in this case wood pulp. She was broken up locally in 1928. *[J. and M. Clarkson]*

Below: *Poolton* (yard number 88) seen with H.H. Poole and Co. Ltd., London, was built for Kennaugh as *Stanley Force* (2), their third from Williamsons. She too proved to be a remarkable survivor. Sold to Italy in 1925, she had an oil engine fitted in 1952, and was not broken up until 1972. *[National Maritime Museum P12418]*

Alfred Rowland of Liverpool was an early customer with *Black Rock* (above, yard number 96). Another long-lived steamer, as *Empire Lethe*, she had the dubious distinction of being the oldest ship to carry an Empire name. As *Eleth* she foundered off County Down on 1st February 1952. Before that, *Black Rock* was followed by sister *Bell Rock* (number 99) and by the larger *Brest Rock* (117), below as *Claretta* in the ownership of J. H. Monks (Preston) Ltd. after 1912. She too was a collision victim, off the Longships on 31st August 1930. *[Both: Bristol Series/J. and M. Clarkson]*

Above: Unusually, *Queenie* (yard number184) kept the name given to her by Alfred Keep, London in 1905 through several owners until sent for demolition at Troon by John S. Monks and Co. Ltd., Liverpool, in whose ownership she i seen. *[World Ship Society Ltd.]*

Above: Next in yard number sequence to *Queenie*, but launched almost 18 months later, *Shad Thames* (yard number 185) was also for a London owner, coal merchants M.A. Ray and Sons. She survived the grounding shown, but not a collision with a Norwegian steamer off Hartland Point on 15th March 1918. *[Roy Fenton collection]*

Left: Another Cumberland owner, the Carr family of biscuit fame, ordered two small coasters, *Eden* (yard number 139) and *Nith* (140) to move grain from Liverpool to their mill near Carlisle. *Eden* was photographed, appropriately enough in the Ribble, in the ownership of Seller's Ribble Shipping Co. Ltd, about 1908. After several sales she was broken up during 1946. *[J. and M. Clarkson]*

Below left: Williamson attracted relatively few orders from Glasgow owners, probably because they were well-served by builders on the Clyde. An exception were Mann, Macneal, who took delivery of *Slateford* (yard number 183) in 1903. Photographed at Preston as *Bannmaid* she had seen at least seven owners and 45 years later as Coe's *Bannmaid* she was broken up ther in 1952. *[J. and M. Clarkson]*

Below: Kennaughs liked the name *Stock Force*, using it three times, first for Williamson's yard number 186. As *Tarpeia* she was sunk by *UB 18* in the English Channel on 11th May 1917. *[Author's collection]*

Left: A Kennaugh sister to *Stock Force* was *Colwith Force* (yard number 200). Owned by Mullock and Son of Limerick from 1920 as *Loop Head*, she left Barry with coal for her home port on 27th October 1927 and disappeared. *[Bristol Series/J. and M. Clarkson]*
Right: Built for Murphy and Sandwith (see 'Record' 21), *Wythburn* (yard number 213) was photographed at Preston in Monroe's colours. She was mined and sunk off Barry on 28th October 1940 whilst bringing in bog ore from Buncrana. *[J. and M. Clarkson]*

gers and Bright of Liverpool were also good customers, taking five coasters ween 1906 and 1913. *Lyme Regis* (above) was the third, launched as *Volpone* rd number 206) and is seen in the colours of Harrison, Sons and Co. Ltd., rdiff. As the Cardigan-owned *Continental Coaster* she was torpedoed by an oat off Cromer on 24th September 1940. *[Bristol Series/J. and M. Clarkson]*
n feet longer than *Volpone* was *Volhynia* (yard number 207). Seen as Kelly's *lisle* (below), she too was a Second World War loss, sunk by the Luftwaffe in Bristol Channel on 21st March 1941 with coal from Cardiff for Cork. *[B. and Feilden/J. and M. Clarkson]*

ow: *Skelwith Force* (Yard number 210) was another Kennaugh order stined for a long life. Retained by the company until 1944, she went to nmark three years later and after being dieselised as *Primrose* in 1952 was eted from 'Lloyd's Register' only in 1999.

Above: Kennaughs returned for the *Aysgarth Force* (yard number 214), completed in 1912. She foundered on 28th March 1925 after her ore cargo shifted near the Maas Light Vessel. *[Author's collection]*

Above: Unusual in being built for the East Coast coal trade, and with minimal cargo gear, *Stepney* (yard number 222) was completed for the Commercial Gas Company. As *Kyleburn* she was scrapped at Llanelli in 1957. *[National Maritime Museum P13187]*
Below: Rogers and Bright's *Volana* (yard number 223) was taken over by Coast Lines in 1919 to become *Cornish Coast*. Sold to Turkey in 1951, she survived until scrapped in 2004.*[J. and M. Clarkson]*

Left: Kennaugh deserted Williamsons after taking the second *Stanley Force* (yard number 228) their ninth from the yard. She foundered in the Channel o 14th February 1953. *[J. and M. Clarkson]*
Above: Constantines of Middlesbrough were the last owner to order from Workington, with *Levenwood* (yard number 238) seen 23rd September 1934 She was wrecked as *Devonbrook* on 28th August 1946. *[R.A. Snook/]*

Sodality running trials for F.T. Everard and Sons Ltd., Greenhithe in September 1938. Laid down for Williamsons own account as yard number 243, she was towed to Goole for completion and to have her oil engine fitted. This had to be sat higher than usual to line up with the shaft aperture, designed to suit a stea engine. After almost 20 years in service this engine was removed and the hull sold to T.W. Ward Ltd. She arrived at Ward's yard at Grays, Essex on 23rd July 1958. *[Courtesy K. Garrett]*

Williamsons' significance

Williamsons' yards were the most important and longest lived of any on the coast of Cumberland. Under a number of successive owners, including the Ritsons, Maryport built a number of large sailing ships and steam coasters up to 1914, following a trajectory quite similar to Williamsons', with frequent building on spec. Between 1871 and 1889, the Whitehaven Shipbuilding Co. Ltd. turned out 76 iron and steel hulls, predominantly sailers, but with a number of steam ships which were significantly larger than those produced at Workington. In national terms, Williamsons' output was on the low side, and the accompanying table of output by year indicates that there was annual capacity to turn out just two or sometimes three ships, although many more small barges could be built in the same period. A yard list, which is not totally accurate according to later research, refers to a 'top yard', suggesting there was also a 'lower yard' but also notes that the *Carmanian* of 1907 was the last launch at the top yard. This is born out by an Ordnance Survey map, which was revised in 1898, which shows the yard having just one slipway, launching into Workington's Old Dock, such a limited facility explaining the yard's low output. Nevertheless, the big iron and steel ships and barques which Williamson built made an important contribution to the British merchant fleet and were well regarded. The steam coasters, too, had admirers, particularly the Kennaughs and the diminishing number of local coaster owners, although the output of these was relatively small, especially compared with the major coaster builders in the West of Scotland.

A local historian has wondered if the lack of an engine building facility at Williamsons' yard, or indeed anywhere in Cumberland, might have made the yard unviable when it came to steam ship construction. This seems unlikely, as fitting engines only required the hulls to be towed to the Clyde where there were a plethora of well-established marine engineering companies, including Ross and Duncan of Govan who engined a high proportion of the yard's steam ship hulls. Given that the Workington yard could generally turn out only one or two steamers a year, the investment in the skills and machinery required for an engine works at the

Workington yard was probably seen as unnecessary. There were plenty of yards, even some established around the time of Williamsons' demise, which did very well by concentrating on hull building, the Burntisland Shipbuilding Co. Ltd. (1920-1968) being a classic example. A more likely reason for problems once orders became sparse was the lack of a dry dock at Workington. Although this was not such an issue from the shipbuilding perspective, it diminished the opportunities for taking on repair work, such work often keeping yards going during the many lean periods when orders were scarce.

It has also been questioned whether the yard could have remained open until the outbreak of the Second World War, when it might have proved useful. In fact, the beginning of the end was long before, in 1926, with the final order placed by a customer, Constantines of Middlesbrough. The last three ships were laid down for Williamsons themselves, and by 1932 the workforce would have been completely laid off and the yard allowed to deteriorate. Given the wholesale yard closures elsewhere in the 1920s and 1930s, there were other facilities which could be rejuvenated, and those that did revive were situated in active shipbuilding areas such as the Tyne, Clyde and Tees. The death of Richard Williamson on 8th April 1939 would also have militated against revival.

With Williamson's demise, shipbuilding in Cumberland ceased. Yet, not far away it thrived and continues to this day. At Barrow-in-Furness in north Lancashire, an iron shipbuilding yard was established in 1871 and although its early output was predominantly mercantile, under Vickers ownership from 1891 it very successfully diversified into warship construction, also completing some important and sophisticated merchant ships including passenger liners and gas tankers. As BAE Systems the yard is now the UK's only submarine builder. Clearly, geography did not prevent this yard succeeding, and we must look elsewhere for reasons for Williamsons' ultimate demise. Perhaps they were ultimately too conservative, sticking with one slipway, not investing in a dry dock and not moving on from coasters and colliers to bigger steamers. Neither did they embrace motor ships, of which the only one which could call itself a product of Cumberland was yard number 244, and the installation of its diesel engine had nothing to do with Williamsons. Ships were built mainly for local owners and those in Liverpool, and the decline in ship owning in Cumberland in particular undoubtedly hurt Williamsons.

The yard's manager, Richard Williamson, was well into his seventies when building at his yard stuttered to a halt, and it is quite likely that neither he nor his brother were prepared to invest further in what must have looked like a moribund enterprise in a sunset industry, and one into which, in terms of speculative building, they had already sunk significant capital. Nevertheless, on their deaths both brothers left estates valued at around £500,000.

Output by year

Yard numbers are not a satisfactory guide to yearly output, as the sequence in which they were allocated does not always match the order in which hulls were launched. The table alongside looks at launches at Workington by year, with the total gross tonnage figure giving the best available indication of annual output. Hulls are classified as sail, steam coasters and others – the last-named are barges or lighters unless stated.

* Hull launched for the builder's account.

† Actual tonnage higher, as no figures recorded for some of the barges built that year.

Year	Number	Gross	Sail	Steam	Other
1882	2	3,680	2	-	-
1883	4	5,769	3	1	-
1884	2	4,004	2	-	-
1885	1	1,860	1	-	-
1886	2	3,746	2	-	-
1887	3	4,124	2 (1*)	1	-
1888	2	3,882	2 (1*)	-	-
1889	2	4,373	2	-	-
1890	2	2,885	1	1	-
1891	3	5,401	2	1	-
1892	2	5,057	2	-	-
1893	6	4,517	1*	1	4
1894	6	530	-	1	5
1895	9	4,568	1*	1*	7
1896	17	2,219	2	-	15
1897	5	1,100	-	1	4
1898	4	1,385†	-	2	2
1899	7	2,128†	-	3	4
1900	6	2,314	-	3	3
1901	10	1,452†	-	1	9
1902	4	1,809	-	3	1
1903	2	1,036	-	1 (1*)	-
1904	6	1,729	-	3	3
1905	4	538	-	2	2
1906	7	2,614	-	3 (1*)	4
1907	2	1,090	-	2 (1*)	-
1908	3	1,535	-	3 (2*)	-
1909	1	707	-	1*	-
1910	3	1,748	-	3 (2*)	-
1911	2	1,037	-	2	-
1912	4	2,822	-	4	-
1913	2	800	-	2*	-
1914	-	-	-	-	-
1915	3	2,074	-	3 (2*)	-
1916	2	1,248	-	2	-
1917	2	780	-	1	1 trawler
1918	4	1,619	-	1	3 trawlers
1919	2	408	-	-	2 trawlers
1920	3	2,199	-	3	-
1921	-	-	-	-	-
1922	-	-	-		-
1923	1	803	-	1	-
1924	-	-	-		-
1925	1	870	-	1*	-
1926	1	881	-	1	-
1927	-	-	-	-	-
1928	1	870	-	1*	-
1929	-	-	-	-	-
1930	1	1,131	-	1*	-

Output by type from both yards	
Wooden sail	37
Composite sail	5
Iron and steel sail	59
Iron and steel coasters	59
Other steamers	6 trawlers 1 dredger, 1 tug
Barges, lighters, hoppers	61

Williamsons as ship owners

Ship ownership amongst the members of the Williamson family goes back at least as far as the foundation of the Harrington yard in the 1830s. The founder, Richard Williamson, built for himself and other family members, of whom Thomas continued the tradition right up to the iron ship *Cumberland* (79) of 1884. Thereafter the second Richard Williamson (the son of Thomas, who shared an address at 'Oakhurst' in the market town of Cockermouth) continued the tradition. With a Robert Hardy Williamson (his son or brother, and again sharing an address) Richard was to jointly own five sailing vessels and seventeen and a half steam coasters, all but one built at the Workington yard. Some of these were operated only until market conditions improved and a buyer could be found. Indeed, in the case of *Holmecrag* (110), the first *Voreda* (188) and *Petriana* (209), this was only a matter of months.

The first vessel built in the name of Robert and Richard Williamson, the iron ship *Silverdale* (86) is said to have been sold after only one voyage, but if so it was clearly a very lengthy one, stretching from April 1887 to June 1889. Quite likely, a 'voyage' had been reckoned in terms of her first return to a United Kingdom port, as when in London on 18th June 1889 she was sold for £18,500 to Robert Thomas of Criccieth and was quickly re-registered as *Criccieth Castle*. Under both names she became quite celebrated, and was painted by the highly-collectable painter William Yorke flying Williamson's flag (several publications err in referring to her as being built for Robert Thomas). To digress a little, her end under this successful North Welsh sailing ship owner was both tragic and probably preventable. Having brought a cargo of wheat to Peru in 1912, she loaded guano for Antwerp. In the South Atlantic she sustained moderate damage to her hull, but the pumps could not control the ingress of water, as they were continually blocked by the remains of the previous wheat cargo in the bilges. Attempts to clear the pumps were prevented by the suffocating atmosphere created by the guano, and on 15th July she was abandoned and subsequently foundered. In a remarkable small boat voyage, the master, Captain Thomas, his wife Catherine and the other survivors of the crew reached the Falkland Islands, but 15 men were lost. At the subsequent enquiry, the Board of Trade censured one of her mates for not ensuring the remains of the previous wheat cargo were removed from the bilges.

The four other sailing vessels gave Williamson longer service; until her wreck off Japan in 1900 in the case of *Iranian* (101), and their sale to German or British owners in 1900 and 1901 for the *Silvercrag* (89), their last build the *Carmanian* (107) and their 'centenary' ship *Centesim*a (100).

Williamson's first financial interest in a steamer was taken in the *Holme Force* (84) of 1887, jointly owned by Richard and William S. Kennaugh of Whitehaven. The latter had his *Scale Force* (77) built by Williamson in 1883 and for this, his second ship, he appears to have needed Williamson to partly finance her. Interestingly, *Scale Force* was bought by Williamson from Kennaugh in 1891, the only second-hand ship to join the fleet in Richard Williamson's lifetime. Normally such a transaction might have the objective of winning an order for a new ship but, if so, Williamson missed out as Kennaugh's next order, *Aira Force* (349/1891), went very unusually to a yard in South Wales.

In the lean years of the first decade of the 20th century speculative builds of five other steamers – *Galava* (193), the second *Voreda* (201), *Calatum* (191), *Glanoventa* (212) and *Calcaria* (211) - kept the yard open, and they were run until conditions improved just prior to the First World War. Trading coasters was obviously felt to be worthwhile, as the next three completions – *Deventia* (217), *Arleia* (220) and *Galacum* (224) – could have been readily sold at an immense profit during the First World War, yet were retained in the fleet. That this was a mistake must have become quickly apparent in the 1920s, as freight rates plummeted and with them the value of ships. Three further buildings for the Williamson fleet, *Ravonia* (239), *Corinia* (241) and *Silvonia* (242) just had to be traded under very depressed conditions until they were wrecked or became war losses.

Prior to 1925, the ships were under the ownership of Robert and Richard Wiliamson, but they were then transferred to the newly-formed Northwest Shipping Co. Ltd. The family continued to manage them until Richard's death in 1939, when management passed to the Constantine family of Middlesbrough. They persisted with the venture, even adding a second-hand, Williamson-built steamer, the *Kylebrook* (240) in 1942. Her sale and the loss of the *Ravonia* in 1944 ended the existence of Northwest as ship owners, although they continued for some time as shipbrokers.

Evidence from loss data and photographs suggests the Williamson/Northwest Shipping steamers engaged in many of the United Kingdom's typical coasting trades. Two larger coasters, *Stepney* (222) and *Ravonia* (239), had been built for the East Coast coal trade to London and Southern ports, and post-war the three completions for the fleet were also employed in this trade, where bigger ships were generally used than on the Irish Sea.

Fleet list

Includes ships part-owned by Williamsons. Hulls are steel unless stated.

1. SILVERDALE 1887-1889 Iron ship
O.N. 79127 1,920g 1,877n.
263.9 x 39.0x 23.7 feet.
10.3.1887: Launched (Yard No. 86).
2.4.1887: Registered in the ownership of R. Williamson and Son, Workington as SILVERDALE.
18.6.1889: On completion of maiden voyage, sold to Robert Thomas and Company, Criccieth, Caernarvonshire and subsequently renamed CRICCIETH CASTLE.
31.8.1892: Transferred to Ship Criccieth Castle Co. Ltd. (Robert Thomas and Company, managers), Criccieth.
15.7.1912: Abandoned in position 54 south, 61 west whilst on a voyage from Ballistas Island, Peru to Antwerp with a cargo of guano.
4.9.1912: Register closed

2. HOLME FORCE 1887-1899 Iron and steel
O.N. 79128 269g 92n.
144.0 x 23.0 x 10.2 feet.
T.3-cyl. by Dunsmuir and Jackson, Govan; 55 NHP.
22.6.1887: Launched (Yard No. 84).
27.7.1887: Registered in the ownership of Richard Williamson, Cockermouth and William S. Kennaugh, Whitehaven as HOLME FORCE
14.11.1899: Transferred to the Holme Force Steamship Co. Ltd. (W.S. Kennaugh and Co., managers), Liverpool.
9.2.1905: Transferred to the West Coast Shipping Co. Ltd. (W.S. Kennaugh and Co., managers), Liverpool.
6.4.1906: Sold to Preston Corporation, Preston.
27.7.1928: Sold for £400 to T.W. Ward Ltd., Preston for breaking up and arrived at their quay the next day.

Silverdale as *Criccieth Castle* *[State Library of Victoria H99.220/4292]*

Williamsons' first steam coaster, *Scale Force*, was bought back from Kennaugh in 1891 and later renamed *Holme Wood*. She is seen at Bristol whilst with Bain of Portreath. *[Author's collection]*

3. SILVERCRAG 1888-1901 Ship
O.N. 79130 1,939g 1,897n.
264.0 x 39.0 x 23.6 feet.
29.3.1888: Launched (Yard No. 89).
2.4.1888: Registered in the ownership of Richard and Robert Williamson, Workington as SILVERCRAG.
31.5.1900: Sold to the Deanmount Sailing Ship Co. Ltd. (Robert Ferguson and Company, managers), Dundee.
20.2.1902: Renamed DEANMOUNT
11.9.1906: Sold to the British and Mexican Shipping Co. Ltd. (W.C. Jarvis and Sons, managers), Liverpool.
3.10.1910: Wrecked at Aviles Bay whilst on a voyage from Iquique to Bilbao with a cargo of sodium nitrate.
4.11.1910: Register closed.

4. SCALE FORCE/HOLME WOOD 1891-1899 Iron
O.N. 84636 229g 90n.130.0 x 21.2 x 8.8 feet.
C. 2-cyl. by J. and T. Young, Ayr, 50 NHP.
7.1883: Launched (Yard No.77).
29.8.1883: Registered in the ownership of William S. Kennaugh and Company, Whitehaven as SCALE FORCE.
7.1891: Acquired by R. Williamson and Son, Workington.
30.5.1894: Reregistered as HOLME WOOD.
23.12.1899: Sold to William H.H. Hutchinson, Hull.
25.10.1904: Sold to the South Coast Steamship Co. (1904) Ltd. (Kennedy, Collingwood and Co., managers), London.
24.10.1905: Sold to Bain, Sons and Company, Portreath.
1924: Sold to British shipbreakers.
5.11.1924: Register closed.

5. CENTESIMA 1893-1901 Four-masted barque
O.N. 95403 2,949g 2,796n.
308.0 x 46.2 x 25.8 feet.
11.9.1893: Launched (Yard No. 100).
27.9.1893: Registered in the ownership of Richard and Robert Williamson, Workington as CENTESIMA.
31.7.1901: Register closed on sale to Rhederei Visurgis A.G., Bremen, Germany and subsequently renamed NAUARCHOS.
17.4.1908: Sank at Antofagasta after fire broke out in the nitrate cargo she was loading.

6. QUEEN'S CHANNEL 1894 Iron and steel
O.N. 102130 370g 128n.
153.2 x 23.6 x 9.0 feet.
C. 2-cyl. by Dunsmuir and Jackson, Govan; 60 NHP, 350 IHP, 10 knots.
2.1894: Completed.
24.2.1894: Registered in the ownership of John Edwards, Liverpool and Richard Williamson, Workington as QUEEN'S CHANNEL.
21.4.1894: Transferred to the Queen's Channel Steamship Co. Ltd. (John Edwards and Co., managers), Liverpool.
12.10.1907: Sold to George Webster and Company, Glasgow.
12.12.1907: Transferred to the Steamship Drumalla Co. Ltd. (George Webster and Co., managers), Glasgow.
22.11.1911: Sold to John Stewart and Walter Fulton, Glasgow.
29.11.1911: Sold to John Emlyn Jones and Evan Williams, Cardiff.
1.2.1912: Renamed EMLYN.
4.3.1912: Transferred to the Emlyn Line Ltd. (Emlyn, Jones and Williams, managers), Cardiff.
5.12.1916: Managers became Emlyn Jones and Co. Ltd., Cardiff.
18.11.1919: Sold to the British Dominions Steamship Co. Ltd. (Thomas W. Pritchard and Jonathan M. Smith, managers), Cardiff.
15.6.1920: Sold to Rees G. Reynolds, John Evans and Samuel L. Greville trading as the Burry Port Shipping Co., Burry Port.
21.6.1920: Transferred to the Pembrey Steamship Co. Ltd. (Francis J. Evans, manager), Burry Port.
1920: Renamed PEMSCO.
1.3.1922: Left Burry Port for Dublin with a cargo of coal and disappeared.
5.4.1922: Posted missing.
21.1.1924: Register closed.

7. IRANIAN 1895-1900 Four-masted barque
O.N. 95404 2,958g 2,798n. 308.3x 46.2x 25.8 feet.
11.3.1895: Launched (Yard No. 101).
27.3.1895: Registered in the ownership of Richard Williamson and Son, Workington as IRANIAN.
3.4.1900: Wrecked on Redfield Rocks, off the Idzu Peninsula, Japan whilst on a voyage from New York to Yokohama with a cargo of kerosene. Her crew was rescued.
8.6.1900: Register closed.

8. HOLMECRAG 1895
O.N. 95405 390g 133n.
153.2 x 23.6 x 9.1 feet.
C. 2-cyl. by Dunsmuir and Jackson, Govan.; 60 NHP, 350 IHP, 10 knots.
25.6.1895. Launched (Yard No. 110).

Queen's Channel was jointly owned by Williamson and Edwards for her first few months. She is seen under Cardiff ownership as *Emlyn. [Author's collection]*

Holmecrag was quickly sold by Williamsons to Spanish owners, but in 1902 returned to British registry under her last Spanish name *Enriqueta. [Author's collection]*

27.6.1895: Registered in the ownership of Richard and Robert H. Williamson and Son, Workington as HOLMECRAG.
7.1895: Completed.
8.11.1895: Register closed on sale to S. de Aldecocea, Bilbao, Spain and renamed CANTABRICO.
1896: Sold to Compania 'La Peninsular' de Navegacion a Vapeur, Bilbao.
1898: Sold to Ballesteros y Compania, Gijon, Spain and renamed ENRIQUETA.
20.12.1902: Registered in the ownership of Coast Transit Co. Ltd. (James Bogle, manager), Falkirk as ENRIQUETA.
6.4.1905: Sold to Robert Kay, Glasgow.
4.9.1905: Sold to Samuel P. Jackson, Grangemouth.
7.9.1905: Sold to George Webster, Glasgow.
16.11.1905: Transferred to Steamship Enriqueta Co. Ltd. (G. Webster and Company, manager), Glasgow.
11.10.1912: Sank off Portland following a collision whilst on a voyage from Hull to Kingsbridge with a cargo of coal.
15.11.1912: Register closed.

9. CARMANIAN 1897-1901 Ship
O.N. 95406 1,867g 1,773n.
260.0x 38.7 x 23.6 feet.
19.4.1897: Launched (Yard No. 107).
19.5.1897: Registered in the ownership of Robert and Richard Williamson, Workington as CARMANIAN.
5.7.1901: Sold to the Andrada Sailing Ship Co. Ltd. (Edmund F. and William Roberts, managers), Liverpool.
19.8.1910: Register closed on sale to A/S Bark Carmanian (K. Olsen), Stavanger, Norway.
25.4.1916: Captured, shelled and sunk by the German submarine U 19, 50 miles south west of the Fastnet in position 50.16 north, 12.02 west whilst on a voyage from Buenos Aires to Falmouth with a wheat cargo.

10. PYLADES 1903
O.N. 95407 681g 222n.
182.8 x 27.9 x 12.3 feet.
T. 3-cyl. by Ross and Duncan, Govan; 85 NHP, 650 IHP, 9.5 knots.
11.8.1903: Launched (Yard No. 187).
15.9.1903: Registered in the ownership of Richard and Robert H. Williamson and Son, Workington as PYLADES.
2.12.1903: Sold to the City of Cork Steam Packet Co. Ltd., Cork.
22.2.1919: Sold to Matthew Taylor, Methil.
12.11.1937: Foundered after developing a leak twelve miles north of Veulettes whilst on a voyage from Havre to Antwerp with a cargo of zinc concentrates.
18.11.1937: Register closed.

11. VOREDA (1) 1906-1907
O.N. 95410 679g 252n.
182.2 x 27.8 x 12.2 feet.
T. 3-cyl. by Ross and Duncan, Glasgow.
9.5.1906: Launched (Yard No.188).
2.7.1906: Registered in the ownership of R. Williamson and Son, Workington as VOREDA.
23.10.1906: Register closed on sale to Sociedad Nacional de Buques y Maderas, Valparaiso, Chile and renamed MAULLIN.
1915: Sold to Compania Carbonifera y Fundicion Schwager, Valparaiso, Chile.
22.4.1917: Wrecked on Rapel Reefs whilst on a voyage from Coronel to San Antonia with a cargo of coal.

12. GALAVA 1906-1908
O.N. 124391 400g 111n.
141.4 x 23.9 x 10.6 feet.
C. 2-cyl. by Ross and Duncan, Govan; 81 NHP, 520 IHP, 9.5 knots.
20.9.1906: Launched (Yard No.193).
26.10.1906: Registered in the ownership for R. Williamson and Son, Workington as GALAVA.
18.5.1908: Sold to Davies and Fehon Ltd., Sydney, New South Wales.
8.4.1909: Sold to the Galava Steamship Co. Ltd. (C.G. Warburton, manager), Sydney.
1919: Managers became Eliot and E.O. Warburton.
26.3.1920: Sold to Abermain Collieries Ltd., Sydney.
8.2.1923: Transferred to Abermain Seaham Collieries Ltd., Sydney.
5.2.1924: Sold to Jones Brothers Coal Ltd., Sydney.
8.2.1927: Foundered off Terrigal, New South Wales whilst on a coasting voyage with a cargo of coal.
9.8.1927: Register closed.

13. VOREDA (2) 1907-1912
O.N. 124392 559g 196n.
164.5 x 26.6 x 10.9 feet.
T. 3-cyl. by Renfrew Brothers and Company, Irvine; 69 NHP, 500 IHP, 10 knots.

23.9.1907: Launched (Yard No. 201).
31.10.1907: Registered in the ownership of Richard and Robert H. Williamson, Workington as VOREDA.
11.1907: Completed.
1.10.1912: Register closed on sale to Vve. Gaston Levasseur et Fils, Rouen, France and renamed FIGARO.
1917: Sold to Société d'Importation du Nord et de l'Est (M. Ramet, manager), Paris, France.
26.1.1918: Mined and sunk nine miles off Hanois Lighthouse in position 49.04 north by 02.43 west whilst on a voyage from Brest to Rouen with a cargo of coal.

14. RAVONIA (1) 1908-1915
O.N. 124393 703g 277n.
182.7 x 27.9 x 12.3 feet.
T. 3-cyl. by Ross and Duncan, Govan; 114 NHP, 600 IHP, 9.5 knots.
4.2.1908: Launched (Yard No. 208).
9.3.1908: Registered in the ownership of Richard and Robert H. Williamson, Workington as RAVONIA.
15.2.1915: Sold to the Commercial Gas Company, London.
26.3.1919: Sold to the Wandsworth, Wimbledon and Epsom District Gas Company, London.
5.11.1923: Sold to Stephenson, Clarke and Co. Ltd., London
28.11.1923: Renamed LANCING.
2.5.1928: Owners became Stephenson, Clarke and Associated Companies Ltd.
27.7.1933: Sold to John Netherwood and Co. Ltd. (Peter Bossalini, manager), London.
2.8.1933: Register closed on sale to G. Balzano fu Achille, Genoa, Italy and renamed GIANNINA.
1935: Sold to Giuseppe Agrifoglio, Genoa and renamed ALVERNIA.
1936: Sold to F. Italo Croce, Genoa and renamed RINA CROCE.
1937: Sold to Alberto Maria Volpe, Naples, Italy and renamed GIGLIOLA.
1939: Sold to Mario Veronesi, Trieste, Italy.
9.1943: Seized by Germany.
8.2.1944: Sunk by Allied air attack at Zara.

15. CALATUM 1908-1913
O.N. 124394 270g 55n.
120.5 x 22.1 x 9.6 feet.
C. 2-cyl. by Ross and Duncan, Govan; 57 NHP, 375 IHP, 9 knots.
24.9.1908: Launched (Yard No.191).
22.10.1908: Registered in the ownership of R. Williamson and Son, Workington as CALATUM.
26.7.1913: Register closed on sale to A. Rodriguez, San Juan, Teneriffe, Spain and renamed SAN JUAN.
1918: Sold to Felgueroso y Figaredo, Gijon, Spain.
1922: Sold to Manuel Campos Pena, Seville, Spain.
1943: Sold to J. Gallego Urrestarazu, Larache, Spain.
1954: Sold to Jose E. Gomendio Ochoa, Madrid, Spain.

Designed as an up-river (or 'flat-iron') collier, *Ravonia* was clearly intended to be chartered to one of the London gas companies, probably the Commercial Gas Company to whom she was sold in 1915. She was photographed at Shoreham in 1932 as Stephenson Clarke's *Lancing. [G.A. Osbon/World Ship Photo Library]*

30.5.1960: Wrecked at Punte de Taliarte, off Melenara, whilst on a voyage from Puerto de la Luz to Villa Cisneros.

16. PETRIANA 1909
O.N. 124395 707g 280n.
182.7 x 27.9 x 12.3 feet.
T. 3-cyl. by Ross and Duncan, Govan; 90 NHP, 585 IHP, 9.5 knots.
22.2.1909: Launched (Yard No. 209).
20.3.1909: Registered in the ownership of R. Williamson and Son, Workington as PETRIANA.
24.11.1909: Sold to William Eadie, Vancouver, British Columbia, Canada.
16.12.1910: Sold to the Canadian North Pacific Fisheries Co. Ltd., Toronto, Ontario, Canada.
24.5.1911: Renamed GRAY.
26.10.1915: Sold to the Victoria Whaling Co. Ltd., Toronto, Ontario, Canada.
15.5.1919: Sold to the Consolidated Whaling Corporation Ltd., Toronto, Ontario, Canada.
10.5.1943: Sold to Union Steamships Ltd., Vancouver.
1946: Sold to the Canadian Transport Co. Ltd., Vancouver and sunk as a breakwater.
19.10.1948: Register closed.

17. GLANOVENTA 1910-1914
O.N. 128966 401g 156n.
141.6 x 24.3 x 11.0 feet.
C. 2-cyl. by Ross and Duncan, Glasgow.
13.1.1910: Launched (Yard No. 212).
15.2.1910: Registered in the ownership of R. Williamson and Son, Workington as GLANOVENTA.
1914: Sold to John Harrison Ltd., London and renamed HORSHAM.
1915: Transferred to the Horsham Steamship Co. Ltd. (Harold Harrison, manager), London.
1917: Sold to Thomas Walker and Co. (Hull) Ltd., Hull.
1924: Sold to Edward G. Willis, London.
1926: Transferred to Guernsey Coasters Ltd. (Edward G. Willis, manager), Guernsey.

The single-hatch *Calatum. [Bristol Series/J. and M. Clarkson]*

1930: Sold to the St. Baldred Shipping Co. Ltd. (A. Tate and Co., managers), Newcastle.
1932: Sold to John S. Monks and Co. Ltd., Liverpool and renamed CRESTVILLE.
1936: Sold to Osborn and Wallis, Bristol and renamed SNEYD.
7.6.1957: Arrived at Newport, Monmouthshire to be broken up by John Cashmore Ltd.

18. CALCARIA 1910-1915
O.N. 128969 569g 224n.
164.8 x 26.6 x 11.0 feet.
T. 3-cyl. by Ross and Duncan, Govan; 88 NHP, 375 IHP, 9.5 knots.
20.9.1910: Launched (Yard No.211).
27.10.1910: Registered in the ownership of R. Williamson and Son, Workington as CALCARIA.
7.1.1915: Sold to Alfred J. Smith Ltd., Bristol.
3.2.1915: Transferred to the Calcaria Steamship Co. Ltd. (Alfred J. Smith Ltd., managers), Bristol.
31.3.1937: Transferred to Calcaria (Bristol) Ltd.
5.1939: Arrived at Briton Ferry to be broken up by T.W. Ward Ltd.
15.9.1939: Registration closed.

19. DEVENTIA 1913-1929
O.N. 133261 800g 364n.
186.3 x 29.4 x 12.4 feet.
T. 3-cyl. by Ross and Duncan, Govan; 85NHP, 575 IHP, 9.5 knots.
20.5.1913: Launched (Yard No. 217).
27.6.1913: Registered in the ownership of Richard (32/64) and Robert H. Williamson (32/64), Workington as DEVENTIA.
14.5.1923: Transferred to Northwest Shipping Co. Ltd. (Richard Williamson, manager), Workington.

Glanoventa under her three subsequent names: *Horsham* sailing from Goole (top), as *Crestville* of John S. Monks and Co. Ltd. at Preston (middle) and as *Sneyd*, owned by Osborn and Wallis, Bristol and as which she lasted until 1957, apparently never acquiring a wheelhouse (bottom). *[Top: M. Barnard/J. and M. Clarkson; World Ship Society Ltd. (x2).]*

Calcaria at Torquay whilst owned by a single-ship company managed by Alfred J. Smith of Bristol. *[David Eeles]*

As far back as 1903 with *Pylades* (yard number 187), Williamson had begun to build larger coasters over 180 feet and probably intended for the East Coast coal trade. *Deventia* was a slight enlargement of this design, and reflecting her size had an extra mast and derrick aft. *[Bristol Series/J. and M. Clarkson]*

12.2.1929: Wrecked on Bolt Tail whilst on a voyage from Fleetwood to London with a cargo of soda ash. Subsequently refloated and broken up.
22.3.1929: Register closed.

20. ARLEIA 1915-1929
O.N. 133262 795g 368n.
186.3 x 29.4 x 12.4 feet.
T. 3-cyl. by Ross and Duncan, Govan.
18.1.1915: Launched (Yard No. 220).
2.1915: Completed.
2.3.1915: Registered in the ownership of R. Williamson and Son, Workington as ARLEIA.
14.5.1923: Transferred to the Northwest Shipping Co. Ltd.
3.1.1929: Sold to the Brunswick Steamship Co. Ltd. (Pollexfen and Co. Ltd., managers), Liverpool.
3.1.1929: Renamed POLGLEN.
7.6.1940: Sold to Charles Strubin and Co. Ltd., London.
15.5.1948: Mined and sunk 14 miles east north east of Borkum whilst on a voyage from Hamburg to London with a cargo of pitprops.
5.7.1948: Register closed.

21. GALACUM 1915-1943
O.N. 133263 585g 243n.
165.7 x 26.6 x 11.0 feet.
T. 3-cyl. by Ross and Duncan, Glasgow.
14.9.1915: Launched (Yard No. 224).
11.1915: Completed for R. Williamson and Son, Workington as GALACUM.
1923: Transferred to the Northwest Shipping Co. Ltd.
1943: Sold to the Derwent Steam Shipping Co. Ltd. (Anthony and Bainbridge, managers), Newcastle-upon-Tyne.
12.9.1951: Sold to the Satco Shipping Co. Ltd., London and renamed SATCO PREFECT.

Arleia (above) was a repeat of *Deventia* as was *Ravonia* (2), but unlike her sisters she found a buyer with the Liverpool-based Pollexfen family, who renamed her *Polglen* (below) and used her in the coal trade, as seen here at Portsmouth. *[Bristol Series/J. and M. Clarkson]*

Galacum (below) reverted to a more modest 166 feet. *[World Ship Society Ltd]*

28.7.1952: Sold to Tyson, Edgar Shipping Ltd., London.
10.4.1954: Arrived at Redhaugh, near Gateshead to be broken up by C.W. Dorkin and Company.

22. RAVONIA (2) 1925-1944
O.N. 140833 813g 378n.
186.5 x 29.4 x 12.4 feet.
T. 3-cyl. by William Beardmore and Company, Coatbridge; 99 NHP, 500 IHP, 9 knots.
26.1.1925: Launched (Yard No. 239).
28.3.1925: Registered in the ownership of R. Williamson and Son Ltd., Workington as RAVONIA.
4.1925: Completed.
2.5.1925: Transferred to the Northwest Shipping Co. Ltd. (Richard Williamson, manager), Workington.
23.9.1944: Sank following a collision with H.M. Trawler EROICAN about 10 miles off Spurn Point in position 53.31.18 north, 00.24.12 east whilst on a voyage from Sunderland to Cowes with a cargo of coal.
11.11.1944: Register closed.

23. CORINIA 1928-1941
O.N. 140835 870g 426n.
188.3 x 30.2 x 12.4 feet.
T. 3-cyl. by William Beardmore and Company, Coatbridge; 99 NHP, 500 IHP, 9 knots.
1928: Launched (Yard No. 241). During the launch, the ways collapsed and she was deposited on the beach. Jacked up, with fresh ways laid, and relaunched 30.8.1928.
16.10.1928: Registered in the ownership of the Northwest Shipping Co. Ltd. (Richard Williamson, manager), Workington as CORINIA.
10.3.1941: Mined and sunk about 15 miles south of Beachy Head in position 50.55 north, 00.35 east whilst on a voyage from Blyth to Cowes with a cargo of coal.
7.8.1941: Register closed.

24. SILVONIA 1930-1935
O.N. 161186 1,131g 581n.
211.3 x 33.4 x 13.1 feet.
T. 3-cyl. by William Beardmore and Company, Dalmuir; 108 NHP, 550 IHP, 9 knots.
12.2.1930: Launched (Yard Number 242).
25.6.1930: Registered in the ownership of the Northwest Shipping Co. Ltd., Workington as SILVONIA.
7.1930: Completed.
6.5.1935: Struck rock and sank off Hubaut Rocks, St. Brelades Bay, Jersey whilst on a voyage from Sunderland to Jersey with coal.
2.10.1935: Register closed.

Seen at Bristol on 1st November 1935, *Ravonia* (2) had already been transferred to the Northwest Shipping Co. Ltd. She was to be sunk following a convoy collision with an armed trawler off Yorkshire in September 1944. *[J. and M. Clarkson]*

Corinia, the biggest steamer yet built at Workington caused problems during her launch. *[Author's collection]*

The short-lived *Silvonia* was the Williamsons' largest steamer. *[World Ship Society Ltd.]*

25. KYLEBROOK 1942-1944
O.N. 147785 870g 426n.
193.9 x 30.2 x 12.4 feet.
T. 3-cyl. by William Beardmore and Co. Ltd., Coatbridge.
20.10.1926: Launched (Yard No.240).
7.1.1927: Registered in the ownership of the Joseph Constantine Steamship Line Ltd., Middlesbrough as HOMEWOOD.
1939: Sold to the Kyle Shipping Co. Ltd. (Monroe Brothers, managers), Liverpool and renamed KYLEBROOK.
1942: Acquired by the Northwest Shipping Co. Ltd., Workington.
1944: Sold to Ellerman's Wilson Line Ltd., Hull.
1946: Renamed DYNAMO.
1956: Sold to the Holderness Steamship Co. Ltd., Hull and renamed HOLDERNOOK.
18.8.1959: Arrived at Haarlem, Holland to be broken up by M.C. Hoole.

Homewood seen above after sale to Monroe Brothers in 1939, was sold to Ellerman's Wilson Line in 1944 as *Dynamo* (right) to replace an earlier Williamson ship of the same name. *[J. and M Clarkson; Fotoflite inc. Skyfotos]*

Names of Williamson's ships

Names chosen by Williamsons were an eclectic mixture including local place names, often of Roman origin, with some names from Greek mythology or the ancient Greek language, and some which sounded Roman but whose derivation is not known.

Arleia	Gaelic name meaning 'promise'.
Calatum	Probably from Calacum, a Roman fort on the River Lune, near Casterton, Lancashire.
Calcaria	Roman name for Tadcaster, Yorkshire, meaning 'lime kilns'
Carmanian	Inhabitant of an ancient region of Iran, which approximates to the modern province of Kernan.
Centesima	Spanish for 'hundredth'. *Centesima* was yard number 100.
Galava	Roman fort near Ambleside.
Glanoventa	Roman fort near Ravenglass.
Holmecrag	House and garden near Witherslack in the southern part of the Lake District.
Holme Wood	A mixed woodland on the banks of Loweswater.
Petriana	A Roman fort on Hadrian's Wall, now just outside Carlisle.
Pylades	A relative of Agamemnon involved in the Trojan Wars.
Silvercrag	A modest hill which separates the upper and lower reaches of Ullswater.
Silverdale	A village on Morecambe Bay.
Silvonia	A name which fitted in with the others, and which may derive from an area of the Val Gardena in the South Tirol.
Voreda	Roman fort near Old Penrith, Cumbria.

WHALE FACTORY SHIPS FEEDBACK

Ships in Focus published Ian Hart's magnum opus 'Whale Factory Ships and Modern Whaling 1881-2016'in 2016, and it has the distinction of being our first book to have been reviewed (and favourably) in the Society for Nautical Research's academic journal 'Mariner's Mirror'. The absence of additions or corrections upholds our view that Ian did an excellent job. However, there is always room for more details and explanations, and regular contributor Malcolm Cooper has supplied the following, mostly based on his own work in London registration documents in the National Archives, Kew. Malcolm's notes are numbered according to the order the ships appeared in Ian's book, a 232-page hardback which remains available from Ships in Focus at £29.50 (end of unashamed plug).

8. ADMIRALEN 1869 ex-GIBRALTAR, ex-ARIADNE

John Ryde, the only partner in John Ryde and Company, entered the South American trade in 1869 and built up a fleet of four vessels of which the *Ariadne* was one, all of which sailed under the trade name the Ryde Line. After winning a mail contract for two routes (one to Brazil and the River Plate, and one around the Horn to Valparaiso), he ordered four new vessels, floated the Belgian Royal Mail Co. Ltd., and transferred his existing fleet to the new concern. Thus, the *Ariadne* was not sold to an outside concern, but transferred in return for shares in that company. The transfer value of the *Ariadne* was £22,000, but as Ryde had only retained 8/64th shares in her, he only received £2,750 worth of shares for that part of the transfer. The Belgian Royal Mail Co. Ltd. struggled from the start, and was wound up after only two years, when its vessels were sold. The registration opening and closing dates for the vessel are as follows:

8. ADMIRALEN 1869

2.11.1869: Registered at London (226/1869).

9.7.1875: Sold to John Hall Junior and Company (22/64), London and renamed GIBRALTAR.

26.10.1890: John Hall dies and his 22 shares pass to Sir William Gray, West Hartlepool and George Septimus Warmington, London.

16.12.1897: Sold to Henry John Purvis and Adam Stuart Kettelwell, London.

6.10.1903: Register closed after sale to Chr. Christensen.

20. SOBRAON 1889

38. AQUILA/THULE 1888 ex-AMY

Neither of these ships was built for Gordon Steam Shipping Co. Ltd. which was not formed until 1897. Along with all the other early ships in the fleet, the *Amy* of 1888 and the *Sobraon* of 1889 were registered at London in the name of Frederick Gordon of Sunderland and owned on the 64th share basis. By 1888, Robert Gordon had established a London office for the family firm at 93 Bishopsgate, but the registered manager for the ships was still Frederick Gordon in 1897. The registration opening and closing dates for the two vessels are as follows:

20. SOBRAON 1889

4.10.1889: Registered at London (166/1889).

9.5.1907: Sold to Alexander McDougall, St. John's, Newfoundland.

11.5.1907: London register closed on transfer to St. John's, Newfoundland.

38. AQUILA/THULE 1888

3.9.1888: Registered at London (159/1888).

17.5.1910: British register closed.

23. ORN/FALKLAND (2) 1883 ex-FLORIDA

25. BOMBAY/PROFESSOR GRUVEL 1882

Like Frederick Gordon above, Nelson and Donkin registered their ships at London, but were not themselves based there. Henry Nelson lived at Westoe, South Shields, and Richard Sims Donkin at North Shields throughout the 1870s and 1880s. The registration opening and closing dates for the two vessels are as follows:

23. ORN/FALKLAND (2) 1883

15.1.1883: Registered at London (6/1883).

2.3.1909: British register closed.

25. BOMBAY/PROFESSOR GRUVEL 1882

8.9.1882: Registered at London (153/1882).

9.6.1909: British register closed.

41. FALKLAND (1) 1890 ex-CARNARVONSHIRE, ex-GAEKWAR

The 1906 change of name was the consequence of Brocklebank acquiring 50% of the goodwill of the Shire Line in May 1906 and transferring ships to what was in effect a joint venture.

97. PELAGOS

102. OLE WEGGER

111. KOSMOS

112. SOLGLIMT

There is some confusion about naval numbers assigned to the German commerce raiders *Thor* and *Pinguin*. All merchant ships taken over by the Kriegsmarine were given Schiff (ship) numbers, while those converted into auxiliary cruisers received a second H.S.K. (HANDELS-STÖR-KREUZER – literally Trade Disruption Cruiser) number. Thus the H.S.K. number (33) attributed to *Pinguin* is in fact its Schiff number, its H.S.K. number being H.S.K.5. Note also that the Kriegsmarine did not use roman numerals, and that the number for *Thor* was H.S.K.4, not H.S.K. IV. To add to the mix, the ships were known to the British by alphabetical Raider letters, assigned in the order in which the vessels were first detected. For the sake of clarity, the basic data for the seven raiders which had sailed by the end of 1940 is outlined below.

Raider	Ex-Commercial name/Owner	Tons/ Built	H.S.K.	Schiff	Sailed	British Name
ORION	KURMARK/Hamburg-Amerika	7,021/30	1	36	6.4.1940	Raider A
ATLANTIS	GOLDENFELS/D.D.G. 'Hansa'	7,862/37	2	16	31.3.1940	Raider C
WIDDER	NEUMARK/Hamburg-Amerika	7,851/29	3	21	6.5.1940	Raider D
THOR	SANTA CRUZ/Oldenburg-Portugal	3,862/38	4	10	6.6.1940	Raider E
PINGUIN	KANDELFELS/D.D.G. 'Hansa'	7,766/36	5	33	22.6.1940	Raider F
KOMET	EMS/Norddeutscher Lloyd	3,287/37	7	45	9.7.1940	Raider B
KORMORAN	STEIERMARK/Hamburg-Amerika	8,736/39	8	41	3.12.1940	Raider G

Index of ships

All ships' names in the text are listed, including proposed or other names not actually used, which are shown in brackets. Dates of build or other information are given to identify individual merchant ships.

(Californier) 31
(Granville Stuart)(1943) 85
(War Tummel) 10

A.J. Cassatt (1944) 90
Accruity (1935) 103
Achille (French) 97
Ada Burton (1933) 100
Ada Iredale (1872) 124
Adelsö (1936) 39
Adelsö(1937) 40
Admiralen (1869) 141
Aegean Navigator (1954) 114
Aethelberht (1876) 124
Aethelstan (1876) 124
Afamia (1979) 89
Agate (1878) 75-6
Aghios Georgios II (1916)103
Aghios Marcos (1910) 79
Aghios Spyridon (1883) 105
Agia Varvara (1945) 110
Agios Markos 84
Agios Spyridon (1883) 105
Agnes C. James (1859) 76
Ahrensburg (1956) 58-9
Aigburth (1882) 124
Aigle (French) 97
Ainderby (1925) 30
Aira Force (1891) 132
Airey Force (1873) 123-4
Akri Hill (1924) 29
Al Farwaniah (1972) 83
Aldebaran (1888) 124
Alderpool (1936) 40
Aldershot (1897) 17,22
Algeciras (French) 97
Almirante Cervera (Spanish) 110

Alnmoor (1922) 28
Alston (1903) 23
Alvernia (1908) 135
Amacuro (1945) 46
Amalia Vlassopulo (1890) 105
Amber Star (1965) 63
Amersham (1906) 33
Amethyst (1870) 75
Amsteldiep (1943) 80
Amy (1888) 141
Andelana (1889) 123-4
Andreas K. (1903) 79
Angelina S (1965) 13
Anglier (1900) 25
Angola (1912) 25,83
Ann Gambles (1862) 122
Ann M (1926) 6
Anna Maria (1947) 112
Anneliese (1905) 26
Annike (1929) 86
Antenor (1972) 84,87
Antinous (1925) 38
Antiope (1898) 33
Antiope (1904) 32
Anton Ivovic (1895) 14
Apsley (1906) 32
Aquila (1888) 141
Aradous I (1965) 13
Archangelos (1896) 106
Ardclinis (1870) 74
Ardeer (1871) 74-5
Ardenlea (1963) 54-5
Ardgantock (1) (1917) 2,10
Ardgantock (2)(1919 3,5-6,9-10
Ardgarroch (1918) 3-4,12
Ardgarry (1957) 6-7,13
Ardgartan (1918) 3,6,10
Ardgarth (1913) 2,4,8
Ardgarvel (1) (1917) 2,4,9
Ardgarvel (2) (1965) 7-8,13
Ardgirvan (1918) 3,10
Ardglass (1) (1914) 2,8-9
Ardglass (2) (1919) 3-6,10-1
Ardglen (1953) 6-7,12-3
Ardgour (1914) 2,4,9
Ardgryfe (1918) 3-6,11-2
Ardshean (1920) 126-7
Argonaute (French) 97
Ariadne (1869) 141
Aristea (1965) 63
Arleia (1915)126,132,138,140
Arlon (1903) 32
Armonia (1924) 28
Arncliffe (1906) 32
Arranmead (1915) 26
Arranmoor (1915) 26-7
Ascot (1902) 17,36
Ashby (1896) 19
Ashby (1927) 30
Ashenden (1898) 34
Asian Amigo (1956) 59
Atbara (1899) 25
Atilla (1907) 106
Atlantis 141
August Thyssen (1943) 85
Avalon (1963) 116
Aviemoor (1902) 22
Aylsham (1910) 37
Aysgarth Force (1912) 126,129
Aznar Jose Luis (tug) 46
Aztec (1920) 110

Baldersby (1913) 19
Baleares (1959) 60
Balmerino (1965) 13
Balniel (1886) 73,75
Balsa (1960) 60
Baltenland (1898) 33
Baltenland (1915) 83
Bande Nawaz (1948) 112
Banglar Polyxeni (1958) 80,82
Bannmaid (1903) 128
Barbalis (1945) 110
Barracuda (1960) 63
Barton (1899) 23
Barton (1903) (tug) 71
Basuta (1897) 25
Baygola (1912) 25,83
Baygowan (1905) 25
Baynyassa (1915) 25
Baysarua (1913) 25
Beaconsfield (1938) 42-3
Beckenham (1901) 36
Beckenham (1937) 42-3
Bedeburn (1896) 23
Bell Rock (1893) 126,128
Bellaport (1878) 123-4
Belle (1974) 84,88
Belle Rose (1974) 84,88
Ben Rossal (1929) 51
Benan (1890) 105
Bermeo (1964) 80,83
Berwick (French) 97
Betelgeuse (1936) 99
Bharatkesari (1948) 112
Bickerstaffe (1897) 67-8
Birgitte (1924) 28
Birgitte Basse (1948) 86
Black Boy (1854) 95-6
Black Diamond (1864) 72-3,78
Black Rock (1891) 123,126,128
Blackheath (1911) 36
Blackheath (1936) 42-3
Blair (1819) 75
Blakemoor (1901) 20
Bleamoor (1902) 22
Blue Fruit (1956) 59
Blue Ocean (1953) 58
Blythmoor (1922) 28
Boadicea (1887) 124
Boaz (1943) 81
Bogen (1911) 26
Boheme (1911) 32,35
Bohemia (1902) 94
Bolbec (1918) 3,10
Bolton Abbey (1958) 118
Bombay (1882) 141
Boren (1947) 111
Boro (1912) 126
Boulderpool (1928) 30
Boutry (1919) 84
Bow Fell (1882) 75
Braeside (1900) 126
Bratton Castle (1920) 99
Brest Rock (1896) 126128
Bridgepool (1924) 30
Bright Fruit (1956) 59
Brighton Belle (1900) 68
Brookby (1905) 19
Brunsberg (1960) 60
Brunstal (1959) 60
Bucentaure (French) 97
Burnby (1905) 19
Burnholme (1904) 32

Cairo (1882) 18
Calatum (1908) 126,132,135,140
Calcaria (1910) 126,132,136-7,140
Caledonia (1898) 49
Caledonia (1921) 100
Caledonia II (1932) 37
Calli (1) (1943) 84-5
Calli (2) (1957) 86
Cambria (1895) 97
Campden Hill (1918) 99
Canby (1911) 36-7
Cantabrico (1895) 134
Cap Domingo (1958) 59
Cape Ora (1937) 39
Cape York (1902) 126
Capito (1918) 12
Captain Anastassis (1960) 90-1
Captain Giorgis (1919) 84
Caradoc (1892) 124
Cargan (1873) 74
Caripito (1945) 46-7
Carlotta (1914) 9
Carmanian (1897) 123-4,127,130,132,134,140
Carmen (1930) 41
Carnarvonshire (1890) 141
Carol (1907) 101,107
Carol Dorian (1907) 107
Carperby (1928) 30
Castlemead (1906) 26
Castlemoor (1906) 26-7
Castlemoor (1922) 28
Centaur (1964) 116-8
Centesima (1893) 124,132-3,140
Cetus (1920) 102,109
Chapayev (1967) 64
Charger (1856) 74
Charles Doran (1917) 50
Charlie (1924) 28
Chassiron (1913) 50
Chatham (1902) 23,33
Chatham (1904) 21,23
Chatham (1910) 34,36-8
Cheng Cheng (1956) 59
Chertsey (1) (1898) 21,23
Chertsey (2) (1900) 23,33
Chesham (1906) 36
Cheshire Witch 72
Chilliwack (1917) 9
Chislehurst (1912) 32,36
Chiswick (1896) 33
Chiswick (1904) 23
Christine (1910) 101,106
Christine Marie (1910) 106
Christine Marie (1919) 101,108
Cibou (1932) 37
City of Cairo (1915) 16
City of Edinburth (lifeboat) 50
City of Exeter (1974) 89
City of Portsmouth (1943) 80
City of Reims (1888) 25
Clacton Queen (1897) 65
Claretta (18960 128
Clearpool (1935) 40
Cliburn (1916) 126
Cliddesden (1899) 23
Cliffmore (1880) 74
Clifton (1904) 23
Clinton (1899) 23
Clodmoor (1902) 20
Clonlee (1920) 102,110
Clydevalley (1886) 73
Coalby (1911) 36-7
Coath (1882) 95
Coath (1897) 95
Coleby (1907) 19
Colombier (1910) 106
Colwith Force (1906) 126,129
Comeric (1898) 23,34
Conishead (1892) 124
Continental Coaster (1907) 129
Cookham (1906) 32,36
Coral Sea (1960) 61
Corinia (1928) 126-7,132
Cornish Coast (1913) 129
Cosmopolit (1972) 84
Costa Rica (1919) 109
Cragpool (1928) 30
Cragside (1898) 33
Craigendoran (1899) 18
Crestawave (1888) 65
Crestville (1910) 136
Ellena (1921) 50
Criccieth Castle (1887) 132-3
Cromerton (1908) 108
Crosfield (1877) 124
Crown of England (1883) 124
Cruden Bay (1899) 49
Crux (1958) 59
Crystal Sea (1961) 61
Cultra (1884) 1,77
Cumberland (1884) 124,132

Daghild (1916) 44
Daleby (1900) 19
Daleby (1929) 40-1
Dalemead (1909) 26
Dalemoor (1909) 26
Dalemoor (1922) 28
Danae (1953) 58
Danapris (1924) 28
Danby (1937) 40-1
Darnley (1907) 32
Dartford (1930) 38
Datchet (1898) 23,33
Datchet (1918) 36
David M (1933) 6
Daybeam (1920) 110
Deanmount (1888) 133
Deerpool (1930) 36
Demarg (1964) 80,83
Denaby (1900) 25
Denham (1906) 36
Deptford (1931) 38
Derwent (1883) 126-7
Despina (1890) 79
Despoina (1940) 80
Deuterornis (1954) 114
Deventia (1913) 126,132,136-8
Devonbrook (1923) 130
Diamant (1919) 98
Dimitros (1936) 40
Dirfus (1947) 111
Domby (1932) 36-7
Domira (1905) 25
Domira (1924) 31
Dongola (1898) 25
Doonie Braes (1918) 51
Doonie Braes (1946) 51
Dorington Court (1939) 39
Dorothy (1896) 106
Drageren (111) 99
Dragor Maersk (1961) 62
Drakepool (1924) 30
Dreadnought (1907) 49
Droöonby (1900) 18-9
Drover (1923) 100
Dublin (1905) 32
Duchess of Kent (1897) 65
Duguay-Trouin (French) 97
Dulwich (1893) 21
Dulwich (1931) 38
Dunbar (1900) 23
Dunbarmoor (1903) 20
Dundalk Bay (1936) 94
Dunolly (1901) 32
Dunster (1954) 114
Dynamo (1920) 126-7
Dynamo (1927) 140
Dynomene (1882) 73
Earlford (1883) 77
Eastmoor (1922) 28
Eastpool (1925) 40-1
Eastville (1902) 23
Eastville (1925) 40-1
Eccles (1905) (tug) 71
Eden (1896) 126,128
Efcharis (1) (1943) 80
Efcharis (2) (1958) 80,82
Efdemon (1943) 80
Efdromos (1943) 80
Eftychia (1943) 80-1
Egham (1906) 36
Electrician (1887) 17
Elena Margareta (1890) 105
Eleth (1891) 128
Eliza (1792) 75
Elka (1881) 105
Ellen (1835) 75
Ellesborough (1921) 100
Elmmoor (1910) 20
Emlyn (1894) 133
Empire Bank (1941) 5,14
Empire Bittern (1902) 94
Empire Lethe (1891) 128
Empire Pattern (1945) 102,110
Empire Soar (1924) 28
Empire Tees (1920) 102,110
Empros (1889) 16
Ems (1937) 141
Enriqueta (1895) 134
Epsom (1901) 36
Erika (1947) 111
Erinier (1898) 25
Ernst (1885) 124
Espadon (1962) 63
Esso Chelsea (1945) 46,48
Esso Fulham (1945) 46,48
Esso Guiria (1943) 45
Esso Lambeth (1943) 46-8
Esso Lancashire (1962) 48
Esso Wandsworth (1943)46-8
Estro (1979) 89
Evangelia (1960) 91
Everilda (1897) 25
Eversley (1896) 23
Exe (1887) 95
Exmoor (1912) 26
Explorador (1891) 78

Falkland (1) (1890) 141
Falkland (2) (1883) 141
Fenwell (1912) 32
Fernimoor (1935) 42
Fernmoor (1894) 19-20
Fernmoor (1922) 28,35
Fernmoor (1958) 80,82
Fexl Glory (1956) 95
Figaro (1907) 135
Finchley (1892) 23-5,33
Finchley (1912) 21,36,42
Firby (1926) 30
Flimston (1925) 97
Florence (1879) (paddle tug) 123
Florence (1881) 105
Floriana (1964) 80,83
Florida (1883) 141
Forcados (1945) 110
Forestmoor (1910) 20
Formby (1899) 126
Formidaable (French) 97
Fort Astoria (1943) 90
Fort Dauphin (1949) 57
Fort Richelieu (1951) 57
Fort Richepanse (1949) 57
Fougueux (French) 97
Foy (1902) 126
Franchina Fassio (1953) 58
Fred (1899) 126
Freshet (1915) 126
Friars Crag (1890) 124
Fulham (1905) 36
Fusilier (1888) 65

Gadsby (1899) 19
Gaekwar (1890) 141
Galacum (1915) 126,132,138

Galava (1906) 126,132,134,140
Garston (1883) 123-4
Garthwray (1889) 125
Gaspesian Park (1945) 80
Geest Star (1973) 97
Geestcape (1966) 97
Geestcrest (1972) 97
Geesthaven (1966) 97
Geestland (1972) 97
Geest-tide (1971) 97
Geltwood (1876) 124
Gemlock (1914) 27
General Botha (1916) 51-2
General Gordon (1899) 25
George Bewley (1877) 124
Georgios P. Bouboulis (1890) 105
Gerrit Fritzen (1910) 37
Ghadeer (1969) 115
Gianfranco (1915) 39
Giannina (1908) 135
Gibraltar (1869) 141
Gigliola (1908) 135
Gilwen Park (1906) 32
Gipsy(1899) 126
Glanoventa (1910) 126,132,135,140
Glen Clova (1976) 55
Glen Rosa (1877) 97
Glenaan (1884) 1,77
Glenby (1900) 18-ö9
Glengarnock (1870) 74
Glenmoor (1894) 19-20
Glenmoor (1906) 26-8
Glenmoor (1928) 28
Glenstruan (1958) 53
Glofield (1906) 32
Golar Freeze (1968) 63
Golar Frost (1968) 63
Golar Fruit (1965) 63
Golar Nel (19680 63
Golden Seagull (1960) 91
Goldenfels (1937) 141
Goldfinder (1847) 75
Golfo Degliangeli (1949) 57
Gowanburn (1905) 25
Graanhandel (1910) 106
Grace Wetherby (1917) 49
Grangemoor (1911) 20
Granny Suzanne (1930) 41
Grasby (1946) 51
Grassendale (1) (1882) 123-4
Grassendale (2) (1885) 124
Gray (1909) 135
Greenwich (1899) 21
Greenwich (1904) 23,36
Greystoke Castle (1886) 124
Grigorios C.(1890) 105
Guanche (1904) 126-7
Guarico (1943) 46-7
Guiria (1943) 45
Gullpool (1928) 30
Gutrune (1895) 14
Gwladys (1908) 108
Gyda (1920) 109
Gyda C (1920) 109

Hai Da (1964) 116
Hai Yu (1914) 27
Haider A (1962) 114
Hainaut (1948) 86
Hallaren (1929) 86
Hallmoor (1910) 26-7,35
Hamm (1900) 126
Hamm (1910) 79
Hampstead (1896) 33
Hampstead (1906) 34,36
Happy-go-Lucky 72
Harpalyce (1958) 80,82
Hawnby (1895) 19
Hawnby (1936) 40
Haxby (1892) 23-5
Haxby (1929) 30
Hazelmead (1894) 26
Hazelmoor (1894) 26
Headcliffe (1915) 83
Helena (1907) 106
Helena Margareta (1890) 101,105
Helena Margareta (1915) 101-3,108
Heliopolis (1906) 79
Helka (1881) 105
Helka (1903) 105
Helka (1912) 101-2,106-7
Helka (1947) 104,112
Helmsdale (1907) 107
Hendi (1896) 106
Hendi (1947) 111
Hendrik (1908) 101-2,108
Hendrik (1946) 102-3,110-1
Henley (1894) 17,21
Henry van Dyke (1943) 80
Henzee (1948 103,113-4
Heronspool (1929) 30
Heros (French) 97
Hesperia (1919) 108
Hibernia (1889) 16
Highbury (1912) 21
Highgate (1901) 33-4
Hindpool (1928) 30
Holdernook (1927) 140
Hollandia (1951) 7
Holme Force (1887) 126-7,132
Holme Wood (1883) 133,140
Holmecrag (1895) 126,132-4,140
Homewood (1927) 126-7,140
Hopemoor (1911) 20
Horn (1901) 126
Horsham (1910) 135
Hounslow (1899) 23,33-4
Howard D (lifeboat) 98
Humanity (1954) 114
Hurliness (1899) 25
Hydra (1902) 25

Ilford (1901) 36
Imperator Alexander II (1885) 124
Implacable (HMS) 97
Inca (1897) 23
Inchmead (1900) 26
Inchmoor (1900) 26
Indoceanique (1963) 116
Indomptable (French) 97
Induna (1898) 18
Induna (1925) 31
Ingertre (1954) 87
Inglemoor (1912) 20
Inglewood (1875) 124
Ingman (1907) 107
Ingola (1925) 31
Ingramar (1954) 84,87
Ingrid 1 87
Ingstad (1910) 126
Innesmoor (1928) 28
Intra Triumph (1958) 82
Intra Trophy (1958) 82
Intrepide (French) 97
Invella (1924) 31
Iowa (1902) 94
Iranian (1895) 124,132-3
Iris II (1940) 80
Irlam (1903) (tug) 71
Iro (1899) 79
Iron Chief(1930) 40-1
Iron Shield (1917) 9
Irthington (1897) 18
Ise Maru (1902) 22
Islemoor (1907) 26-8
Isleworth (1896) 21,23
Italia (1869) 73
Ivanhoe (1888) 25

J.C. Ertel (1920) 109
Jane Bacon (1865) 73-4
Janeta (1929) 16,31
Jangdaesan (1974) 88
Jarlshof (1963) 54
Jayem (1956) 90
Jean L.D. (1936) 99
Jeanara (1907) 16,18
Jedmead (1913) 26
Jedmoor (1913) 26-7
Jedmoor (1928) 28
Jerryeverett (1960) 61
Jerseyman (1883) 77
Jerseymoor (1901) 17,20
Jerseymoor (1915) 26-7
Jobshaven (1916) 10
Joh. Gorthon (1947) 57
John Gambles (1874) 124-5
John Gillman (1917) 50
Jose (1900) 26
Jubilee Queen (1897) 65
Jumbo (1940) 80

K 56 (Russian) 33
Kalimba (1914) 25,35,39
Kalpogiorgos (1953) 12
Kamourska (1911) 37
Kandelfels (1936) 141
Kassala (1897) 25
Kassanga (1899) 18
Katanga (1901) 32
Katharina Dorothea Fritzen (1916) 44
Katuchka (1965) 63
Kelsomead (1914) 26-7
Kelsomoor (1914) 26-7,41
Kepbay (1984) 87
Kettara V (1932) 37
Khalij Crystal (1965) 92-3
Kinaldie (1914) 51
Kindiesel (1936) 4-5,8,14
Kinsale (1896) 25
Kirkby (1891) 1819
Kirkless (1865) 73-4
Kirkpool (1928) 30
Kirriemoor (1935) 22,42
Kis (1972) 84
Kitty Taylor (1929) 40-1
Knud (1903) 26
Komet 141
Kopernik (1914) 9
Kormoran 141
Kosar (1907) 106
Kosmos (1929) 141
Kotovskiy (1968) 64
Kronprinz Wilhelm 19
Kurmark (1930) 141
Kyklades K (1972) 87
Kyle Castle (1919) 5,11
Kylebrook (1927) 132,140
Kyleburn (1916) 129
Kylecastle (1919) 5,10-1

La Marguerite (1894) 69
Lackenby (1928) 30
Lady Brassey (1913) (tug) 39
Lady Clarendon (1853) 2
Lady Evelyn (1900) 68
Lady Orme (1888) 65
Laila H. (1965) 13
Lake Hallwil (1907) 107
Laleham (1904) 36
Lamington (1907) 33
Lamorna (1910) 106
Lancaster Castle (1884) 124
Lancing (1908) 135
Lanercost (1865) 122
Larenberg (1915) 108
Laurentic (1964) 93
Laurice Fidelity (1954) 114
Ledsund (1919) 109
Lefkipos (1936) 40
Leila (1969) 115
Leneverett (1960) 60
Lethe (1962) 63
Levenwood (1923) 126-7,130
Lewisham (1898) 21
Lexington (1906) 32
Lifland (1919) 14
Linda Woermann (1895) 14
Lindekerk (1943) 80
Lindsay (1866) 72
Lingfield (1910) 32,37
Linkmoor (1913) 26-7,35
Linkmoor (1914) 20
Lisbeth (1891) 123
Lise (1920) 109
Little Nota (1953) 12
Liza (1968) 64
Lizzie (1857) 75
Lizzie Gardner (1873) 75
Llangorse (1904) 32
Loch Brora (1958) 53
Loch Dee (1937) 39-40
Loch Don (1937) 39-40
Loch Lomond (1934) 32,40
Loch Maddy (1934) 40
Loch Ranza (1934) 40
Lodes (1898) 126
Londoner (1886) 73
Loop Head (1906) 129
Lord Talbot (1917) 50
Lovaine (1898) 23
Lowmead (1902) 26
Lowmoor (1902) 26
Lowther Castle (1886) 124
Lubna (1953) 13
Luddick (1898) 126
Ludwig Nobel (1888) 99
Ludworth (1907) 106
Luna (1895) 14
Lupata (1875) 124
Luso (1912) 34
Lyme Regis (1907) 129
Lynburn (1917) 126
Lynton (1899) 23

Madura (1901) 18
Maestro (1979) 84,89
Magdala (1895) 16
Maidenhead (1914) 32,36,42
Majestic (1921) 100
Mallsgate (1877) 124
Maltby (1889) 16
Maltby (1906) 19
Mangara (1889) 18
Mansepool (1928) 30
Maple Branch (1906) 25
Margaret Morrice (1917) 49
Margarete (1898) 34
Margo (1895) 5-6,14
Marguerite (1883) 127
Maria A. Hinde (1883) 78
Marianthi (1953) 12
Marie Lamey (d) (tug 12
Marinda (1948) 84,86
Maritsa (1943) 80
Mariyos Hope (1965) 13
Marko Polo (1958) 59
Marlindo (1946) 111
Maronia (1949) 57
Marquis of Bute (1868) 68
Marstonmoor (1906) 20
Marthara (1905) 16,25
Marthara (1926) 16,31
Martin (1895) 19
Mary Emily (1904) 126
Mary Walton (1925) 108
Masarua (1913) 25
Mascara (1912) 18
Masunda (1909) 18
Masunda (1929) 31
Mater Misericordiae (1884) 124
Maullin (1906) 134
Maylands] (1907) 26-7
Maymead (1907) 26-7
McElwain (1912) 126
Meadowfield (1904) 18
Medmenham (1904) 32,36
Memnon (1947) 111-2
Menhir (1868) 74
Meraggio (1889) 16
Merannio (1891) 16,25
Mereddio (1897) 18
Mersario (1906) 16,22,25
Middlemoor (1915) 26-7,41
Mijdrecht (1912) 107
Millisle (1908) 129
Millpool (1906) 35
Millwall (1896) 106
Minnie Hinde (1891) 78
Miriella (1913) 107
MNG Tahiti (1990) 121
Modesta (1917) 102,109
Moerdyk (1965) 47
Mofreeze (1962) 63
Molesey (1899) 23
Molesey (1912) 21,23
Mona's Isle (1882) 70
Mona's Queen (1885) 70
Monkshaven (1911) 32
Mont Blanc (French) 97
Montegiove (1924) 29
Moorby (1936) 40
Morning Light 72
Morning Star (1895) 49-50
Mortlake (1898) 23,33
Mortlake (1904) 36
Mortlake (1925) 38,42
Moto (1920) 109
Mottisfont (1913) 84
Mount Ard (1931) 50-1
Mount Ithome (1943) 90
Mount Keen (1936) 50,52-3
Mount Parnassus (1915) 83
Mount Rhodope (1919) 83-4
Mount Taurus (1920) 99
Mountby (1898) 19
Möwe 18-9
MRS 12 94-5
Muskoka (1891) 97
Myriel (1913) 101-2,107

Naderi (1902) 22
Naftilos (1946) 111
Nauarchos (1893) 133
Nefertiti (1948) 112
Nellie (1913) 83-4
Neni (1953) 12
Nentmoor (1903) 20
Neotsfield (1913) 38
Neptune (French) 97
Neree (1918) 12
Nestor (1948) 114
Netley Abbey (1915) 95
Neumark (1929) 141
Nevada (1878) 105
Newby (1890) 1622
Newlands (1902) 25
Newlands (1921) 100
Newnham (1901) 33
Newquay (1914) 32
Newtonmoor (1907) 26-8
Ngakoa (1938) 6
Nicholaston (1902) 26
Nikolaos S. (1974) 89
Nikolay Shchors (1969) 64
Nile (HMS) 102
Nith (1897) 126,128
Norbiton (1911) 34-6,38
Nordöst (1919) 6,14
Normanton (1899) 79
Norsea (1987) 118-9
Norseman (1891) 78
North Briton (1894) 50
North Wave (1954) 115
Northland Prince (1963) 116
Northmoor (1928) 28
Nots (1913) (USN) 107
Nour (1974) 84,89
Nürnberg (1936) 94-5
Nyanza (1897) 18
Nyanza (1928) 31
Nyassa (1897) 18
Nyassa (1915) 23,25

Oakby (1897) 19
Oakhurst (1879) 123-4
Ocean Dawn (1956) 54-5
Oceana (1906) 25
Olderfleet (1880) 76
Ole Wegger (1914) 141
Olga (1948) 113-4
Opaline Bay (1962) 63
Ophir (1907) 6
Orangemead (1911) 26
Orangemoor (1911) 17,26
Orangemoor (1923) 28
Orion 141
Orn (1883) 141
Otterpool (1926) 30
Overdale (1903) 32
Owain Tudur (1882) 76
Oweenee (1879) 124
Oweenee (1891) 97

P. Margaronis (1913) 79
Pandias (1912) 83
Pandias (1984) 84,87
Pantelis (1945) 80-1
Parkhomenko (1968) 64

Parkmore (1880) 74
Parnassos (1984) 87
Parthia (1874) 122,124
Patagonia (1958) 80,82
Patdoris (1913) 8
Patria (1919) 108
Patricia (1982) 118
Pearl (1897) 66
Pearl Sea (1930) 61
Pearlmead (1905) 26
Pearlmoor (1905) 26
Pearlmoor (1923) 28
Peggy Grieve (1882) 76
Pelagos (1901) 141
Pembroke Cormorant 100
Pembroke Mallard (1933) 100
Pembroke Pelican 100
Pemsco (1894) 133
Pendennis Castle (1958) 118
Pendragon Castle (1891) 123-4
Pentelikon (1960) 61
Perseus (1906) 79
Peter (1932) 37
Petersham (1) (1899) 21,23
Petersham (2) (1898) 23,33-4
Petriana (1909) 126,132,135,140
Petrolea (1888) 99
Peveril (1882) 23,25
Phoenix (1913) 94-5
Phoevos (1974) 89
Pikepool (1910) 39
Pinguin 141
Plantagenet (1869) 44,73-4
Plantagenet (1883) 44
Planudes (1900) 123
Plod (1960) 61
Pluton (French) 97
Point Lynas (1900) 123,126
Polglen (1915) 138
Polyxeni (1) (1945) 80
Polyxeni (2) (1958) 80,82
Polyxeni (3) (1972) 80,83
Poolton (1920) 127
Port Launay (1965) 92
Portland House (1918) 12
President Bunge (1905) 32
Preveza (1924) 28
Primrose (1908) 129
Prince George (1891) 69
Princess Irene (1891) 95
Princess Sophie (1891) 95
Prinz Eitel-Friedrich 19
Professor Gruvel (1882) 141
Pungué (1895) 14
Purley Downs (1908) 108
Putney (1899) 23,33
Putney (1904) 33
Putney (1913) 38,42
Pylades (1903) 126,134,137,140

Queen Elizabeth (1907) 26-7
Queen Mary (1936) 48
Queen of the North (1895) 68
Queen's Channel (1894) 126,133
Queenie (1905) 126,128
Queenmead (1903) 26
Queenmoor (1903) 17,26
Queenmoor (1924) 28,35

Radiation (1957) 54-5
Ramko (1965) 13
Ravonia (1) (1908) 126,135
Ravonia (2) (1925) 126,132
Red Cap (1899) 25
Red Rover 72
Redoubtable (French) 97
Reedpool (1924) 30
Remenham (1903) 36
Remenham (1911) 32-3
Retlaw (1902) 25
Reynolds (1898) 21,23
Rhodes (1878) 101,105
Richmond (1904) 21
Rijperkerk (1915) 94-5
Rina Croce (1908) 135
Ringvard (1968) 91
River Trent (1906) 32
Riveton (1943) 80-1
Rixton (1905) (tug) 71
Robert Burns (1857) 75
Rochdale (1906) 32
Rock Channel (1898) 126
Rockpool (1912) 19
Rockpool (1927) 29-30
Rokeby (1899) 23
Rollesby (1906) 19
Romanby (1908) 19
Romanby (1927) 30
Romford (1898) 21
Rookley (1940) 80
Roquelle (1918) 32
Rose-Julie M (1941) 14
Rosemoor (1914) 20
Rosyth Castle (1918) 99
Roxby (1923) 30
Roxen (1948) 112
Royal Kris (1969) 115
Royalmoor (1924) 28-9
Ruby (1897) 66
Ruckinge (1925) 38,42
Rudby (1924) 30
Rushpool (1928) 30
Ruth (1909) 26
Rutherglen (1906) 18
Rydal Fell (1881) 75
Ryoei Maru (1972) 61

Sadikzade (1945) 41
Safina-e-Barkat (1974) 89
Sagittarius (1896) 106
Sahara (1897) 25
Salamanca (1912) 23
Salatis (1906) 79
Salmonpool (1913) 19
Salmonpool (1924) 29-30
Salvia (HMS) 102
Samara (1906) 18
Samaritan (1943) 85
Samhain (1943) 80
Samos Sea (1965) 63
San Juan (1908) 135
Sandhurst (1897) 17,21,23
Santa Alicia (1964) 90
Santa Ana (1944) 90
Santa Barbara (1984) 87
Santa Calli (1943) 84-5,90
Santa Constance (1960) 90-1
Santa Cruz (1938) 39,141
Santa Despo (1943) 90
Santa Despoina (1957) 90
Santa Madre (1944) 90
Santa Maria (1956) 90
Santa Pola (1968) 90-1
Santa Rosa (1943) 90
Santa Venetia (1944) 90
Sapphire (1898) 66
Satco Prefect (1915) 138
Saxilby (1914) 35
Saxon (1881) 23,25
Scale Force (1883) 123,126-7,132-3
Scawby (1911) 19
Scheldestroom (1903) 105
Scipion (French) 97
Scottish Trader (1962) 47
Seagull (1902) 126
Sebastian (1920) 110
Sedgepool (1918) 22,39
Selamet (1920) 110
Selby (1895) 19
Senator (1936) 5,14
Sergey Lazo (1968) 64
Shad Thames (1902) 126,128
Shropshire (1968) 97
Shuntien (1934) 102
Sideris (1) (1943) 84-5
Sideris (2) (1972) 84,87
Sierra Morena (1903) 79
Signe (1907) 107
Silkeborg (1915) 106
Silvercrag (1888) 123-4,132-3,140
Silverdale (1887) 124-5,132-3,140
Silvermoor (1925) 28-9
Silvonia (1930) 126-7,132,140
Sinchion Reefer (1947) 57
Singapore (1906) 32
Skelwith Force (1908) 126,129
Skerryvore (1897) 95
Slateford (1903) 126,128
Sletter (1936) 14
Slingsby (1892) 22
Snaefell (1876) 70
Sneyd (1910) 136
Snowdon (1892) 69
Sobraon (1889) 141
Socrates (1913) 79
Sodality (1938) 126-7,130
Solbulk (1972) 87
Solglimt (1900) 141
Solitaire (1969) 115
Somersby (1913) 30
Somersby (1930) 36
Southville (1904) 23
Spennymoor (1915) 18,20
St Helena (1) (1963) 116-7,119
St Helena (2) (1990) 119-21
St Helena Island (1963) 116
St. Dunstans Hill (1918) 12
St. Rollox (1866) 75
Stagpool (1905) 39
Stagpool (1930) 40-1
Stainburn (1903) 126
Stanley Force (1) (1890) 126
Stanley Force (2) (1920) 126-7,130
Star of Alexandria (1911) 35,38
Star of Cairo (1910) 37-8
Star of Victory (1917) 50
Stefanos M (1947) 111
Steiermark 141
Stepney (1916) 126,129
Stock Force (1905) 126,128-9
Stonepool (1928) 30
Strachans (1956) 51
Strait Fisher (1917) 6
Strathdare (1974) 89
Strathtay (1962) 84,88
Streambank (1958) 80,82
Sunlight (1868) 74
Sunwind (1979) 89
Swainby (1917) 39
Swiftpool (1929) 30-1
Swiftsure (French) 97
Sylfaen (1883) 76-7

Tadmor (1965) 13
Talavera (1896) 21,23
Tantallon (1898) 23
Tantallon Castle (1954) 99
Taplow (1896) 21,23
Taplow (1905) 21
Tapton (1904) 32
Tarantella (1947) 56-7
Targis (1915) 94-5
Tarpeia (1905) 128
Tarpon (1960) 63
Tartar, HMS 10
Tees (1920) 110
Teesdale (1904) 19
Teespool (1905) 39
Telamon (1945) 81
Telfair Trader (1968) 91
Temple Arch (1969) 115
Temple Hall (1945) 80-1
Temple Lane (1954) 114-5
Terica (1962) 104,114
Theme (1884) 77
Theseus (1899) 23
Thesis (1887) 77
Thetis (1919) 5,11
Thirlby (1898) 19
Thirlby (1928) 30
Thistleglen (1924) 39
Thomas Connolly (1837) 78
Thor (1938) 39,141
Thornaby (1889) 19
Thule (1888) 141
Tintagel Castle (1954) 99
Tintern Abbey (1910) 106
Titov Veles (1962) 104,114
Tolka (1867) 77
Topic (1881) 77-8
Topic (1889) 78
Torca (1875) 73
Torrid (HMS) 99-100
Tortona (1883) 105
Tottenham (1906) 21,36
Triton (1945) 59
Troutpool (1903) 30
Troutpool (1927) 30
Trujillo (1945) 46
Trunkby (1896) 19
Tugela (1900) 23,25
Tullochmoor (1899) 18,20
Tullochmoor (1924) 28,42
Twickenham (1912) 36
Twinhorse (1938) 43
Twinkling Star 54
Twyford (1905) 36
Tyne Bridge (1925) 108
Tynedale (HMS) 110

U 8 19
U 16 21
U 19 134
U 20 18
U 24 18
U 28 79
U 33 19
U 34 105
U 34 (Austrian) 21
U 35 17-8,20-1
U 38 (WW1) 17-20
U 38 (WW2) 32,38
U 39 17,19-21
U 41 20
U 44 20
U 46 21
U 48 19
U 53 25
U 60 19-20
U 62 18
U 70 19
U 82 19,21
U 84 18
U 89 41
U 91 20
U 94 19
U 99 22
U 100 32
U 103 18
U 107 (WW1) 20
U 107 (WW2) 83,102-3,108
U 124 38
U 559 102
U 568 102
U 607 84
U 613 30
UB 16 18
UB 18 128
UB 19 77
UB 21 18
UB 30 50
UB 40 20
UB 50 18
UB 51 20
UB 57 18
UB 72 21
UB 80 20
UB 81 21
UB 91 19
UB 95 18
UC 3 19
UC 17 21
UC 18 19
UC 27 19
UC 31 19
UC 37 18-20
UC 49 19
UC 53 18
UC 54 21
UC 65 9
UC 67 20-1
Uganda (1905) 25
Uganda (1927) 31-2
Ullapool (1927) 30
Ulva (1878) 105
Umlazi (1918) 99
Union (1939) 122
Urania (1929) 84,86
Uskmoor (1912) 20
Uskmoor (1924) 27-8,42

Vaishnavi (1948) 112
Valdona (1898) 33
Valemead (1907) 26-7
Vandalia (1943) 84-5
Velba (1947) 111
Venango (1943) 85
Ventmoor (1900) 20
Verdala (1968) 96-7
Victoria (1887) 18
Victoria Reefer (1962) 62-3
Vigilant (1902) 50
Ville d'Alexandrette (1895) 14
Vinci (1883) 105
Vinemoor (1924) 27-8
Virgilia (1970) 96-7
Voce (1961) 62
Volana (1913) 126,129
Volhynia (1908) 126,129
Volpone (1907) 126,129
Volscian (1898) 126
Volturnus (1912) 126
Voreda (1) (1906) 126,132,134,140
Voreda (1971) 96-7
Voreda (2) (1907) 126,132,134-5,140
Vortigern (1891) 124
Vrontados (1956) 84-5
Vrontados (1979) 84,86,89

W. Hendrik (1925) 101-2,108
W.L. Burton (1921) 100
W.S. Caine (1883) 76
Wabana (1911) 37
Wallace (1905) 32
Wandby (1899) 30
Wans Fell (1882) 75
Wanstead (1928) 33
War Earl (19180 99
War Gulf (1919) 84
Warlaby (1927) 30
Watford (1928) 33-4,38
Wearpool (1936) 40
Wendover (1928) 33
Westmead (1915) 26-7
Westmoor (1911) 20
Westmoor (1924) 27-9
Westonby (1901) 19
Westra (1912) 32
Westsee (1924) 29
Widder 141
Wieldrecht (1913) 107
Willem Frederik (1883) 105
Willerby (1912) 19
Willesden (1905) 36
Willesden (1925) 38-9
William Brocklebank (1872) 75
William Hinde (1880) 78
William McAllum (1906) 79
Willowpool (1925) 29-30
Windsor (1903) 17,22-3
Winslow (1903) 34,36
Witte Zee (tug) 59
Wokingham (1906) 32,36
Wolfram (1915) 94
Woodburn (1905) 36
Woolwich (1887) 17,21
Wragby (1901) 19
Wray Castle (1889) 124-5
Wye Valley (1901) 20
Wythburn (1911) 126,129

Yacu Mama (1946) 111
Yaratilda (1857) 122
Yarborough (1900) 25
Yearby (1929) 30
Yolac (1922) 106
Yorkdale (1914) 9
Yorkminister (1913) 8
Yorkmoor (1912) 20
Yorkmoor (1925) 28
Yorkvalley (1901) 20
Ythan Braes (1917) 49

Zak (1962) 84,88
Zealandic (1965) 92-3
Zenith (1974) 89
Zonguldak (1903) 105
Zurichmead (1910) 26
Zurichmoor (1910) 26-7
Zurichmoor (1925) 28

St Helena, at Cape Town 21st October 2015, used as the background on the cover of 'Record' 2018. *[Ian Shiffman]*